SO NEW YORK
Angela A. Phelan

So New York

...why you'll never pay retail in the Big Apple again

Published by
Eiresol Publications SA

Author: Angela Phelan

Design: Cobalt Design

Illustrations: Eva Byrne

Printed by Elkar-mccgraphics, Spain.

Published by Eirosol Publications SA, Edificio Arnoya, 001 Planta 1, Campos de Guadalmina, San Pedro de Alcantara, Marbella, Spain.

ISBN: 0-9547238-0-5

For

Laura

Acknowledgments

Most of my close friends share my passion and together we have hunted down and bagged great bargains over the years. I would like to thank the following savvy shoppers who have always been the best fun as we have pursued our prey all over the city, usually in convulsions of laughter.

Big hugs and thanks for all those special shopping days to my daughter in law Andrea, a native New Yorker and our Princess, Laura, my granddaughter, who is now 20 months. Everyone agrees she has inherited the shopping gene and the wonderful memories of the two of us heading over to Madison and Fifth Avenue for Christmas shopping 2003 will always be precious. Then eighteen months I watched her run through the legendary FAO Swartz toy store, sadly now gone, to source her much loved Grover, who has hardly been out of her sight since. She learned to hail her first cab that day on Madison at 57th and is now a real New Yorker when it comes to calling cabs. Another day she went through the rails in Bloomies Children's Department like a real pro, only settling for anything pink. When a cool navy blue dress was suggested, it was dismissed with a decisive no! no! no! While the pink baseball cap got an immediate "please." And of course not forgetting son Tim, an Upper East side expert.

And then there's my friend Manny Luxemburg who knows more about New York than, I would suspect, anyone else anywhere. Whether it's history, architecture, museums, theatre, shopping, restaurants, who lives or lived where, Manny is a walking encyclopaedia about the city, as it is now and has been for the past seventy years.

For endless laughs, sharing bargain secrets and being the best company ever thanks Sue Phelan who tracks down the best deals in equestrian and golf gear and David Phelan, who when he can't make it to New York, emails his very detailed shopping lists that have taken me to places I had never heard of. Mary Dooley, the coolest sister ever, and a switched on shopper too has regularly joined the odessey.

Special thanks to John Fitzpatrick of Manhattan, Hamptons, Chicago and Dublin for his friendship and constant encouragement and thanks to everyone at Fitzpatricks Manhattan Hotel who know how to make me feel totally at home. Eithne and Orla Healy and I have shopped until we literally dropped. In Century 21 before Christmas years ago, we had so many shopping bags, we sat down for a second to regroup, when one of the charming store managers asked us to leave " because you have too many bags." We needed two cabs to get home that day. Orla has worked at American Vogue and was deputy editor of Instyle so knows her shopping inside out. James Bailie, Ireland's top florist introduced me to the Flower

District and Tom Moran and Ed Kenney of Mutual of America Insurance, do these boys know the best places to eat in New York? Karen Higgins, John Redmond and I have scoured Woodbury Common together with brilliant results.

The Kennedy gals, PR guru Caroline and designer Louise Kennedy and I have done the Madison Avenue mile and a half as our credit cards can prove. Cathy Reynolds was gobsmacked by Canal Street, Mary Crotty and Derek Sherwin from Dublin, Jenine Dillon from Beverly Hills, Dubliners Siobhra Rush and Kathleen Reynolds, both super shoppers, all did the business in Tanger Outlet Center on a great day out. Margaret Luccibello from London and Marbella discovered the joys of Peter Duffys fur salon. Jen Kelly and Garret Fitzgerald shared shopping secrets in the Hamptons.

Celia Larkin is another smart New York shopper. I introduced her to Chanel and Suarez. Lee Roarty from St. Louis is a great lover of the St John label and knows where to get the best discounts too. It's always fun to be with the glamorous Roma Downey from Malibu who shares her New York shopping skinny regularly. What laughs I've had and bargains I've bagged on Sunday afternoon shopping sessions in SoHo with my dear friend Mary B. Maguire, born and bred in Manhattan and the great laughs we have had in the 'foot rub' places!

George and Helen Kallos from New Jersey have so often made my day in New York. Mary Ellen Vicar, now in North Carolina, also shared her many Manhattan shopping secrets over the years. Limerick born Mike Neville now with Liffey Allied in New York, has much to answer for. He introduced me to the ease of shipping bigger items back home. And huge thanks to Brian McGuire and Bruce Sneider of the one and only 21 Club who always give me a great welcome and an even better table in my all time favourite restaurant.

A big thank you to Kevin Gurry and Brendan Mc Carthy of Cobalt Design, Dublin. Always literally super cool, they totally entered into the spirit of this project and never flapped at any stage and thanks to Brian Hession of Cobalt for the celebratory drink when we signed off.

Special thanks to Dan Loughrey and Bernie Kenny, now both departed from Aer Lingus but both hugely cooperative always and Gillian Culhane at Aer Lingus HQ in Dublin Airport, not forgetting Warren Mc Nally and everyone at Aer Lingus at Kennedy Airport who have always facilitated the fruits of these expeditions, all that luggage!

And all those other special friends - you know who you are - thank you. I look forward to doing it all with you again, very soon.

Contents

Introduction

Every Black Belt Shopper has a Little Black
Book, this is mine! It covers the stores I love in
the city I adore, New York City, which many
consider the biggest shopping center in the
world. Known just about everywhere as 'The
Big Apple' an even more descriptive moniker
could be 'The Big Bargain' because New York
has long since overtaken that other shopping
paradise, Hong Kong as the best and biggest
discount shopping experience in the world.
Anyone can stroll into a department store and
throw their favourite credit card around like a
boomerang to bag their purchases. But in New
York the cognoscenti agree that only the clueless
and tourists, pay retail. At posh Park Avenue
parties there are far more kudos to be gained if
you can boast you got your coat/rug/ring/lamp
at 60% off retail than admitting you paid full
price. This brings a whole new dimension to
'insider trading.' Because in the right circles
everyone knows somebody who has a contact on
7th Avenue, a vendeuse who tips them off to
secret sample sales, a favourite web site that
updates on special offers and sales. Let me be
your contact in New York.

For me locating the latest hot deals is a work in progress that has been ongoing since my student days nearly thirty years ago when my love affair with New York first started. And after all this time it's still unrequited. Like all love affairs it has it's ups and downs, at times blowing hot and cold. But it has never been boring because the City is constantly changing just as retailing is a constantly evolving business. Stores and boutiques are often as changeable as fashion itself. They come and go, often lucky to last a few seasons while others brave the vagaries of the ever changing retailing world and hang on to their own particular niche market.

More often than not New York, the financial capital of the world, dictates the international fashion and design pace too. Most people would expect new trends to emanate from the ritzy designers' lofts atop Seventh Avenue, in fact the germs are actually planted a little further down town. All the way down to Wall Street, in fact. There the daily fluctuations of the New York Stock Market, the Dow and Nasdaq, determine the spending power of millions of everyday shoppers. A one time rule of thumb was the higher the stock market, the higher the hem line reflecting a sense of high fashion exuberance and extravagance. The better the markets perform the more designers are inspired to produce ultra luxurious collections and ever-changing, new ranges. This causes stores to constantly clear stock to ensure they have the latest, up to the nano-second fashions. Bingo! Bargains are born.

When the Dow is down, fashion is similarly restrained and stores are even more eager than usual to turnover their stock and get those bucks in the bank. So those great 50%-75% 'Blow Out' signs begin to mushroom everywhere. So you see which ever way the wind blows, it's a win win situation for bargain hunters.

This is not a general shopping guide to New

York City, it is my bargain bible, specifically a guide to getting more for less. It's an insider's guide to how, where and when to buy that little suit or dress at up to 90% cheaper than in the major department stores. I have personally checked out all the listings and my comments reflect my own experiences. Some of the stores are nothing short of grotty with staff who are so rude they defy description, but the bargains make it all worth while. Because trends now reflect the economic landscape, and especially since September 11 2001, constant change is the norm. This means that stores come and go. Indeed in the four months I've spent writing this guide I've lost at least a dozen of my favourite places. Additions and deletions are made regularly to my listings. When I'm not physically pounding the pavement checking out stores and searching for new discount places, I'm surfing the net checking out the latest cyberbargains.

Sites like www.samplesale.com provide instant up to the nano-second news on all sample sales in the city: in addition to the more main stream sales. If possible definitely log on before you leave home.

At time of writing all information is correct.

More than anything I love the adrenaline pumping experience that comes from finding a great bargain. The thrill of tracking down a pair of $800 Manolo Blahnik shoes, unworn, in the Resale Shop on East 82nd Street where the price tag was much more inviting, $90, and this within a week of first seeing them in Manolo's Holy of Holys on West 54th Street.(By the way Manolo's biannual sales are a must for every aspiring Imelda Marcos. The last days of these sales are particularly frenetic when merchandise is reduced by up to 75%. Check 212 582 3007 for details.)

And the excitement of seeing 100 brand new Charvet shirts on the rails in the Memorial Sloan

Kettering Thrift store on Third Avenue, at 10 bucks apiece!!! (Sometimes you will have to put up with the indignity of someone else's initials on the breast pocket or shirt cuff.) In their spiritual home in the Place Vendôme in Paris, these Sea Island cotton creations would have been priced at least $750 a pop !! Or how about finding that Chanel jacket that you coveted in the 57th Street store but felt that $3,300.00 was a bit excessive. In the Chanel outlet in Woodbury Common it was on sale for $1,650.00 with a further 30% discount on the day of my visit. I also found a Chanel swimsuit that had a $560.00 price tag in ManhattanI, I preferred the $120.00 plus a further 25% discount.

And what about those Ralph Lauren shoes that I had to have. I saw them in the flagship store, the Rhinelander Mansion on Madison Avenue at 72nd Street, priced $ 489.00(plus 8.25% tax). The following day I bought them in the Ralph Lauren Outlet in Woodbury Common. They were marked $110.00 and there was a 50% discount on all ladies shoes that weekend, making them an irresistible $55.00.

But rules apply to bargain shopping:

• The golden rule is if you don't need it, it isn't a bargain. Even if it's the most exquisite Gucci gown, that is the tiniest tad too small, it's a 99% certainty that you won't ever lose that elusive five or ten pounds and you will never wear it. I've learned the hard way myself.

• Always check merchandise carefully. Discount stores are often used to dump irregular stock. Frequently flaws are so tiny they are barely noticeable but you could well find a garment with a major flaw that makes it unwearable.

• When shopping for others make sure you have their correct sizes (check conversion table on page XX for US sizes.) Also it really helps to have a good idea of what they want. I have spent days with girl friends dithering over a shirt or jacket, "do you think he'd like it?... do you think this would fit him?"

• Never blow your budget on a bargain, that is the first step down the slippery slope to becoming a shopaholic. But then again rules are made to be broken so I guess I'd better come out with my hands up here.

Some people go to New York for business, others for the wonderful museums or the colourful Broadway shows that are synonymous with the Big Apple. But increasingly people from all over the world and especially the Euro zone and the UK, are targeting New York as the biggest bargain basement in the world: a place where, if you know where to find it, just about anything can be bought at a discounted price.

In this guide I will take you through the streets and avenues of Manhattan and to the boroughs where unbelievable bargains are waiting for you. You will also find everything you need to know, in advance, about the out of town Outlet Centers.

I've listed the major Discount /Off Price stores throughout the City. Then I've sliced the Apple up into different districts where the best bargains are served up. Since Manhattan is essentially a series of linked neighbourhoods, shopping by district is undoubtedly the best way to go. This is especially the case if you have limited time and/or budget. It cuts out a lot of unnecessary pavement pounding. It also cuts down on cab and bus fares.

Downtown, Chinatown, Soho, Orchard Street, Midtown, the Upper East Side, the Lower West Side, have all been picked over to discover the latest, best bargain opportunities. Miscellaneous specialty stores around town are also included.

Major department stores and their out of town warehouses form another chaper. At certain sale times, usually January and July, the big department stores have unbeatable bargains and year round the store warehouses are always worth a visit. Even better still, try the warehouses when they have their own special sale times.

My own all time favourites and possibly New York's best kept secrets, the Upper East Side Thrift Stores and Resale Stores, are literally treasure troves without parallel anywhere. Native New Yorkers have been blown away when I have taken them "Thrifting" and finds have included Victorian furniture, paintings, sculpture, a baby grand piano, silver objets as well as unworn designer clothes, bags and shoes, all unbelievable bargains.

The guide includes fashion for everyone of every age. I have also included some of my favourite dress fabric outlets, buttons and trimming stores. Furnishing fabrics are a steal in several downtown stores and increasingly overseas shoppers and interior decorators are discovering that it's cheaper and so much quicker to have your curtains and other furnishings made to measure in New York and shipped home. The quality of the workmanship is extremely high.

You will also find the best bookstores, records and toy stores. I'm an Uptown Girl myself and I love sharing my own neighbourhood hideaways on the Upper East Side. I can guarantee, whether it's your first visit or your umpteenth, this guide will throw open a Big Apple you will never have known before.

Obviously, over a few days in the City, you will not be able to check out everywhere in this guide. But if you read it carefully before you travel, you can match the stores with your shopping list. Plan your shopping geographically, i.e. downtown/lower eastside on one day, midtown another, a visit to an outlet center on another.

But before we hit the sidewalks check out this important info.

US Sizes

APPAREL CONVERSION CHART

WOMEN

US	6	8	10	12	14	16
UK	8	10	12	14	16	18
Euro	38	40	42	44	47	50

MEN

US	36	38	40	42	44	46
UK	36	38	40	42	44	46
Euro	46	48	50	52	54	56

MEN'S SHIRTS

US	14	14.5	15	15.5	16	16.5	17
UK	14	14.5	15	15.5	16	16.5	17
Euro	36	37	38	39	41	42	43

SHOE CONVERSION
WOMEN

US	5	6	7	8	9	10
UK	3	4	5	6	7	8
Euro	35	36	37	38	39	40

New York City Sales Tax

A sales tax of 8.625% on clothes or shoes. Remember tax is not included in the listed price. There are two tax free periods annually. There is no fixed date for them but they tend to be in August and just after Christmas. They are well flagged in newspapers. Remember there is **NO TAX** on clothes or shoes in New Jersey.

Store Opening Times

Most stores are open from 10.00am until 7.00pm Monday to Saturday with one late evening opening... usually Thursday or Friday. Sunday: Noon to 6.00pm. But times differ from store to store. Extended shopping hours operate at big sales and holiday times. NB Jewish owned stores especially in the Lower East Side are closed from early afternoon on Friday, all day Saturday and for all major Jewish holidays.

However most are open all day Sunday.

How can I check the beat on the Street? Where will I get the best shopping overview?

If your mission is to buy up all the latest, hip fashions for men, women or children or household goods I always suggest a visit to Bloomingdales at Lexington Avenue and 59th Street on arrival. This store is an Alladin's Cave of all the latest lifestyle temptations. Fashions are no sooner off the catwalk than they're walking off the rails in Bloomies. The store provides the City's best overview of all things fashionable, including furniture and home items. It also has one of the best cosmetic halls in the City. Once you see what's available you can then check out the discount stores for the same garments. It also has wonderful sales several times during the year. Their July shoe sale is a must and I particularly love the Labor Day Sale (the last weekend in August) The swim wear sale is unbeatable with reductions of up to 90%. They also have a big imported rug Blow Out once a year when to die for rugs that usually require a mortgage, become manageable on even miniscule bank accounts. Check out the local newspapers for details.

A few last tips

When possible try to shop during the week. During the holiday season... from the second last week in November until after Christmas, it's important to get to the shops as early as possible, particularly at the weekends. Wear loose clothes that are easy to change in and out of. Most important wear sneakers or your most comfortable shoes.

Make sure you have your wallet in a safe place, ideally in a bag which you can wear not to your side but to your front, where you can see it at all times. Separate your credit cards from your cash and don't carry pin numbers with credit cards. Always carry picture ID, your drivers license is acceptable, if you don't want to carry your passport around.

Credit cards

Credit cards are the most usual form of payment, Visa and Mastercharge are almost universally accepted. American Express, Diners and Discovery are also popular. "Major Credit Cards" usually refers to Visa, Mastercharge, American Express
Cash can cause problems and delays in department stores where assistants all seem thrown by large amounts of cash and never seem to have cash for change. Most shop assistants have very short fuses, many speak little English and paying with Travellers Cheques can turn into a nightmare causing an endless delay as several hierarchies of managers are called.

Finally...

Do make frequent stops for water, tea or coffee. In the winter the stores are all so hot it's easy to become dehydrated: in the summer the AC is so cold you could use a cashmere sweater.

So now it's time to rock and roll.

Discount /Off Price Stores

You will soon know the score on Woodbury Commons and Tanger Outlets but what many shoppers don't realize is that you don't need a car to reap outlet bargains. Below, a list of discount/off price/outlet shops within the city limits.

These stores receive surplus current season stock as well as previous season's merchandise from the manufacturers and sell it on at little more than wholesale price or less! They also have their own sales when stock is reduced by up to a further 60%. Some stores offer a larger range of well known designer's fashions than others. At the outset it must be said that the merchandise changes constantly. On one visit you might well want to buy the entire store while on the next you could wonder what all the fuss is about and just where are the bargains?' Like life it's all about timing and persistence.

Let's go gang!

Burlington Coats

www.burlington
coat.com
Where
116 W 23 Street at
6th Ave.
Ph: 212 229 1300
or 1-800 444 COAT
Hours:
Monday-Saturday
9.00am-9.00pm
Sunday
10.00am-6pm
Credit Cards
Major credit cards

This store is very deceptive. It looks less than inviting from the outside and inside it isn't a lot better either. The ground floor has a vast area of ladies fashions. Most of the stock is immediately forgettable. You will see a lot more than coats, though if you are looking for a classic coat, it's likely you will find it here at the best possible price. Ladies lingerie: beach and sportswear: can be great buys. Men's designer labels: Upstairs the store looks a little more inviting. Again a huge space dedicated to men's fashions. The prices are terrific, but, again, you have to look for them. Most of the top US sportswear designers are here as well as some Italian and French labels. There is an enormous selection of men's suits in a huge range of sizes. The value is superb here year round, and the prices during sale time are simply amazing. There is also an enormous range of men's overcoats in varying lengths, fabrics and sizes. Basic shirts are well priced here as are some nice looking ties. Excellent baby and children's department. A good selection of Baby Dior, Baby Ralph Lauren, Baby Donna Karan etc. There is a terrific nursery furniture and accessory section.

Value 8   Range 6   Service 5

MY BEST BUY: Baby Ralph Lauren sweater, jeans and polo shirt all for $47.00. Sweater alone in Bloomies $120.00

Century 21

22, Courtland St.
bet Broadway and
Church Sts.
Ph: 212 227 9092
Hours
Mon-Wed
7.45am-8.00pm
Thurs
7.45am-8.30pm
Fri
7.45am-8.00pm
Sat
10.00am-7.30pm
Sunday
11.00am-6.00pm
Credit Cards
Major Credit cards

Following September 11 Century 21 was rebuilt and is now a mini department store and is light years away from the bargain packed, hole in wall that was the ultimate magnate for all bargain hunters. Still much loved by thrifty guys and gals, it doesn't do much for me anymore, though I have bought great Armani jackets, Michael Kors suit, Escada and Givenchy evening dresses. That was before I discovered Woodbury Common which I find far better value for time, not to mention money. Those were the days when we were wannabe savvy wall Street types who descended on the store before 8.00am. And we still laugh at the memory of the preChristmas shopping spree there about ten years ago when with Eithne and Orla Healy, we were aksed to leave the store because we had too many shopping bags! Nobody ever suggested that you need to graduate from charm school to get a job at Century 21. The mens department is usually better on designer labels than the ladies. Great for children and baby wear. Good for bed linen, towels, luggage.

Bargain Barometer

		Value	Range	Service
🛍️	Ladies	6	6	2
🛍️	Men	9	9	4
🛍️	Children	10	6	4
🛍️	Household	10	9	4

My Best buy: Divine La Perla lingerie and a Valentino swimsuit all for $76.00, at least 90% less than elsewhere in Manhattan. Also Leonard ties for $29.00 (two hundred quid in Harrods)

Conway

Ph: 212 967 5300
(H.Q)
Where:
Main Store: 1333
Broadway at
35th Street
Ph: 212 967 3460
Also at 11 West
34th Street 5th and
6th Avenues
Ph: 212 967 1370

Also at 49 West
34th Street 5th and
6th Avenues
Ph: 212 967 6454

Also at 225 West
34th Street
between 7th and
8th Avenues
Ph 212 967 7390

Also at 450 7th
Avenue at
35th Street
Ph 212 967 1371

Also at 201 East
42nd Street at
3rd Avenue
Ph 212 922 5030

Also at
45 Broad Street
Ph 212 943 8900

Hours at all stores
Monday-Friday
8.00am-8.00pm
Saturday
9.30am-8.00pm
Sunday
10.30am-7.00pm

To be quite honest this is not part of my regular beat and I'm not too sure why. To be sure the stores are jam packed with clothes for everyone: men as well as Big and Tall men, ladies: petites and plus sizes, teens and tots, bed and bath, body beautiful, toys and jewellry and the prices are hard to beat. It's not designer label central but it carries a huge range of every season's basics at rock bottom prices. Baby wear and kids clothes are so inexpensive, they could be almost disposable. Wear them once and bin them! But I have yet to find anything I couldn't live without here. Yes, they do have a very good household linen section and there is great value especially in bed linen and towels. The range of merchandise differs from store to store. The Broadway store is the flagship and is a vast warehouse type building, stocked to the rafters with just about everything. Merchandise is chaotically strewn all over the place. This store is always unbearably hot and humid. Queues for checkouts always seem to be not only a mile long but take a veritable age to surmount. If I had a buck for every time I have given up and walked away from a queue here, I would now be worth a pretty penny. The main store reminds me of a bazaar in Casablanca, everyone seems to be totally stressed out, hysterically screaming in a myriad of different languages. I'm so grateful I speak Spanish, otherwise you wouldn't know what is going on here.Shoppers always appear as stressed out as the sales assistants, a recipe for fireworks at the check out Why do all toddlers seem to think this store is a playground? The store at 3rd Ave and 42nd St. is far more civilized. But shoppers still seem to be having hissy fits as do the sales assistants - a recipe for fireworks at the check outs.

Main Store
Departments: Kids, mens, ladies, plus sizes health and beautycare, toys, bed and bath, fine jewellry

Credit Cards All credit cards

11 West 34th Street 5th and 6th Avenues
Departments: Kids and ladies

49 West 34th Street 5th and 6th Avenues
Departments: Health and beauty, bed and bath, photo developing department

225 West 34th Street between 7th and 8th Avenues
Departments: Kids, ladies, mens, Big and Tall, Womens, Body Beautiful

450 7th Avenue at 35th Street
Departments: Kids, ladies, mens

201 East 42nd Street at 3rd Avenue
Departments: Kids, mens, ladies, plus sizes and fine jewellry

45 Broad Street
Departments: Kids, mens, ladies, plus sizes, bed and bath

 Value 9   Range 8   Service 4

Daffys

www.daffys.com
135 E. 57th Street
(Lex and Park
Avenues)
212 376 4477
462, Broadway at
Grand in Soho:
212 334 7444
1311 Broadway at
34t Street and
Herald Sq.
212 376 4477
335 Madison at
44th Street
212 557 4422

• Good fashion departments for men, kids.
• It can be terrific for ladies, especially small and sample sizes. There are plenty recognizable designer labels If you're lucky you might hit it when the terrific evening gowns are there with price tags of $500 and below for Armani, Valentino, Donna Karan and Ferre couture. Regular retail prices would be well up to $5,000 or more. But be prepared for lots of rubbish too.
• Good shoe department for ladies and great shoes for kids.
• Excellent lingerie section.
• Men's department is very reliable for basics if light on top designer labels. Usually a good selection of American designers and lots of

111 5th Ave at 18th
Street
212 529 4477
Hours
Mon-Sat
10.00am-9.00pm
Sunday
Noon-7pm
Credit Cards
Mastercard and
Visa Only

Italian and French designers that I've never seen or heard of before.

• The 57th Street store is the flagship and is better laid out than the others. last Fall they had to die for Italian shaerling coats for $700 that were being snapped up in London and Milan for about $5,000.

Value 7   Range 6   Service 4

MY BEST BUY: YSL black cocktail dress $69.00 Clements Ribero cashmere sweater $39.00

Eileen Fisher

Where: 314 E. 9th
Street
Ph: 212-529-5715
Hours: Monday-
Saturday
Noon- 8.00pm
Sunday
noon- 7.oopm
Credit Cards: All
Major Credit Cards

Fisher's simple mix-and-match cotton and linen separates are comfortable, casual, and always roomy. The East Village clearance location offers bargains on casual work-to-weekend staples like boat-neck tank dresses and cropped crepe pants. Samples start at 20 percent off; seconds start at 35% off.

Value 9   Range 6   Service 6

Find Outlet

www.findoutlet.com
361, West 17th
Street at 9th
Avenue
PH: 212 243-3177
Hours: Thurs - Sun:
12 PM - 7 PM
Mon -Wed: CLOSED
Credit Cards: Visa,
Mastercharge. NO
Amex

This simple little shop is to Century 21 what Scoop is to Bloomingdale's - it has choice women's fashion without distractions. Labels on the color-coordinated racks change frequently, and very nicely priced too with reductions of at least 50%.

I've spotted Katayone Adeli, Helmut Lang, and Paige Novick - (mostly under $100). The downside? With miniscule dressing rooms and a perpetual crowd of intrepid bargain hunters, Find isn't for the claustrophobic. Prices start as

And at
229 Mott Street
near Prince Street
Ph: 212 226 5167

low as $5! $40 dresses from Miki P (spotted in recent issue of Lucky for $385)! Leather pants were $500 at Bendels' are $69 here!. Shopping tip: leave those talons at home, this store is incredibly sane even if it does get unbearably crowded at lunch time when the savvy fashionistas swing by for a trawl.

See you there! All sales are final, so hit those fitting rooms!

 Value 8   Range 7   Service 8

Filenes Basement

www.filenes.com
620 6th Avenue at
18th Street
Ph: 516 365 6224
1 800 727 2919
Hours
Monday-Saturday
9.30am-9.00pm
Sunday
11.00am-7.00pm
Credit Cards
Major Credit Cards

I can still remember how excited I was the first time I discovered Filene's basement in Boston. But that was over twenty years ago and bargain basements were few and far between anywhere in the United States then. In this New York branch you need patience because you will have to rummage. It is possible to find terrific bargains especially men's and women's wear. The usual American designers, Ralph Lauren, Nautica, Gant etc and lots of unheard of labels too are stuffed everywhere. It's not as good as the original store in Boston but there are some nice bits and pieces in the household section. This place is a total nightmare from Thanksgiving until after Christmas.

 Value 7   Range 6   Service 5

BEST BUYS: Aquascutum man's raincoat $129.00. £425 in London. Man's cashmere crew neck sweater $59.00. $499 uptown. Ladie's long, white linen coat $29.00 $365 uptown

H&M

www.hm.com
640 Fifth Avenue at 51st
Street
Ph: 212 489 8777
Hours:
Mon-Sat
10.00am-9.00pm
Sun
11.00am-7.00pm
Also at:
125 West 125th Street
Ph: 212 6658300
Hours:
Mon-Sat 10am-8pm
Sun 11am-7pm
Also At:
435, Seventh Avenue
34th Street &
7th Avenue
Ph: 212 643 6955
Hours: Mon-Sat
10am-9pm
Sun 11am-7pm
Also At:
34th Street at
Herald Square
Ph: 646 4731165
Hours: Mon-Sat
10am-9pm
Sun 11am-8pm
Also at:
558 Broadway at Prince
Ph: 212 343 2722
Hours: Mon-Sat
10am-9pm
Sun 11am-8pm
Also At:
515 Broadway
Ph: 212 965 8975
Hours: Mon-Sat
10am-9pm
Sun 11am-8.00pm

Credit Cards
Major credit cards

For fashionistas, gals and guys, this is a must. Technically this is not a discount store but I have included it in this section because prices here are literally unbeatable. High fashion at great prices and I rank it a must stop shop. It's also a must stop for fashion magazine editors and trend spotters. In March 2000 this new Swedish department store opened on 5th Avenue, the crowds shopping here have been so vast that police barricades are regularly in situ outside, especially at lunch-time and at weekends. The store receives new stock daily and it seems that staff work here 24/7 transforming the place at the end of each day from a virtual war zone to a hip emporium by opening time the following day. H&M, which caters for teens, men, women, larger sizes and children, has already been dubbed the biggest retailing success New York has seen for years. When I was there in January 2004, they had great suede jeans for gals, in several colours for $49.00. They also had great little cashmere cardies for $39.00 and up to the minute Prada style coats were walking out of the store for $69.00. Apart from Pucci in Milan, this is where I first saw Pucci like print dresses, skirts and shirts long before the end of 2003. Now we are swamped. The men's floor is equally directional and again well chosen pieces can give that Esquire look to an outfit. I have a friend, a top fashion stylist who is addicted to Prada. He buys most of his wardrobe in Milan and supplements it with shirts, sweaters, teeshirts etc from H&M. He swears that everyone is quite sure that the H & M gear is also Prada. They also do brilliant collections for kids, Tweenies and super size gals.

 Value 10   Range 10   Service 8

Best Buys: Prada type tops $8.99, black beaded evening dress $39.00, long suede skirt $39.99, Shantung silk coat $39.99, Pucci look alike silk jacket $29.00

Jacks 99 cent Store and Jack's World

110, West 32nd
Street between 6th
and 7th Avenues
Ph 212 268 9962
And at
16, East 43rd
Street between 5th
and Madison
Avenues
Ph 212 696 5767
Hours Monday
Friday 7.30am
7.45pm
Saturday 10.00am
7.45pm
Sunday 10.00am
6.45pm
Credit Cards
Mastercharge,
Visa, Discover NO
American Express

This is quite a recent find for me. Much loved by Village People it's just a few blocks north of the Flower District. It literally has all kinds of everything on two floors. Much of the first floor is a 99 cents mecca, with foodstuff, kitchen gadgets, and general bric a brac all costing under $1.00. Before you dismiss this out of hand, it's extremely fertile, stocking filler territory for the holidays. I was particularly impressed with how clean and how well laid out all the aisles were and what a dedicated following this store has. Upstairs is more upmarket. Garden furniture, some small electrical appliances, infants and children clothes, toys and glass and china are all at way below wholesale cost. If you are looking for Barbie, Action Man, Head tennis racquets, towels, lamps and upmarket bric a brac, this is about as good as I have seen. At 8.00am, when I've been there, it's positively buzzing. It has got to be a nightmare later in the day.

Value 10   Range 9   Service 9

Loehmanns

101 7th Avenue at
16th Street
Ph: 212 352 0856
1 800 813 7734
(freephone general
number)
Hours
Monday-Saturday
9.00am-9.00pm
Sunday
11.00am-7.00pm
Credit Cards
Mastercard and
Visa only

There is usually a great selection of everyday clothes for women, men and children at equally great prices. However I have always found the store so chock a block with merchandise, piled up everywhere, and so poorly displayed, that it's quite overwhelming. There isn't a breath of air there, the ceilings seem very low and it feels like being in a rather dingy basement. It's hard to believe that this was the original, legendary Barneys, in it's heyday the most exclusive store in the whole United States. But that was before the Pressman family moved the business to Madison Avenue where they lost the plot and lost the store as well.

• The Back Room is where you will find the major designer labels for ladies. Sometimes the selection is fantastic and you want to buy everything, especially evening wear, beaded creations etc. while at other times there is nothing to excite that credit card. I've been very lucky with evening dresses here but the Beverly Hills, California store is so much better than this New York one.

Value 8   Range 7   Service 5

BEST BUYS. Waterford Crystal Millennium Champagne Flutes $29.00 for two. Ralph Suede Jacket (men's) $159.00, Dior Cashmere coat (ladies) $98.00, Cashmere twinset (two pieces) $85.00

National Wholesale Liquidators

**632 Broadway
between Bleeker
and Houston
Ph: 212 979 2400
Hours
Monday-Saturday
9.30am-8.30pm
Sunday
11.00am-7.00pm
Credit Cards
Major Credit Cards**

This store doesn't exactly draw you inside, it looks quite junky. However once inside this warehouse like emporium, you will discover that it is packed to the gills with houseware, health and beauty aids, lighting, some clothes and bed linen as well as dried foods, all discounted by at least 60%

There are also small electrical and battery operated appliances at amazingly inexpensive prices.

Value 8   Range 8   Service 7

Odd Job Trading

**66, W.48th Street
between 5th and
6th Avenues
465 Lexington
Avenue between
45th and 46th**

This started out life as one pretty grotty store and has mushroomed over the past few years. It is one of Manhattans best kept secrets. These off price stores are not especially inviting from the outside but are well worth a visit. Closeouts with class boast the advertisements for Odd Job. Wowsa is a

Streets

10, Cortland Street between Broadway and Church, next to C 21

36, East 14th St., Corner of University Place & 14th St. on Union Square

390 5th Avenue: corner of 36th Street.

169, East 60th Street at 3rd Avenue across from Bloomingdales

601 8th Avenue, Corner of 39th Street

299 Broadway at Duane, near Chambers Street

149, West 32nd Street between 6th and 7th Avenues

Ph: 212 575 0477 for newest location details

Hours

Monday-Saturday 7.30am-8.00pm

Sunday 10.00am-6.00pm

Credit Cards Mastercharge and Visa only

new word in my vocabulary. It's Odd Job's way of describing their ultimate bargains. On my most recent visit it was very Wowsa indeed. Off brands: overruns, returns, rejects etc. cheaper cosmetic brands, perfume, small electrical goods, kitchen ware, glassware, china, cutlery, bric a brac:

• Toys: A great place to find a good selection of Fisher Price and Barbie:

• Garden parasols of every kind, Balinese teak steamer loungers at an unbelievable $79.99, picnic coolers, lanterns under $10.00, folding chairs from $5.00 etc in season (usually from the middle of April)

• Great at Christmas and for other seasonal decorations. They have just about anything you ever wanted for Christmas, especially toys, Valentine's Day, Easter, Halloween 4th July and Christmas stock that begin to appear immediately after Thanksgiving

• Luggage: When you find, as you undoubtedly will, that you need a cheap canvas bag or extra suitcase, you will find it here. Large, like huge, canvas bags, from $9.99. Suitcases from $15.00

• Greeting Cards and wrapping paper for all occasions, gift boxes and bags etc. When I was there last time they had great silver candle holders for $9.99. The identical ones were in a Dublin gift store at the same time for were €59.95. On that visit they also had a great selection of knock down price towels that were even cheaper than the outlets and just too cool was a battery operated scooter for adults for $99.00 that was $500.00 in other Manhattan stores.

• Stock varies from store to store.

• Don't shop in these stores at lunch time. The lines go on forever and shoppers can be very strung out causing World War III to break out at any second.

• The staff in all these store, well the less said the better!

 Value 10   Range 7   Service 3

BEST BUY: Garden furniture, Fisher Price toys, All Clad Saucepans, seasonal decorations, gift wrapping, party plates etc. Electric Scooter

OMG

850 Second Avenue
at 45th Street
Ph: 212 661 6495
Hours:
Monday-Saturday
9.30.00am-9.00pm
Sunday:
10.00am-8.00pm
Credit Cards:
Mastercard, Visa
and
American Express

This little chain has stores dotted around Manhattan. It specializes in designer jeans for guys, gals and kids, particularly Calvin Klein, Levis, Tommy Hilfiger and Donna Karan. It also carries a limited supply of mens shirts, jean jackets as well as ladies skirts, dresses, shirts etc. Limited selection but very good value.

Also at

476 Broadway between Broome and Grand Streets
Ph: 212 343 1164

Also at

546 Broadway between Prince and Spring Streets
Ph: 212 925 9513

Also at

428 Broadway between Canal and Howard Streets
Ph: 212 925 5190

Also at

55 Third Avenue at 11th Street
Ph: 212 533 8549

Also at

1523 Third Avenue at 86th Street
Ph: 212 628 6214

Value 8   Range 6   Service 8

Portico Clearance

www.portico
home.com
233 Tenth Ave.,
near 24th St
Ph: 212-807-8807
Hours:
Mon Sat
10.00am - 7.00pm
Sun
Noon - 6.00pm
Credit Cards: All
major credit cards.

Portico's own line of luxury linens is sleek, contemporary, and sharp enough to add a bit of oomph to your bed. A 300-count sheet set normally runs around $300, but here such fineries can be had for up to 80 percent off. Depending on what's in stock, you can also get great deals on bath accessories, tableware, and even furniture.

Value 9   Range 7   Service 8

Syms

www.syms.com
400 Park Avenue at
54th Street
212 317 8200
40, Trinity Place
(bet Rector &
BatteryPark)
212 799 1199
1, Syms Way,
Secaucus, NJ
201 392 1000
1, Syms Way,
Secaucus, NJ
201 902 0300
Hours
Mon-Wed
9.00am-6.30pm
Thurs-Fri
9.00am-8.00pm
Saturday
10.00am-6.30pm
Sunday
Noon-5.30pm
Credit Cards
Major credit cards

"Brand names! All off price! All the time! Why wait for a sale?" is the boast of this store. If you are looking for high- end designer labels, it's a fair boast some of the time, indeed I have had some terrific finds at the Park Avenue store. If you are looking for run of the mill classics, you should almost always have a great selection. The men's department is consistently good. Shop assistants in this chain are rather pretentiously referred to as 'Educators' and customers are ' Educated Consumers.' They would need to be, in my extensive experience of shopping here, the Educators leave so much to be desired !!!

• The Secaucus New Jersey stores are vast warehouses were prices are even cheaper than in the city. But you have to be prepared to rummage here. Definitely not a place to go if you are tired !!

Value 8   Range 7   Service 5

My Best buys: Ralph Lauren Polo Shirts $19.00, Armani men's dress suit $339.00, Ralph Lauren leather jacket $139.00, Donna Karan couture evening dress $89.00, Ferre silk evening coat $112.00, Frette Sheets $80.00 for queen size set

TJ Maxx

www.tjmaxx.com
620 6th Avenue at
18th Street
Ph: 1 800 926 Maxx
212 229 0875
Hours
Monday-Saturday
9.30am- 9.00pm
Sunday
11.00am-7.00pm
Credit Cards
Major credit cards

This huge store has acres of badly laid out 'stuff'. In addition to what seems like miles of nondescript stock where you can find so, so bargains but you have to spend hours rummaging through the rails, there are also some gems. Top American designers, Ralph, Joseph Aboud, Calvin, Tommy, Gant, Nautica etc. all at really keen discounts. Fashions for women and children. Gifts, houseware, jewellry. Prepare to do battle at holiday times. Some people swear by TJ Maxx. It is not one of my favourites. Why are the men's departments at so many of these discount stores so much better than the ladies? This is the case here too. You will find a very good selection of casual clothes that are now so much in demand for dress down Friday. The prices are pretty dressed down too.

 **Value 7**   **Range 6**   **Service 5**

Best Buys: Beautiful Italian blanket covers Queen Size $ 29.00 each. Interesting hand painted plant containers three sizes from $9.95 to $19.95. Crystal ice bucket $19.00, Log basket $29.99.

Weber

48 West 48th between 5th and 6th Avenues. 475 5th Avenue (corner of 41st Street) 45 West 45th St (between 5thand 6th Avenues) 160, West 32 Street (between 6th and 7th Avenues)

Ph: 212 764 1615

Hours
Monday-Saturday
7.30am-8.00pm
Saturday/Sunday
10.00am-6.00pm
Credit Cards
Major credit cards

This close out center boasts brand name and designer close outs at 50% to 80% off everyday prices. On a recent visit I spotted a consignment of Armani, Canali, Chaps Ralph Lauren and Donna Karan men's shirts all priced at $19.99. A much cooler price tag than the $100.00 or more regular price. But I have to be honest and say that this was my one and only decent find at this chain over a period of six of more years of dropping by there regularly. So I wouldn't exactly go out of my way to find this one. Some of the stores are close to branches of Odd Job Trading, at West 48th and West 32nd Streets, if you have time on your hands, check it out. Frankly, by and large you will find a load of rubbish here but at holiday time it's not bad for Christmas tree ornaments, decorations, wrapping paper and seasonal bric a brac. You can be lucky with toys here and it is always a safe place to get the very cheapest luggage, that should last just about long enough to ferry home all your extra purchases!!!!!

 **Value 9**   **Range 3**   **Service 4**

Sample Sales

Designers showrooms are the ne plus ultra for the most fabulous finds when Sample Sales Show Me The Showroom! Save Me More Money many of New York's top designers throw their showrooms open to the public for their biannual sample sales. Reflecting the fact that New York City is the fashion capital of the world, designers regularly hold what they call Sample Sales in their showrooms and elsewhere. Some designers advertise in the New York Daily News or the New York Post. Others will be listed in the Sales and Bargains section of New York Magazine or Time Out New York, while many designers don't even need to advertise, the grapevine works so efficiently. The best listings come on www.nysale.com (as before)

Merchandise can vary, but it usually consists of surplus stock, sample collections, frequently part of the current collection and you can even be lucky enough to find samples from the next season's collections.

Listed below are sales that I have attended myself. There were others that were so trashy that I wouldn't waste your time including them. Because the dates and locations of these sales

can differ from one sale the next, I have
included phone numbers of the designer's retail
stores. If you see a designer that you are
interested in, phone when you arrive in the city
to see if they have a sale on. But be warned:
most of these sales are like a cattle mart on a
busy fair day and expect to be treated
accordingly. They are usually held in the
Garment District, 7th Avenue from 34th to 40th
Street, in showrooms or warehouse spaces that
are not at street level. Flyers are often handed
out to the public outside the buildings where the
sales are held. If you see the HQ of your
favourite designer, ask the doorman if there is a
sale on. These guys know everything that moves
in the District and can direct you to some fab.
impromptu sale that hasn't been flagged
anywhere.

• Savvy sample shoppers should start at the
Garment District Information Booth, beside the
gigantic needle and button on the north east
corner of 7th Avenue and 39th Street. The gals
that man this booth are extremely helpful to
ordinary punters They have encyclopedic
knowledge of where you will find what and they
also provide a listing of the current sample
sales. On a recent visit I wanted to buy ivory,
Chantilly lace. They supplied me with a three
page print out of all the lace outlets in the
district which included one lace sample sale. It's
that specific.

However at these sales
• Don't expect service of any kind and you
won't be disappointed.
• Trying-on facilities are iffy at best. At times it
can seem as if you are trapped in a heaving
mass of female flesh. Most shop assistants have
extremely short fuses.
• Be prepared to rummage
• Check return policies. Usually all sales are
final and there are No Returns.
• Cash is often the only currency accepted at
these sales

Aeffe's Sample Sales

30 West 56th Street bet. 5th and 6th Avenues:
1st Floor
Ph: 212 632 9300
(Sale dates every 3-4 months, call for information on particular dates and designers.)
Hours Usually 10.00am- 5.30pm
Credit Cards
Major credit cards

This company's sales features designers like Alberta Ferretti, Moschino, Paul Gaultier, Rifat Ozbek and Narcisco Rodriguez for men, women and children. Small and medium sizes only at a fraction of original prices.

Value 9   Range 9   Service 8

Badgley Mischka

Where: 123 West 18th Street (4th Floor Gallery)
Ph: 212 921 1585
Hours: Check for dates and hours
Credit Cards:
Major Credit Cards

You will always see some of the major players in Hollywood dolled up in their Badgley Mischka when red carpet fever breaks out. The ball gowns and bridal wear are simply stunning. So are the prices but at sample sale time you can dress like a millionaire and pay pence. Think 90% discounts. At this sale there are usually great shoes and accessories too.

Value 10   Range 9   Service 9

Bernardaud, Christofle, Vivre

Where: 560 7th Ave. (Parson's School of Design) (corner of 40th St.)
2nd Fl.
Ph: 718 747-1656
Hours: Check for dates and hours
Credit Cards:
Major Credit Cards

Introduce a touch of class to your home and wardrobe with premium accessories from top name brand designers. At up to 70% off retail, you'll just love the divine Bernardaud limoges porcelains, Christofle cutlery, gifts, crystal glasses and barware as well as luxury clothing, accessories and jewelry for men and women by Vivre.

Value 10   Range 8   Service 8

Burberry

9 East 57th Street.
(This is the retail
store address. Call
the retail store
directly for
information on sale
dates)
Ph: 212-371-5010
Hours
Monday-Friday
9.00am-5.30pm
Credit Cards
Major credit cards

Twice yearly showroom sales but just how much more Burberry can we take? Since Rosemarie Bravo revolutionized the rather staid company and turned it into the hottest fashion house, everyone and his/her dog, owns something in the distinctive plaid. Great staff make this an extremely pleasant shopping experience.

Value 9   Range 8   Service 10

Calvin Klein Couture Sample Sale

260 5th Ave, (btwn.
28th & 29th Sts),
Ground Fl
Ph: 212 725-5400
(check for dates
and times)
Hours: Mon-Sat
10am-7pm
Sun 12pm-7pm
Credit Cards:
Major Credit Cards

Nothing should come between you and your Calvins especially with up to 75% off retail! Never has this been truer than at Misorena's designer sample sale featuring the Calvin Klein Couture line for men and women at 50-75% off retail prices. The spring fashion extravaganza presents men's suits, shirts, sweaters and leather. Women will find stylish skirts, sweaters, knits, dresses, pants, leather, shoes and eveningwear. Of course no wardrobe's complete without the proper accessories. Misorena offers an array of extraordinary accompaniments for any and all outfits. Check out Men's suits now $395, retailing at $2,200, shoes now $95, retailing at $525 or leather jackets now $395, retailing at $1,800

Value 10   Range 8   Service 8

Cashmere Fifth Avenue & Co.

www.curlisto.com
Location: 242 W.
36th Street
Ph: 212-502-4040

Cashmere has the quintessential luxury men and women sweaters and accessories at 1/2 price. Once you've worn it nothing else will do and when it's cheaper than scratchy wool, as it is here, then there's no contest.

Value 10   Range 7   Service 8

Cristina Arzuaga Couture Bridal Sample Sale

Cristina Arzuaga creates alluring bridal gowns that are not only beautiful but sensual as well. Her collection is sold in the finest salons. The collection includes full A-lines, small A-lines, drop waist and empire tops, some with detachable trains.These couture quality gowns are made from exquisite silk duchesse satin, silk organza and chiffons (either embroidered or solid). Prices at the sale will range from $500-$1,500. Sizes available at this sale include 6-10. Please Note: To ensure more personal attention, this sale is By Appointment Only.

Value 10   Range 7   Service 10

E.V.A. Diffusion, Inc.

E.V.A. is Louis Feraud's exclusive discount outlet and stock sells at wholesale price or less. If you are a LF fan, this is like an Alladin's Cave full of goodies. Other French designers also stocked here.

Value 8   Range 7   Service 7

Fernando Sanchez

5 West 19th Street
(5th and 6th
Avenues) 7th Floor
Ph: 212 929 5060
Hours
Monday-Friday
10.00am-4.00pm
Credit Cards Major
credit cards No
American Express

Sales twice a year: Wonderful evening wear and really beautiful lingerie. Original prices are extremely high but well worth a visit during sale time. Extremely helpful staff. If you want to be the belle of the ball or the boudoir this is the place to help make it happen.

 **Value 8**   **Range 8**   **Service 9**

Genny USA Inc.

650, 5th Avenue,
18th Floor
Ph: 212 245 4860
Hours
Monday-Friday
9.00am-5.00pm
Credit Cards
CASH ONLY

The famous Versace line at its best and certainly at prices you will not have seen before. A wide selection of day, sports and evening wear as well as separates.

 **Value 7**   **Range 9**   **Service 8**

Gottex Showroom

Where:
1411 Broadway, (
between 39th and
40th Streets Main
entrance to
building is on 39th
street between 7th
Ave and Broadway)
29th Floor
Ph: 212 354 1240
Hours
Monday-Friday
9.00am-5.00pm
Credit Cards Major
credit cards

This fab swim and beachwear company offers discounts of up to 60% Great for wraps and accessories. If you want to be the belle of the beach on a budget, check out this one. I've shopped here on at least four occasions. The stock has always been terrific. The biggest problem is trying to decide what not to buy. Service, however is very patchy. I have been love bombed on a few occasions and endured extremely hostile service on another. But when swim suits that normally costs well over $100.00 are going for $20.00, who am I to complain?

 **Value 10**   **Range 10**   **Service 8**

Hanro

40 E. 34th Street
(5th and Madison
Avenues) 2nd Floor
Ph: 212 532 3320 -
Call for time and
dates.
Hours
8.30am-3.30pm
(for the duration)
Credit Cards
**Cash or Checks
only**

One sale a year. (November/December timeframe) Legendary Swiss underwear for him and her at crazy prices. Once you wear Hanro, everything else seems ill fitting and uncomfortable. It really is the Rolls Royce of very fine cotton underwear and lingerie. The place is always packed and stock literally disappears in front of your eyes.

 Value 10   Range 8   Service 7

Malo Cashmere

712 5th Avenue at
56th Street
Ph: 212-265-4166
Hours: Call for
details
Credit Cards: :
Major credit cards

Usually two sample sales are held during the year. The quality is to die for. Once you wear a Malo cashmere sweater you will find it impossible to settle for anything else. Reductions are usually at least 60% which menas that instead of paying the bones of $1,000 for a fab. sweater you will get it for $400 or less. Sample sales are held in different locations around the Garment District. For sample sale information call the above number. Staff are extremely helpful.

Value 10   Range 7   Service 9

Michael Kors

550 7th Avenue
(39th and 40th
Streets) 6th Floor
Ph: 212-201-8100.
Hours
Monday-Friday
9.00am-6.00pm
Credit Cards
Cash only

Since Michael became darling of the Park Avenue Princesses, his clothes are now de rigeur for all younger best- dressed women. His clothes really are beautiful and he now also designs a stunning collection for Celine in Paris. Wonderful value but I found that sizes tended to be on the small size - 10 and under. He is also designing a great range of shoes and accessories. Look out for great prices. Sales twice a year. Call for details.

 Value 9   Range 7   Service 7

Nice Price

493, Columbus
Avenue between
83rd and 84th
Streets
Ph: 212 362 1020
Hours Monday
Saturday 1.00am
6.15pm
Sunday Noon
6.0pm
Credit Cards Visa,
Mastercharge,
American Express
and debit cards

This stock sale store carries a large inventory from different designers. Deep discounts can be as much as 80% depending on the time of year. Call for details of sales and discounts.

 Value 8   Range 8   Service 6

Patricia Underwood Hats

498, 7th
Avenue,(36th and
37th Streets) 24th
Floor
Ph: 212 268 3774 -
Call for dates.
Hours
Monday-Friday
9.00am-5.30pm
Credit Cards
Mastercharge,
Visa, No American
Express

You know what they say: if you want to get ahead, get a hat !!!!! At the twice yearly sales here I bought several hats including my all time favourite Derby and Royal Ascot hats. Patricia Underwood's simplicity is her greatest strength. I have had some of her plain straw hats dressed by my florist, not only do they end up the envy of everyone who see's them, they actually look like a piece of impressionist art. See her hats in Bergdorf Goodmans for up to $800, then get lucky and find the same ones at the sample sale for $150.00 or less.

 Value 9   Range 9   Service 9

Robert Marc

782 Madison
between 66th and
67th Streets
Ph: 212 737 8000
And 190 Columbus
Avenue between
67th and 68th
Streets
Ph: 212 799 4600
Hours: Check for
dates and hours
Credit Cards:
Major Credit cards

Who can complain about huge discounts at sale time here. Certainly not Cindy Crawford or Meg Ryan who are big fans. And you think they pay retail?

Value 10   Range 8   Service 8

$$$ Sample Sales

www.clothingline.com
261, West 36th
Street between 7th
and 8th Avenue
2nd Floor.
Ph: 212 947 8748
Hours: Usually
Monday to
Thursday
10.00am 6.00pm
but check hotline
for sales schedule.
Credit Cards Visa,
Mastercard,
American Express.
There is also an
ATM on the
premises

This company has been providing space for sample sales for top designers for the past ten years. Sales feature a different designer each week. You need all your energy to get up the stairs and traipse along endless corridors. The warehouse type space isn't exactly inviting though the merchandise and prices, at least 50% off retail, can make you forget these inconveniences very quickly. Some of the sales are worth the awful surroundings, like the Tocca, Darryl K and Cynthia Rowley sales. So either log on or call in for details.

Value 8   Range 8   Service 5

Soiffer/Haskin

www.soiffer
haskin.com
Ph: 718 747 1656
for details and
dates

If you have to remember one 'phone number this is it. This company specializes in sample sales and end of season stock sales for most of the top European designers at the most

wonderful prices. Indeed there is a move away
from designers organizing their own sample
sales in their own showrooms. Instead many of
them pass their inventory on to this company
who are the acknowledged specialists in the
area. Max Mara, Armani, Escada, Sulka,
Valentino, Donna Karan, Yves St. Laurent are
just some of the names. The sales are usually
held Tuesday to Saturday in the second floor
hall at Parsons College of Design, 7th Avenue at
West 40th Street (Phone: 212 229 8900).
Weekdays 9.00am to 5.00pm: only on sale
dates. Log on or 'phone either when you arrive
or before you leave home, for details of
upcoming sales. The value is terrific at these
sales. Merchandise is top quality and in pristine
condition. At a recent Escada sample sale,
couture gowns that had originally sold for from
$4,000- $8,000 were reduced to from $199 -
$599. My only gripe here is the changing room
conditions are awful but staff are very helpful.

Value 9   Range 9   Service 6
(can differ from sale to sale but in general)

Tahari Sample Sales

Sales twice a year: Amazing selection of day
and evening wear as well as separates. This
American label manufactures extremely well cut
clothes that have a distinct look of Armani
about them. They use superb fabrics, are
understated and always look terrific.

Value 10   Range 10   Service 8

Tocca

Where: 261 West 36th Street bet.7th and 8th Avenues
Ph: 212 929 7122
Hours: Check for dates and hours
Credit Cards: Major Credit Cards

I love the very pretty dresses and coats here. There are also great separates. This sales boasts discounts of up to 90%. Tocca's perfumed candles are among the best I have bought anywhere. Not great discounts on these, pricey but definitely worth it if you want that discreetly scented room.

 Value 10   Range 8   Service 6

The Mystery Sale

318, West 39th Street (11th Floor)
Ph: 212 239 7272
Hours: Check for dates and hours
Credit Cards: Major credit cards

I am on a bit of a wing and a prayer here. I attended this sale once and it was quite amazing. Lots of Miu Miu, Robert Clergerie and other designers too cool to be in a bargain warehouse. I don't know if it was a one off. It's worth checking out.

 Value 10   Range 9   Service 7

Yves Saint Laurent

543 Madison Avenue (54th and 55th Streets) 3rd Floor
Ph: 212 832 7100
Hours: Call for details
Credit Cards: **Cash only**

What can I say about YSL that hasn't already been shouted from the rooftops by fashionistas all over the world. I have got some beautiful, classic jackets and dresses here that over a decade later I refuse to throw out. I've also found great costume jewellery, belts and scarves. Everything at half price or less. Call for dates and times.

 Value 10   Range 8   Service 8

Log on Baby !!

Most of the larger stores now have great web sites so you can do a bit of virtual "window shopping" from your own armchair. It's also worth noting that stores post details of special sales on line and often hold clearance sales on line that are not held in the stores. Great web sites track all the special sales and bargains. In addition, some of these sites also monitor not only regular sample and showroom sales but also impromptu sales that pop up all over the place. This, or word of mouth, is the only way to find out about them.

www.nysale.com

This is the most important site for NYC bound bargain hunters. It lists, in separate categories, sales of every kind that are held in the City. It covers store, sample, warehouse and impromptu sales. In addition it lists sales on the day you log on as well as sales being held that week, that month and the next month. So it gives you plenty of time to do your home work.

www.bluefly.com

This is an online shopping site with discounts of up to 90% on normal retail prices. This site has a great selection of men's ladies, kids and maternity fashions and also has a home and gift section. Goods can be returned for a full refund within 90 days and delivery within the United States is usually one to two business days.

www.clothingline.com

Another resource for discounted design gear.

The site posts pictures of what's in stock at 2 locations in the City: Garment District Showrooms and SSS Sample Sale, 261, West 36th Street, 2nd Floor and Nice Price, 493, Columbus Avenue between 83rd and 84th Streets. The Sample Sale store features a different designer sale each week, check online for details and store hours which change regularly. Nice Price is an off price store and is open seven days a week.

www.dailycandy.com

Currently one of the easiest ways to track all up to the minute sales, this funky site charts every major as well as itty bitty sample sales. Just by loggin' on regularly, you can become a mine of information about just about anything that grooves in the Big Apple. It also includes updates on the latest 'in' bars and clubs and restaurants. This is a hip, fun site that will make you feel like a real Sex in the City gal or guy. Register, it's free, daily emails will keep you totally clued in.

www.overstock.com

Brilliant site for deep discounts on serious designer labels. Think Vera wang at up to 90% discount as well as St. John, Ralph Lauren and Badgley Mischa.

www.stylebug.com

A relatively new site. It has fab. deals on top designers like Vera Wang, Yves St. Laurent, Badgley Mischa at discounts of up to 90%

www.designerbargain.com

It's in the bag at www.designerbargain.com where you will find only the finest fashions and accessories passed on to you at discounts of up to 70%. Expect to find top European designers. You have thirty days to decide if your purchase is the killer buy you expected, if not you can return it for a full refund. Prada and Fendi were top of the pops the last time I logged on.

www.newyork.com

This is the New York Visitors and Convention Bureau site and it carries a ton of terrific info. including a designer sample sale section. This usually flags a dozen or more sales at any one time. The site also includes hotels rates, you can book on line, as well as the main events, sporting, entertainment etc. It's well worth a visit in advance of your trip.

www.nymetro.com

If you can only remember one web site, make sure it's this one. This New York Magazine site has possibly the best sales and bargains info. Click on Sales and Bargains. The column lists a good cross section of the week's bargain sales. New York magazine is published weekly, every Monday and costs $2.99. It also carries a good what's on listings section, restaurant guide as well as some very good, provocative writing on topical subjects.

www.polo.com

This is a newish site that carries all the latest from Ralph Lauren. It also features a fab. clearance warehouse where you can buy all kind of Ralph goodies for discounts of up to 50% The downside to this site is they do not accept non US based credit cards which really doesn't make any sense since all their stores accept all major credit cards regardless of what country they were issued in. When I complained they told me it was a regulatory regulation. Not so, because so many other web sites in the US accept all major cards regardless of where they are issued. However they did arrange for me to collect my order from the Madison Avenue / 72nd Street store in NYC, where I paid for it with my Irish issued American Express Card. Go figure!

www.soifferhaskin.com

VVIP: If you can remember two web sites, then make sure you file this one carefully. This site provides all the low down on major designer sample sales. In recent times many designers have discontinued holding their sample sales in their own showrooms. Instead they contract Soiffer Haskin, a company that specialises in Sample Sales, to conduct their sale instead. The company operates a terrific web site which details all sales at least a week in advance. Sales are usually flagged on line for the current month. Sales are held at Parsons College of Design on 7th Avenue at West 40th Street, 2nd Floor Auditorium, usually from Monday to Friday, unless otherwise specified. Staff are extremely helpful, but changing facilities barely exist. Major credit cards are usually accepted. The sales are always packed from 11.00am to 3.00pm. Best to get there earlier. As the week progresses there are even further markdowns. Merchandise is in pristine condition and includes current season, past season and even next season's samples. They usually have a very good range of sizes.

www.timeoutny.com

Time Out New York - Shoptalk Section is always right on the money when it comes to the latest sales. The Just Opened section tracks the newest stores in town. When it comes to tapping into the pulse of New York it's hard to beat TONY. It is great for current What's On listings. Published weekly. Cost: $2.99.

www.ebay.com

Ebay is a legend in it's own short but vastly profitable lifetime. Fashion is now the biggest business on ebay. Vintage accessories, Hermès Birkin and Kelly bags, Gucci, Fendi, Louis Vuitton are all available. If you are a gambler, you'll love ebay. Leave placing your bid until the last half hour of the items life span, that's when all the action starts. I have bought loads of things this way and I've never been disappointed. Of course good can be shipped anywhere in the world.

Fall/Winter Sales Calendar

Shopping is easy; bargain-hunting is hard, but so much more fun! Want to avoid paying top dollar for everything from great cashmere sweaters to belle of the beach bikinis? It's all a matter of timing and location. For details see Sample Sales section

November

MaxMara
Sleek, sophisticated women's fashion made from the most luxurious fabrics can be yours for half off at the company's massive, supremely popular sales.

Aeffe
Imagine half-price Narciso Rodriguez, Alberta Ferretti, Moschino, and Jean-Paul Gaultier, all under one roof. This sale, packed with women's clothes, bags, shoes, and even swimsuits, is the real deal.

Chaiken
Our favorite all-purpose urban fashion for work and for play, the clothes at this sample and stock sale are always sleek, chic, and amazingly well-priced (don't miss the $10 sample racks!).

TSE
Sure there are oodles of cashmere goods here, but there's also much more: cotton, silk, things for your house, and divine cashmere for your baby bambino. Get on line early, though—this place gets seriously packed.

Calvin Klein
Iconic American style—from Madison Avenue–priced Calvin Klein Collection all the way down to the mall-priced CK Jeans line. At the sample sale, it's all more than half off.

The News

Downtown hipsters don't need to trek all the way uptown for their street-chic staples. They all go on sale around now at this gallerylike showroom—Diesel, Margiela, Clements Ribeiro, Costume National, and more—at half the regular prices.

Beth Bowley

Cute, cute! That's what all the young women say when they see Bowley's sweet, festive, reasonably priced clothes. At Bowley's annual fall sample sale, they're a steal.

Elie Tahari

Great pants, classic shirts, mix-and-match suiting pieces that are serious enough for work and hip enough that you don't want to hide when you're wearing them. At the sample and stock sale, they're all more than half off.

December

Vera Wang

The No. 1 name in weddings is also a doyenne of classic, always-correct eveningwear. At her sample sales, you'll find it all for less than half what you'd pay in the store. But why are the sizes soooo small?!

Nicole Farhi

Nicole Farhi is one-stop shopping for intensely cuddly knitwear, gorgeous wool coats, and sleek pants. At the sample sale, all can be had for less than half what it fetches in the store.

One of a Kind Bride

Designer Candice Solomon's gowns are in the dreams of every would-be princess-bride. And if you stop by the sale, one can be yours for way less than the usual regal price.

Leigh Bantivoglio
Half off the daintiest, most delicate, and utterly divine underwear around. Just in time to give yourself a little pre-Christmas treat. Straight from Sex in the City girls!

Vivienne Tam
It may seem like your ordinary, old-fashioned store sale. But here's the thing: This one happens before New Year's Eve. Which is when you're planning on wearing those gorgeous party clothes, isn't it?

Inca
Whether you're heading for the islands or just thinking ahead to next summer, this is the time to pick up bright, bold bikinis, beach mats, and other sunny gear. It's all half off, after all.

Area
Huge discounts on our favorite neutral, ultra-luxe modern bed linens. I never miss this one.

Patch NYC
For gifts or for you, this reasonably priced sale (everything's under $100) of trendy bags, jewellry, and other accessories is a winner.

Liz Lange
Attention, all hip, urban mums-to-be: The ultimate in not-too-cute maternitywear can be yours at serious discounts if you stock up here now.

Roberta Chiarella
Fun, frivolous, crystal-embellished jewelry can do wonders to spruce up last year's basic black dress. At the sale, it's always a steal—practically everything's under $100.

Catherine Malandrino
Bright, sexy, and just-trendy-enough frocks and other festive fare—you've seen this collection at every high-end department store in town—are half-price when you buy them here.
A huge showroom packed with downtown-chic

designers from both sides of the Atlantic—
Imitation of Christ, Ghost, Erickson Beamon,
and more—this place cleans house around now,
marking everything down to less than half the
retail prices.

Meryl Waitz
Stocking stuffers galore—picture frames, bath
accessories, jewelry, and so on—at prices that
let you buy in pairs.

Stuart Weitzman
Imelda Alert! The more you buy, the more you
save at Weitzman's annual holiday shoe
blowouts. So don't choose: Get the stiletto boots
and the crystal-adorned sandals. Get the lot girls!

Autumn Cashmere
I just love it. Wouldn't evrn consider flyinmg
first class without my cashmere blanket! The
best cashmere doesn't always come in the
trimmest, most-figure-skimming shapes. Which
is the case here, where vast amounts of stock go
on sale for less than half of what you'd pay
elsewhere.

Daniel Levy
Daniel Levy's cool tone-on-tone modern
pottery—tableware, vases, and so on—is perfect
for gifts and a steal at his annual winter sale.

Miguelina
A festive addition to any hipster's wardrobe,
these bright, itsy-bitsy women's fashions are
half off at the sale.

Jay Strongwater
Delectably ornate, uptown-chic little picture
frames, boxes, and so on can be a serious deal if
you find them at a sale.

Vivienne Westwood
The queen of British fashion's annual winter
sale means more than half off everything from
perfectly cut pants to outrageously patterned
ensembles!

January

Martin
Most fashion that goes on sale in January is already so last season. But pick up something at half off here, and we pretty much guarantee that next season, you'll wear it twice as often as anything new.

ABC Carpet and Home
The winter clearance sale is not to be missed if you're in the market for top-quality linens, lamps, furniture, and more. This time of year, you can usually find them for up to 75 percent off. This is a must for anyone redecorating or especially for anyone who loves a great bargain.

Suarez
J'adore Suarez! In love with an iconic French handbag maybe a Kelly or Birkin?? You can find a snazzy look-alike—and many other chic, beautifully made styles—at Suarez's annual sale. In addition to the classics which are reduced the high fashion seasonal colours are a real steal.

Michèle Saint-Laurent
Maternitywear need not be boring. Here, it's fun, festive, and almost all from France. And at sale times, it's deeply discounted.

Judith Ripka
Glitzy, glamorous stone-encrusted jewelry is Ripka's forte—and finding it at her blowout half-off sales is good fortune indeed.

Sigerson Morrison
Nolita's original shoe store is always crazy busy. "Crazy Sale" time, when things are all under $250, is downright insane.

Diesel
Essential for any self-respecting teen hipster

and an instant way to add a touch of cool to an adult wardrobe. Diesel's denim and good old casual clothes are more than half off at the company's sample sales.

February

Rafe
By far the hippest bags for the price that we've seen, Rafe's wares are even more covetable at sale time, when they're up to 80 percent off.

Joël Name Optique
No need to keep saving for expensive designer eyewear. You can find it at this annual sale for up to half off.

Broadway Panhandler
Major Bargain Alert! This is as close as you will get to heaven if you are a kitchen lover. The lovably chaotic downtown pots-and-pans store takes about half off when it puts some of its top-end lines on sale. A lot of chefs shop here. You should, too.

Flight 001
No more boring luggage! Flight 001 furnishes the kind of travelers who swear by JetBlue and Virgin Atlantic with equally chic bags and accessories. Stock up at sale time, and you'll have cash left for the plane ticket.

Fetch
Sometimes even a dog could use a fashion fix. Millie and Molly just love their cool canine fashion from here. But these savvy bitches insist on shopping at sale time too!

Varasolona
All the gizmos, gadgets, and cute home accessories that you never knew you needed and had to have the second you saw them, on sale around now.

Leigh Bantivoglio

You've seen this label on the city's prettiest, most feminine lingerie, at stores like Bergdorf's. Get yours for next to nothing when Bantivoglio has one of her frequent sample blowouts.

March

Edmundo Castillo

Gloriously sexy, decadent footwear at half off!

David Saity

Turquoise-jewelry fans will find discount nirvana in this midtown source for Native American baubles and more.

Yeohlee

Ultra-sharp, trend-proof women's clothing (at stores like Bendel's) is more than half off if you buy it at the designer's showroom sale.

Boucher

Pretty, modern jewelry is surprisingly affordable at this cute downtown shop. At the sale, it's even more so.

French Connection

Who doesn't need great pants, a well-cut trench coat, the perfect turtleneck sweater? These and more are always available in abundance at this chain shop's massive blowout warehouse sales.

Wearkstatt

Just-hip-enough bridalwear is a steal if you fall in love with a sample at one of this company's sales.

Paula Varsalona for the Bride

Brides with princess fantasies and commoners' budgets can find dreamy dresses at a Varsalona sale for up to 70 percent off.

Triple Pier Antiques Show

There are deals and there's some serious dealing to contend with at this massive annual furniture market. Bargain hard! It's not the easiest place to get a bargain.

Paul Stuart

A classic for well-tailored American clothes for men and women, this Madison Avenue shop takes up to 80 percent off at seasonal sales.

Store Wars

New York City is blessed with some of the best and most beautiful department stores in the world some of which are a worldwide by word for directional fashion and luxury and are the yardstick by which department stores all over the world judge themselves. So what are they doing in a book about bargains? Well if you have tired of discount stores and want to blow the rest of your budget on one divine deal you will hit the jackpot in one of these stores. Take yourself off to any of New York's major department stores. Everyone will find just about anything from fashion from size 0 to 60, to dazzlingly beautiful household linen, fabulous furniture, jewels that cost a kings ransom, divine decorations, cosmetics that can do everything from stopping the clock to erasing wrinkles, books by the mile and no self respecting Imelda will be disappointed in the shoe sections.

I am skimming through these legendary stores since apart from sale times, they do not literally qualify as bargain or discount outlets. But that's not to say that there are not mega-bargains to be found during sale times. Sales are widely advertised in the New York Times, New York Post and New York Daily News. In addition the stores are always beautiful at holiday time and the windows in Barneys, Bergdorfs, Saks, Lord and Taylors and Macys are well worth a visit, especially if you have little ones with you.

For bargain hunters, keep an eye out for the many sales that are held during the year. Discounts of up to 80% are available at different times of the year

Barneys

www.barneys.com

Location

660, Madison Ave
between 60th
&61st Streets

Ph: 212 826 8900

Hours

Mon-Fri
10.00am-8.00pm

Saturday
10.00am-7.00pm

Sunday
11.00am-6.00pm

Credit Cards

Major credit cards

Barneys is the highest altar ever of high fashion.
If minimalism at surreal prices is your scene, then
this is the place to shop. Even the doormen wear
Armani here. This really is top of the shop pops.
For me the store has lost just about all of it's
original character during it's traumatic upheavals
in the 'nineties'. In fact I believe once it
transferred up town from Chelsea it was the
beginning of the end for Barneys as New Yorkers
had known and loved it for years.

It's a real see and be seen place, there is usually
some movie or TV star in a state of angst about
whether black is still the new black. If a lone,
black, Jean Muir dress on a seemingly mile long
clothes rack is your thing, then Barneys is for you.
There are some divine clothes at ultra de luxe
prices. The shoes here are stunning but so are the
prices. The cosmetics hall is interesting but not as
hip as Bendels. The Men's Department on the
Ground Floor is well worth a visit. Beautiful
shirts, sweaters and accessories exquisitely
displayed. But, like all the other stores Barneys
also has great sales with terrific discounts. The
windows in Barneys are always worth checking
out. Simon Dooney, chief designer is a living
legend. He regularly creates veritable works of art
in the windows along Madison Avenue.

Tick Tock: If you only have an hour in
Barneys don't miss the stunning shoe section.
Check out Barneys Co-Op, directional fashion at
a fraction of the prices on the main fashion floor
and Barneys Home, seriously luxurious goodies
for your little nest. Now that we have the
Princess, I always detour to the children's
department which has rig outs fit for royalty. Or if
you are totally wrecked from retail, pop down to
Freds in the basement. It's one of the happening
eateries on Madison but make sure the hair and
nails are done, it's all about grooming here. (By
the way the foods fab. too.)

Value 7   Range 6   Service 6

Bergdorf Goodman

www.bergdorf
goodman.com
754 5th Avenue
between 57th and
58th Streets
Ph: 212 753 7300
Hours
Mon-Sat
10am-7.00pm
Thursday
10am-8.00pm
Sunday
noon-6.00pm
Credit Cards
Major credit cards

When it comes to shopping this is Manhattan's pièce de resistance. Bergdorfs, is in my opinion, the most beautiful store in New York. It's also possibly the most exclusive and expensive. I always expect to bump into Edith Wharton here because this store is all about serious money and I think it still reflects everything that was so special about the New York of Wharton's Age of Innocence. Wonderful style, superb service and old money!

Now this is definitely the flip side of bargain shopping since you could drop half a million dollars or more in an hour before lunch. However, like the other stores, it does have splendid bargains at sale times. And even if you haven't won the lottery, it will lift your spirits to see such a magnificently laid out store. It's also worth a visit, even if your budget won't run to a Chanel suit at $10,000, to see the crème de la crème of the world's designer's creations and the Park Avenue princesses who buy them. Bergdorfs has one of the best ladies shoe departments in all of New York and the mark downs at sale times are terrific. They really clear all the old season's stock, often before the season is even over.

Bergdorfs for men is located across straight across 5th Avenue and has one of the best men's stores anywhere. I adore the Charvet section, the best outside the iconic store on the Place Vendôme. The sale assistants are quite so helpful and have great style. So I guess it's the old story, you pay your money and you take your choice! But remember the prices out of sale time here really do require an extremely healthy bank balance. But, as in the main store, the value at sale time is hard to beat. Perhaps that is why so many canny Wall Street types do their shopping here at sale time only. And I know a brace of billionaire's wives who always score their Chanel suits during the sale.

If you are planning to be a blushing bride, the

bridal department here is sheer magic.

 Tick Tock: Only got an hour. Bergdorfs has the legendary John Barrett hair salon. John is from Limerick and is recognized as one of the best locksmith's in the world. But you need an appointment, at least a month in advance. The Susan Ciminelli Day Spa is also among the best in the City. The art of pampering reaches new heights here. A veritable oasis pf calm, appointments needed here too. Otherwise I never pass the shoe department, always make a beeline to the Chanel shop and also always love to check out the cosmetics section downstairs.

Value 9   Range 10   Service 10 (at sale time)

Bloomingdales

www.blooming
dales.com
Lexington Ave
between 59th &
60th Streets
Ph: 212 705 2000
Hours
Mon-Fri 10-8.30pm
Saturday
10-7.00pm
Sunday
11-7.00pm
Credit Cards
Major credit cards
ATM in store

If you want to get a feel for what's hip and happening in New York, be sure to make Bloomingdales your first stop. It provides the best overview of just about everything retail in the City. Cutting edge is the best way to describe the legendary Bloomies on Lex. Whatever is a hit on the cat walks of Paris, Milan, London or New York will be walking out of Bloomingdales within a week, having been copied exclusively for the trend setting store.

The 4th Floor Designer Section has had a multi million dollar make over and is now the ultra luxurious home to just about every major designer. Chanel, Armani, Dolce & Gabana, Sonia Rykiel, Versace, Donna Karan, Ralph Lauren, Calvin Klein, Lagerfeld are only a fraction of the top names that have their own 'in store' stores on this floor. Price tags can look like international telephone numbers on this floor but keep an eye on your favourite outfit and check to see if it's in one of the many sales that are held during the year. If you are in town in the dying days of any of the major sales, take time out to go through the racks. There really are gems to be found at knockdown prices.

There is a terrific Louis Vuitton concession here and I just adore the Lancôme Eyebrow bar where I had the best eyebrow trim ever. A snip at $15.00! And I got so many freebie eye make up samples from my technician that I reckon I ended up making money. I also love the children's department with it's Tommy Hilfigger, Ralph Lauren, Dior, Donna Karan etc departments. Bloomies has a fab. beachwear and lingerie department. As a one stop shop it's hard to beat. Definitely has the best cosmetics hall in the city.

The furniture and rug departments are also well worth a visit and visitors from Europe regularly ship home pieces from these departments that, even with shipping charges, still work out significantly less than at home.Look out for the annual rug blow out!

Tick Tock: An hour in Bloomies should include a visit to either the beachwear or fur departments, a sort of ying and yang thing going on. The men's department here is also well worth a browse. But it's the cosmetics hall, with the possability of a make over that I would most look forward to.

 **Value 9   Range 10   Service 5**

Henri Bendel

www.henri
bendel.com
712 5th Avenue
between 54th
&55th Streets
Ph: 212 247 1100
Hours
Mon-Sat
10.00am-7.00pm
Thursday
10.00am-8.00pm
Sunday
noon-6.00pm
Credit Cards
Major credit cards

This used to be one of my all time favourite stores. Great directional ladies fashion and fabulous cosmetics companies, many designers who made their retail debut in Bendels went on to become international household names. But over the last few years I feel the store has lost it's edge. It is still a great place for every kind of sweater in cotton, cashmere, silk or wool. It does have a good millinery department and great faux jewellery. It is a great store for petites. But woe is me: the great restaurant on the first floor was gone when I last went there. It was a legendary meeting places in the city. I hope this is a temporary little arrangement.

Tick Tock. I was in Bendels for an hour recently and spent most of it checking out new cosmetics companies, cashmere and separates on the ground floor. I had a make over at MAC and tried several new fragrances in the perfume section.

Value 7   Range 6   Service 7

Jeffrey New York

Where:
449 W 14th Street
between 9th/10th
Avenues
Ph: 212 206 1272
Hours:
Monday-Weds
10.00am-8.00pm
Thursday
10.00am-9.00pm
Friday
10.00am-8.00pm
Saturday
10.00am-7.00pm

Not really a department store this is a seriously hip store, way over in the meat packing district of the Lower West Side, now dubbed the New West Coast. Don't let the warehouse feel of the place trick you into thinking that this is anything other than a mega expensive store indeed. The most expensive labels at top dollar - so what is it doing in a bargain guide? Like so many other places, they have mighty good sales here too. It's a great place to pick up your Manolo Blahniks at up to 60% off in the sale. The staff really know their stuff too.

Tick Tock: Make sure the Amex is in cracking good form. In an hour you'll get to check out the entire store but be very afraid of the damage you could do here.

Value 8   Range 7   Service 9   (at sale time)

Lord and Taylor

www.lordandtaylor.
com
424. 5th Avenue
between 38th&
39th Street
Ph: 212 391 3344
Hours
Monday/Tuesday
10.00am-7.00pm
Wednesday
10.00am-7.00pm
Thursday
10.00am-8.30pm
Friday
9.00am- 8.30pm
Saturday
9.00am-8.00pm
Sunday
10.00am-7.00pm
Credit Cards
Major credit cards

Lord and Taylor boasts the largest selection of ladies dresses in New York. Whether it's a bathrobe or a ball gown you will find it here and in every colour, shape and size. It is a vast multi floored department store but it's not a store that I ever feel I have to visit. If I'm walking down that part of 5th Avenue and have time on my hands, I check it out. For me this huge store is over stocked and it's hard to find anything there. Older New Yorkers are loyal to Lord and Taylor. It seems to have a life of it's own away from the hoi aristoi of the fashionistas that frequent Midtown and the Upper East Side. Somehow it reminds me of a provincial or mid west store, it's got that pile 'em high feel, even if they don't exactly sell'em cheap here.

Tick Tock: An hour to spend here would find me on the ground floor perusing the jewellery department. If I am up to my gills in carats I usually check out the lingerie and the cocktail dresses. I surprised my self about seven years ago when on one such visit I bought a fab. red, leather bikers jacket which I still adore.

Value 8   Range 7   Service 7   (at sale time)

Macy's

www.macys.com

Herald Square and
34th Street

Ph: 212 695 4400

Hours

Monday-Saturday
10.00am-8.30pm

Sunday
11.00am-7.00pm

Check extended
hours at sale times

Credit Cards

Major credit cards

ATM in store

11 floors of merchandise has always made
Macy's quite overwhelming for me but, this
store, that claims to be the largest department
store in the world, is a must stop shop for many
of my friends. You will find literally everything
here and walk miles in the process of locating it.
In addition to the major sales, there always
seems to be some one or two day sale here.
Check the newspapers or call for information.
End of season sales boast acres of fantastic
bargains. It's manic at sale time and also during
the holidays. It's got just about any designer of
men or ladies fashion, but I usually get lost
trying to find the department and give up. I
always say you need at least a day in Macys.

🕐   Tick Tock: I love the Cellar at Macys
which has a terrific kitchen department where
you can buy everykind of gadget and gizmo.
There is also a 'London pub' where you can
grab a decent sandwich. I got snowed in there
for a few hours on one occasion and ended up
totally furnishing and equipping an apartment
while the white stuff kept coming down outside.
Kids and tweens are really well catered for here
too.

Value 9   Range 9   Service 9   (at sale time)

Saks 5th Avenue

www.saksfifth
avenue.com

611, 5th Avenue
between 49th and
50th Streets

Ph: 212 753 4000

Hours

Monday-Saturday
10.00am-7.00pm

Thursday
10.00am-8.00pm

I love Saks or SFA as it is locally known. There
is nearly always some kind of sale or promotion
going on in the store and it's major sales are not
to be missed. The Cosmetics Hall that occupies
most of the ground floor is amazing. Every
cosmetic company you ever heard of and many
I'd guess, you haven't, all vie to sell their wares
here. The ground floor shopping hall is always
beautifully decorated with stunning seasonal
flowers. A visit here can be worth while just to
see these beautiful blooms. If you have time on

Sunday
12.00pm-6.00pm
Credit Cards
Major credit cards
ATM in store

your hands treat yourself to a free make up make over. There are usually make up artists at most of the counters only too happy to "reengineer your look for the new season". However be prepared for a hard sell when they finish. It's virtually impossible to escape without being arm locked into buying something. Try an inane line like "I'd love my Honey to see this first" or "Can I see how this reacts to the A/C or humidity" or even "I need to check with my allergist." !!!!!! Don't miss the following:

• Ladies shoe departments are among the best in the City. Chanel, Ferragamo, Manolo, Jimmy Choo, Burberry etc

• Several Fashion Floors cover all the bases from basics to top designer labels.

• Leisure Wear and Lingerie A vast selection of some of the best in the city.

• Men's department covers all the bases for the very well dressed man. A particularly good shirt department with top French, Italian and Jermyn Street shirt makers represented. One of my fave boys buys all his terrific ties here.

• Kids and infants. You can't ever start designer shopping too early

• Own brand cashmere department for gals is always worth checking out.

• SFA Fur Salon, great value at sale time usually around the end of March/beginning of April, mark downs of up to of 75%.

• Café SFA is a great place to have lunch. It looks out over the roof gardens of Rockefeller Center, the spires of St Patrick's Cathedral and 5th Avenue. Food is very good.

• In addition to the major sales there are frequent sales during the year when there are excellent mark downs throughout the store.

Tick Tock: When I only have an hour I usually check out the cocktail/evening dress department. It's one of the best in the City. I also love the handbags/luggage, shoes and the cashmere.

Value 9   Range 9   Service 8   (at sale time)

69

Quintessentially American

So many great fashion companies have started in the United States and spread their style gospel all over the world. Hence devotees of Donna Karan, Ralph Lauren, Calvin Klein, Ann Taylor, Stuart Weitzman, Timberland etc are to be found all over the world. Needless to say New York is HQ for most of them and it is Bargain Central too!

Apartment 48

48,W.17th Street
Ph: 212 807 1391
Hours:
Credit Cards: All
major credit cards

This is the ultimate experiment in retail reality. The store is designed as an apartment and everything is for sale. Some couples get so carried away they hang out here for hours on end. So New York! A mega for singletons, not exactly cheap but certainly cheeky and a bit of a giggle and if you are about to embark on the domestic dive stage of your life, you might just love it.

Ann Taylor

www.anntaylor.com
645 Madison
Avenue at 60th
Street
Ph: 212 832-9114
Hours Monday
Friday 10.00am
8.00pm
Saturday 10.00am
7.00pm
Sunday Noon
6.00pm
Credit Cards:
Major Credit Cards

This chain stocks well made ladies fashions that reflect the season's colours but tend not to be trendy. The range has an Armani feel to it. Excellent tailoring, good fabrics, understated and chic. It carries an extensive range of very small sizes as well as normal sizes. Prices are average, not hugely expensive, good value for what you get. At sale time there are reductions of up to 75%. That's the time to buy the basics, black suits, cotton shirts, coats etc. Call or check web for other branches

Ann Taylor Loft

www.anntaylor.com
1155 Third Avenue
at 68th Street
Hours
Monday Saturday
10.00am 8.00pm
Sunday
11.00am 7.00pm

This is a diffusion range, a similar look to the main Ann Taylor stores but prices and quality are cheaper. Still, it's a smart, well cut, preppy look and it's always 'in' even if it's not exactly directional fashion. It's a safe place to shop, if you are wary of being too high fashion. Call or check web for other branches.

Value 7   Range 7   Service 9

Banana Republic

www.banana
republic.com
625, 5th Avenue at
Rockefeller Center
Ph: 212 974 2350
Hours:
Mon-Sat 10.00am
to 7.00pm
Sunday 11.00am-
6.00pm
Credit Cards: Major
Credit Cards.

This is also part of The Gap chain and there are stores all over the city.

Clothes here are more formal, better quality and more expensive than The Gap. High fashion is affordable here though price tags have got much steeper in recent seasons. Wonderful coats, suits, dresses and separates for women and they also have great mens's stores and home interiors too The new flagship store is at Rockefeller Center on 5th Avenue and is well worth a visit. They will deliver to your hotel or apartment free from here and they will also charge your mobile 'phone while you shop. Check web or call for other branches.

Value 7   Range 8   Service 10

Bebe

www.bebe.com
1127, Third Avenue
at 66th Street
Ph: 212 935 2444
Hours
Monday Friday
10.00am 8.00pm
Saturday
11.00am 7.00pm
Sunday
11.00am 6.00pm

Bebe is one of the hottest, best value chains for all the latest looks with seriously cool price tags. But the clothes favour younger, fitter bodies that are no larger than a small size 12: THE place for the disco divas. Great shoes too. Great sales at the end of each season. Call or log on for other branches.

Value 9   Range 10   Service 10

Club Monaco

www.club
monaco.com
699 5th Avenue at
55th Street
Ph: 646 497 1444
Hours
Monday Saturday
10.00am 7.00pm

This is a relatively new Canadian chain that is a smash hit since it opened in Manhattan some years ago. It was acquired by Ralph Lauren in 2000 so expect to see an explosion of new stores. Really directional fashion for men and women and a great range of cosmetics and skin care products too. Everything is very well priced

Sunday
6.00pm

here and yes, they do have great sales. They are now in some of the outlet centers where the markdowns are mega. They also have great cosmetics and beauty products. Monica Lewinsky loves their lipsticks. Call or log on for other branches around the city.

| | Value 9 | Range 9 | Service 8 |

Crate and Barrel

www.crateand
barrel.com
650 Madison
Avenue
Ph:212 308 0011
Hours:Mon-Fri
10.00am-7.00pm
Sat 10.00am-
6.00pm
Sun12.00pm-
6.00pm
Credit Cards:
Major Credit Cards

Well worth a visit. One of the most popular places for Bridal Lists, so obviously a great place to buy wedding gifts. A wonderful section of homeware, gadgets, furniture and furnishings and now that homeware and furnishings are as season conscious as high fashion, each season has a whole new look and this is the place to see it at it's best. Very good prices and a great place for new décor ideas. They also have a wonderful range of everything you will need to decorate your home at Christmas. I love the upstairs furniture section. great pieces at knock out prices. Log on or call for other branches.

| | Value 8 | Range 10 | Service 9 |

Eddie Bauer

www.eddie
bauer.com
1172 Thirsd Ave
Ph: 212 737 0002
Hours:
Mon -Thurs.
9.00am-7.30pm
Fri 9.00am- 8.00pm
Sat
10.00am-7.00pm

Very popular with the 'dress down Friday' crowd because it stocks a wide range of great casual clothes for men and ladies. Persoanlly I find the ladies section very limited, it's yet another variation on the jeans and chinos look with OK shirts, sweaters, shorts etc. But to be honest there are more interesting places for gals to spend their dollars. Prices are keen year round but you can find some real steals at sale times. Log on or call to check out other branches in the city.

 Value 8 Range 6 Service 8

Gap

www.gap.com
680, Fifth Avenue
Ph:212 977 7023
Hours:Mon-Fri
10.00am-8.00pm
Sat 9.00pm-8.00pm
Sun 11.00am -
7.00pm
Credit Cards: Major
Credit Cards.

Gap now in addition to it's eponymous stores also has separate Gap Kids that caters for 2 year to about 12 year olds and Baby Gap, a must for all newborns to 2 years, Gap Maternity and Gap Body (underwear, perfumes, body lotions etc) around the city. Not all locations have all five stores so call your nearest location for details or check online. This is the flahship store and it has everything. This label has now achieved icon status around the world. It's the ultimate in hip recreational wear and what ever appears in The Gap will have a knock on throughout the fashion world. Jeans, sweat shirts, polo shirts, tee shirts, leather and suede jeans and jackets are all great value and very good quality.

For other store locations and hours log on or call the above number.

Value 10 Range 10 Service 10

Baby Gap Luxe
Details as above

Baby Gap Luxe takes the biscuit, even if you don't have a baby to buy for. If you are looking for a gift for the baby who has everything, why not buy a Cashmere polo shirt, leather jeans or suede mini skirt for a new born !!! What ever happened to the old babygro?

Value 8 Range 6 Service 8

75

Hammacher Schlemmer

www.hammachers
chlemmer.com
147, east 57th St
bet. lex and 3rd
Aves
Ph: 212 421 9000
Hours:
Mon- Sat 10.00am
- 6.00pm
Closed Sunday
Credit Cards: Major
Credit Cards.

The first of the great gizmo and gadget stores. I rarely pass by this one. It's a fun place to browse and a great place for gifts. Whether you are looking for a state of the art bottle opener for less the $100.00 or a bicycle for four at over $10,000 this is the place to shop. Great catalogue and super staff make shopping here the best fun. Try the massage chairs!

Value 8   Range 8   Service 10

Hold Everything

www.hold
everything.com
1311, 2nd Ave (bet
68th and 69th Sts.
Hours
Monday Friday
10.00am 8.00pm
Saturday
10.00am 7.00pm
Sunday
11.00am 6.00pm
Credit Cards Major
Credit Cards

This store literally stocks just about anything that can hold something. Great for bathroom organizers, drawer organizers, kitchen organizers, desk organizers, hatboxes, garment bags, laundry bags and baskets etc. It's one of those places where you nearly always buy something. Extremely helpful staff. Gets crowded at weekends.

Value 8   Range 10   Service 10

Pier 1 Imports

www.pier1
imports.com
1550, Third Avenue
at 87th Street
Ph: 212 987 1746
Hours: Mon-Sat
10.00am - 9.00pm
Sun 11.00am -
7.00pm
Credit Cards: Major
Credit Cards

I fell in love with this store in San Francisco when I was a student out on the West Coast. Back then it really did feel like an import warehouse and was one of the first stores to specialize in wicker and rattan furniture and fixtures and all things oriental. Since then it has become more main stream and the New York stores are very well laid out with the merchandise well displayed. A good selection of well priced china, glassware, furniture, as well as cushions, candlesticks, photoframes etc. In a nutshell everything hip that you will need especially for a first apartment. This store really appeals to first time home and apartment owners. Prices year round are good but are exceptional at sale time. It's also a great place for seasonal goodies, picnic baskets etc during the summer and great Christmas gift ideas from the middle of November on. Check for other branches.

Value 8   Range 8   Service 7

Pottery Barn

www.potterybarn.com
117,E. 59th Street
between Lex and
Park Aves
Ph: 917 369 0050
Hours:
Mon-Sat
10.00am-8.00pm
Sun:
11.00am-7.00pm

A great store for everything to do with homeware, glass and china. There is also a small rug department. This is where furnishings meet fashion with each season's high fashion colours featured in curtains, cushions and other accessories. If you are interested in interior design and décor it's worth a visit to check out all the latest. At sale times there are great bargains. Also a great catalogue.

Value 8   Range 8   Service 10

Ralph Lauren

www.polo.com
867 Madison Ave
at 72nd Street.
Ph: 212 606 2100
Hours: Mon-Sat
10.00am-6.00pm
Thurs: 10.00am-
7.00pm
Sun: 12.00pm-
5.00pm
Credit Cards:
Major Credit Cards.

It started with a tie over 35 years ago now Ralph Lauren rules the world. The ubiquitous polo shirt is probably one of the most copied fashion items anywhere but Ralph has a lot more up his extremely well designed sleeve than these shirts which sport 'My Little Pony'. Stunningly tailored mens suits, egyptian cotton shirts, cashmere sweaters, everything for baby and toddler and an endless collection of ladies fashion. Then there is bed linen, home ware, sportswear. Best go by there and check it out yourself. This is the legendary Rhinelander

Mansion, flagship store. It is the ultimate in aspirational shopping. It seems as if everyone who works and shops here is a bit player in the overall plan to create a perfect Ralph Lauren world. Call or log on for other stand alone stores. Most major department stores all have ralph lauren departments. All these stores have great sales.

Value 6   Range 9   Service 9

Sharper Image

www.sharper
image.com
4, West 57th Street
(just west of 5th
Avenue)
Ph: 212 265 2550
Hours
Monday-Saturday
10.00am-7.00pm
Sunday
11.00am-6.00pm
Credit Cards Major
Credit Cards

This is the ideal place to find all those kooky gifts for that hard to please family member for friend. It is full of gadgets and gizmos many designed by the store and exclusive to it. Ever feel you have to have a CD player in your shower ? Well you will find one here. It is great for telescopes, massage chairs, weird and wonderful audio and video gear. Some of the products seem pricey but since it's not possible to source them anywhere else, if you want them, you just have to pay up.

Value 7   Range 9   Service 10

Williams Sonoma

www.williams
sonoma.com.
1175 Madison
Avenue: 86th Street
and Madison
Ph: 212 289 6832
Hours
Monday Friday
10.00am 7.00pm
Saturday
10.00am 6.00pm
Sunday 12.00pm

The ultimate store for cooks. This has everything you ever will ever need for your kitchen and dining room. Great pots, pans, knives, dishes, tools, books, china and glassware etc. It is the ideal place to find great housewarming and wedding gifts and it is also the place to find the very latest gadgets and gizmos for the chef in the family. Very busy at weekend when so many Manhattan house husbands gather to check the latest All Clad saucepans! Great demonstrations in the store

6.00pm
Credit Cards Major
credit cards

and also great markdowns. All my great suacepans and carving knives have been bought here at mind blowingly cheap prices.

 Value 8   Range 10   Service 9

And clearance store at:

110 7th Avenue, Chelsea
Ph: 212 633 2203
Hours: Monday Friday 10.00am8.00pm
Sunday 12.00pm 6.00p
Credit Cards: As Above

Plucking the Best Bargains on Orchard Street

This was the original bargain, discount rag trade center of New York. It was also home to many Jewish families when they arrived in the New World and indeed many Jews still live and work in the area. The movie the Jazz Singer was filmed on location here. But time has been catching up with Orchard Street and while the original tenements still remain and it is still home to loads of discount clothes stores it is rapidly becoming gentrified and a whole new crowd go there now to check out great art galleries, boutiques and night clubs. Heck, there is even a brand new apartment block on the Houston Street corner that has rents as exorbitant as the Silk Stocking area of the Upper East Side.

Orchard Street intersects a warren of other streets that at one time all had their own specialty, ie ladies fashions, mens suits, furs, fabrics, bedlinen, lingerie etc. Many of the old shops and characters are gone and Chinatown seems to be inching further over here almost daily. Sunday is busiest shopping day. Then Orchard Street becomes a pedestrian zone and takes on a carnival atmosphere. Loads of stalls out on the streets hawk knock off 'designer' watches, bags, baseball caps, luggage and leather goods. The quality is very mixed but you'll find plenty of pressie/stocking filler material here. You will also be quite safe here but be alert for pickpockets. Cash is king here and don't be afraid to bargain.
NB Many stores close early afternoon on Friday and all day Saturday for the Jewish Sabbath.

Altmans Luggage

135 Orchard Street
Ph: 212 254 7275
Hours
Sunday-Friday
9.00am-6.00pm
Saturday Closed
Credit Cards Major
cards but a better
deal for cash

Great place and prices for Haliburton, Samsonite, Tumi, American Tourister. Very good selection here. Staff can be pushy but ignore them. You MUST bargain here too. Also good for Filofax and Mont Blanc pens.

 Value 9   Range 8   Service 5

Fine and Klein

119 Orchard Street
Ph: 212 674 6720
Hours
Sunday-Friday
8.30am-4.30pm
Saturday Closed
Credit Cards
Major credit cards

Good looking bags and shoes made in Italy. This used to be a big favourite of mine but the arrival of the outlets where you can find the original designers at discount prices have made it rather redundant now. I also find it a bit dated so I don't drop by here too often anymore. They also have a shoe section now, good looking shoes but rather overpriced. Pushy, disinterested staff are no incentive to return here.

Value 7   Range 6   Service 5

Fishkin Knitwear

314 Grand Street at
Allen Street
Ph: 212 226 6538
Hours
Monday-Thursday
10.00am-5.00pm
Friday 10.00am-
4.00pm
Saturday Closed
Sunday 9.00am-
4.30pm
Credit Cards Major
credit cards but best
deals for cash

DKNY, Liz Claiborne, Eileen Fisher (great leisure wear) are some of the brands you will find here. About 30% off. The store doesn't look much and the staff are pushy and quite unhelpful. But it does carry a good selection of cashmere in all styles and colours and well priced Pashminas. There is also a small shoe section in the back that's worth casting an eye over if you're in the store but I wouldn't make the trip especially to check it out.

Value 8   Range 5   Service 5

Forman's Apparel

82 Orchard Street
between Broome
and Grand Streets
Ph: 212 777 3600
Hours -
Orchard Street
Sunday-Weds
9.00am-6.00pm
Thursday
9.00am-8.00
Friday
9.00am-2.00pm
Saturday Closed
Credit Cards
Mastercharge and
Visa

In recent years this company has really expanded from its rather humble Orchard Street origins to now having a store on Fifth Avenue. Formans stock a good range of regular, plus and petite sizes. It's great for right up to the minute American designers for ladies only: Jones New York, Adrienne Vittaddini, Dior, Burberry etc. The very same ranges are found in midtown Department Stores but are at least 30% cheaper here. Also great 'on sale' section where reductions run from 30% to 80%. Check the basement. Ignore the v. pushy and unhelpful staff.

 Value 8   Range 7   Service 4

Best Buy: Navy cashmere coat with mink collar: $99.00

Giselle:Sportswear Inc

www.gisellenew
york.com
143 Orchard Street
(between Delancey
and Rivington
Streets)
Ph: 212 673 1900
Hours
Monday-Thursday
9.00am-6.00pm
Friday:
9.00am-4.00pm
Saturday Closed
Sunday
9.00am-6.00pm
Credit Cards Major
credit cards

Major fashion/bargain alert! This is one of the best stores on Orchard Street. Four floors packed to the gills with leading European designers Escada, Valentino, Ungaro, Mondi, Emanuel, Laurel, Iceberg. Sizes 4-20 All current stock at about minimum 20% cheaper...For Euro visitors to New York it is brilliant value now with the strong E. Check the 'on sale' section. They also have knock out sales here. Not the most helpful staff I've ever encountered.

Value 8   Range 9   Service 6

Best Buy: Valentino linen jacket and trousers $130. In Bergdorfs, the same suit was $659.00

Harry Zarin Fabrics

www.harryzarin.com
72 Allen Street at
Grand Street (just
off Orchard Street)
Ph: 212 925 6112
Hours
Monday-Thursday
9.00am-6.00pm
Friday
9.00am-4.00pm
Saturday/ Sunday
9.00am-6.00pm
Credit Cards Major
credit cards
accepted. But cash
is king

One of the biggest selections of every imaginable kind of furnishing fabric can be found in this warehouse. Take your time and poke about. You will more than likely find what you want. Very helpful staff. Best bargain for cash, especially bargain for tax off. They will gladly give you sample fabric swatches here and you can then order by phone. This store ships all over the world. It also makes curtains, bedcovers, cushions etc to order. The quality of the work is first class, extremely good value and is usually completed well within a few weeks or sometimes even days from the order date. If you work for Aer Lingus or a major airline they love you, so tell a white lie and say you're a trolley dolly. See the bargains that await you then!

 Value 10   Range 10   Service 10

Best Buy: 14 yards of toile de jouy for $100. I had almost bought the identical designer fabric in Paris for nearly $200 a meter and in a sale in London, for over £100 a yard.

Joe's Fabric

102 Orchard at
Delancey Street
Ground floor for
trimmings
First floor for
fabrics
Ph: 212 674 7089
or 212 614 6901
Hours
Monday-Thursday
9.00am-6.00pm
Friday 9.00am-
4.00pm
Saturday Closed

Great value here though prices have been creeping up recently as the store becomes posher. Joe is a great character. Tell him you're from Ireland and that you work with an airline , they love the Aer Lingus girls here too, and you'll get an even better deal. Pay in cash and he won't charge tax. This is an Alladin's Cave of furnishing fabrics and trimmings. Great moiré silks for under $10.00 a yard. Great printed organzas, $6.00 a yard. Toile de Jouy $15.00 a yard. Velvets, cottons, towelling, brocades and tapestries. I recently saw wonderful Versace furnishing fabric for $25.00 a yard. Up town the same fabric was $150.00 a yard. Joe now

Sunday 9.00am-
6.00pm
Credit Cards Major
credit cards
accepted but cash
is king

has a good selection of furnishing trimmings. Curtains are made to measure and shipped all over the world.

Value 9	Range 9	Service 9

Best Buy: Silk organza @ $10.00. Uptown the same fabric sold for $40.00 a yard. Moire silk $9.99 a year.

Klein's of Monticello

105, Orchard Street
at Delancey Street
Ph: 212 966 1453
Hours
Monday-Friday
10.00am-5.00pm
Saturday Closed
Sunday 10.00am-
5.00pm
Credit Cards
Mastercharge,
Visa, American
Express

One of the best stores on Orchard Street with a great selection of European designers here. Max Mara, Les Copains, Malo cashmere, Vestimenta. Prices are higher than in the rest of the Street but the stock is always pristine and current, the merchandise well displayed, the store is hip and service is v. helpful. This is one to watch, especially at sale time.

Value 9	Range 9	Service 9

Lea's Designer Fashion

119 Orchard Street
at Delancey Street
Ph: 212 677 2043
Hours: 7 Days
10.00am-5.00pm
Credit Cards Major
credit cards

Louis Feraud, Kenzo, Albert Nippon and other European designers.
Good selection, an older look. Good discounts but be prepared to haggle over the price.

Value 8	Range 7	Service 7

Orchard Corset Discount Center

www.orchard
corset.com
157 Orchard Street
Ph: 212 674 0786
Hours Sunday
Thursday
Friday
Sunday Closed
Saturday
Credit Cards Major
credit cards

This isn't exactly the most inviting lingerie store I have ever been in and if you are looking for La Perla frillies you won't find them here. But you will find most main stream US labels and bras in every size and shape. **Major 'Fashion Moment!** The store also specialises in amazing waist cinchers that knock up to four inches off your waist instantly! Brilliant for brides! Girdles, teddies, bridal lingerie are all stocked and the prices can't be beaten, up to half wholesale. The store is owned by an Orthodox Jewish family,who have run the business for the last 70 years. They have an unerring eye when it comes to guessing your correct bra size, even if this eyeing up can be a little disconcerting.

Value 9   Range 8   Service 5

M&A Decorators Fabric Store

294 Grand Street
between Allen and
Elridge Streets
Ph: 212 226 3910
Hours
Sunday-Friday
9.30am-6.00pm
Saturday Closed
Credit Cards
Mastercharge and
Visa only

All designer fabric, this store boasts uptown quality at downtown prices. The selection is somewhat limited but if you find what you want here, the value is terrific. The staff are all very helpful here.

Value 10   Range 5   Service 8

Mendel Goldberg Fabric

**72 Hester Street
(between Allen &
Orchard Streets)
Ph: 212 925 9110
Hours
Monday-Thursday
9.30am-6.00pm
Friday
9.30am-4.00pm
Saturday Closed
Sunday
9.30am-6.00pm
Credit Cards
Major credit cards**

One of the best dress/ suiting fabric stores in
the city, wonderful wools, cottons, lace and silk.
They have all the 'in' fabrics at a fraction of the
cost. They can also recommend a good tailor.
You will also find a good selection of
buttonsand trimmings in this store.

Value 8   Range 8   Service 7

Sheila's Interiors

**68, Orchard Street
at Grand Street.
Ph: 212 777 3767
Hours
Monday-Thursday
9.30am-5.00pm
Friday
9.30am-3.00pm
Saturday Closed
Sunday
9.30am-5.00pm
Credit Cards
Major credit cards**

A good selection of furnishing fabric, though I
have found the same fabrics further along the
street at Joe's Fabrics, quite a bit cheaper. Very
good value on all wall coverings, silks, hession,
wallpaper etc and blinds down in the basement
are really knock down prices. Staff not
especially helpful.

Value 8   Range 8   Service 7

Soho:

Broadway from Houston Street south to Canal Street

SoHo is So Hot right now. Hip fashion, shoe and lifestyle stores are opening along this stretch every week. Downtown is the new midtown right now. It's now considered the hottest, funkiest retailing area in New York City. Prada, YSL, Chanel are all down here, while most of the chain stores also have a presence, there is still that edgy Village vibe to the area.

1909 Company

63 Thompson
Street
Ph: 212-343-1658
Credit Cards:
Major Credit Cards

Vintage Clothing, so hot right now, is fab. here.

 Value 8   Range 6   Service 5

Alice Underground

481 Broadway
Ph: 212-431-9067
Credit Cards:
Majpr Credit Cards

All the vintage classics: corduroys, embroidered blouses from the forties and fifties, even jeans skirts made from old Sergio Valentis and Calvins.

 Value 7   Range 9   Service 7

Andy's Chee-pees

www.andys
cheepees.com
691 Broadway
Ph: 212-420-5980
Credit cards:
Major Credit cards

If colorful jackets and polyester graphic shirts are what you're after, Andy's delivers the look..

Value 8   Range 8   Service 9

A Detacher

262 Mott St. near
Houston St
Ph: 212-625-3380
Hours:
Credit Cards:

Achingly beautiful fashon, the prices will give you a headache too unless you buy in the sale.

Value 7   Range 8   Service 10

Anna Sui

www.annasui.com
113 Greene St.
Ph: 212-941-8406
Hours:
Mon - Sat
11.30am - 7.00pm
Sun.
12.00pm to 6.00pm
Credit Cards: All
major credit cards

This boutique looks like the boudoir of Cabaret's Sally Bowles. And most of the clothes have that girlie boudoir feel too. It's it's your thing, it's a terrific look but sizes are small. Sale is big.

	Value 6	Range 8	Service 9

Bagutta Life

72-76 Greene St.
Ph: 212-925-5216
Hours:
Mon- Sat
11.00am - 7.00pm
Sun
12.00pm - 6.30pm
Credit Cards: All
major credit cards.

In the great multi-designer-boutique tradition of Colette, Browns, and Corso Como, we now have a vastly expanded Bagutta which is quite stunning. Catch it at sale time or be prepared to give your flexible friend a thorough work out!

	Value 6	Range 8	Service 9

Banana Republic Ladies and Home Store

552,Broadway
between Spring
and Prince Street
Ph: 212 925 0308
Hours
Monday-Saturday:
10.00am-8.00pm
Sunday
11.00am-7.00pm
Credit Cards
Major credit cards

Details as for Midtown store

	Value 8	Range 8	Service 10

Banana Republic Menswear

528, Broadway at
Spring Street
Ph: 212 334 3034
Hours
Monday-Saturday
10.00am-8.00pm
Sunday
11.00am-7.00pm
Credit Cards
Major credit cards

Details as for 5th Avenue store

Value 8   Range 8   Service 9

Canal Jeans

www.canaljean.com
Moved from SoHo
to 2236 Nostrand
Ave, near Ave H.
Ph: 718 421 7590
Hours
9.30am-9.00pm:
365 days a year
Credit Cards: Major
Credit cards

This store still claims to be one of New York's most exciting clothes stores even though it's now moved across to Brooklyn. It has got to be one of the biggest jeans stores anywhere. If jeans, jeans and more jeans is you bag, then this is definitely for you. This five floor jean heaven stocks every brand of jeans, new, vintage, retro; jackets, shirts etc. that you have ever heard of and probably many you haven't. Prices are very competitive year round but at sale times quite unbeatable.

Value 8   Range 10   Service 8

Chanel

www.chanel.com
139 Spring St. near
Wooster St.
Ph: 212 334-0055
Hours:
Mon -Sat
11.00- 7.00pm
Sun:
12.00pm- 6.00pm
Credit Cards: All
major credit cards

Decades after Coco "invented" the little black dress, Chanel is still synonymous with chic. Designer Karl Lagerfeld has updated company signatures like gardenias, tweeds, and quilted bags, and has added a whopping dose of street cred. Always worth a visit if you are a Coco gal, but not to be missed at sale time when Chanel becomes quite affordable. This is quintessential investment dressing, I have suits that are nearly twenty years old and they still get copious compliments. Want to buy something here?

Perhaps a bottle of No. 5 or a lipstick (from $23) may not pack the wallop of a Chanel suit, but there's nothing chicer to whip out of your purse or pocket book. And yes, they do come in those shiny black shopping bags that j'adore.

Value is in the eye of the beholder
Range 10   Service 9 (if they like you)

Chill on Broadway

427 Broadway
Ph: 212 343 2709
Hours
7days 10.00am-
8.00pm
Credit Cards Major
credit cards

If you are under 16 and disco bound this is the place to get the gear. Since I don't qualify it's not my scene but I still check it out regularly and the place is always abuzz with very trendy teens gear. It's that sort of budget JLo look

Value 8   Range 8   Service 7

Club Monaco

121 Prince Street
Ph: 212-533-8930
Hours: Mon Sat
10.00am- 8.00pm
Sunday 11.00am-
7.00pm
Credit cards: All
Major Credit Cards.

This one time, Canadian chain is now owned by Ralph Lauren but its sleek urban basics keep getting better. Always well priced, sale time here is a total winner. Always worth a visit! And don't forget CM do great cosmetics too! Monica Lewinsky buys her lipsticks here.

Value 8   Range 8   Service 10

Costume National

www.costume
national.com
108 Wooster Street
Ph; 212-431-1530
Hours:
Mon-Sat
11.00am- 7.00pm
Sunday
12.00pm - 6.00pm
Credit Cards: All
major cards

The dramatic collection housed in this shadowy shop is sleek and tailored and attracts style hounds from far and wide. Flattering tailoring is worth the premium price tags. But it's got to be sale time when prices are very special.

Value 6   Range 9   Service 10

Cynthia Rowley

www.cynthia
rowley.com
112 Wooster Street
Ph: 212-334-1144
Hours:
Mon- Sat
11.00pm - 7.00pm
Sun
12.00pm-6.00pm
Credit Cards: All
major credit cards

Extremely chic and wearable dresses, and separates. Possibly a bit on the pricey side for what they are but you know when you want that simple little dress and you can't unearth it anywhere. The odds are you'll score it here.

Value 7   Range 9   Service 9

Daffys

www.daffys.com
Where:
462, Broadway at
Grand Street
Ph: 212 334 7444
Hours
Monday-Thursday
10.30am-7.30pm
Friday and Sat.
10.30am-8.00pm
Sunday
12.00pm-7.00pm
Credit Cards Major
credit cards. No
American Express

It can be hit or miss at this Soho branch of Daffys. Somehow or another the windows always look far more appealing than the merchandise available in the store. The basement is extremely disorganized and quite claustrophobic.

Value 8   Range 7   Service 5

Daryl K

21 Bond Street
Ph: 212-777-0713

Dublin born Darryl Kerrigan was one of the hottest names in New York fashion before she sold out to a Japanese conglomerate some years ago. She's back in action in her own right again and she's as edgy and funky as ever.

Value 7   Range 9   Service 6

David Aaron

529, Broadway
between Spring
and Prince Streets
Ph: 212 431 6022
Hours:
Mon/Tues/Wed/Sun
11.00am-8.00pm
Fri/Sat:
11.00am-8.30pm
Credit cards
Major credit cards

Own design, pretty cool shoe shop. A must for funky footwear lovers. Pretty cool prices too.

Value 9   Range 10   Service 10

Eddie Bauer

www.eddiebauer.com
578 Broadway
Ph: 212-925-2179
Credit Cards: All
major credit cards.

You won't set the fashion fires blazing here but these well-made, affordable togs-short-sleeved shirts ($30), sweaters ($48), gabardine pants ($68), and fleece anything-are so comfortable, you'll most likely emerge laden down with bags. A one stop shop for 'Dress Down Friday'. Great value year round becomes a total steal at sale time.

Value 10   Range 8   Service 10

Label

265 Lafayette
Street
Ph: 212-966-7736
Credit Cards: All
major credit cards

If you're in search of a perfect silk party dress,
look no further.

Value 8   Range 7   Service 5

H&M

www.h&m.com
558, Broadway at
Prince
Ph: 212 343 1787
Hours:
Monday-Sat.
10.00am-9.00pm
Sunday:
10.00am-8.00pm

Unless you get there early this store is always
busy. I find it very claustrophic downstairs and
the fashion here is also poorly displayed.
Fashion for guys and gals only at this store.
Other details as before.

Jariel Fabrics

401, Broadway.
(a block south of
Canal Street)
Ph: 212 226 7967
Hours:
Mon- Fri
10.00am 6.30pm
Sun.
1.00pm 6.00pm
Closed Saturday
Credit Cards:
Major credit cards

Don't judge this store by it's exterior, not that
the interior is exactly plush either. But I love the
character of this lower Manhattan store. This is
one of my favourite furnishing fabric stores in
the city. Owner Jack has impeccable taste and
his prices can't be beaten either. He specialises
in end of runs, overruns, cancelled orders etc
and the value here is brilliant. You can find
fabrics that originally sell at a couple of
hundred dollars a yard on sale here for under
$30.00. Of course it helps to have your
window/ sofa etc measurements, but even if you
don't, genius Jack will be able to help you. He
supplies stage, TV and movie sets and ships
fabric all over the world. He is also an
exceptionally pleasant and knowledgeable.

Value 10   Range 7   Service 10

Old Navy

www.oldnavy.com
511 Broadway
between Spring
and Broome
Streets
Ph: 212 226 0838
Hours
Monday-Saturday
9.30am-9.00pm
Sunday
11.00am-8.00pm
Credit Cards
Major credit cards

This is a must shop store for anyone with kids who demand the latest New York gear. Part of the Gap chain the value is terrific in everything for a "relaxed lifestyle " from newborn and kids to adult, guys and gals. Really terrific value all year round but mega value at sale times. If you want to get a feel for the merchandise, check the Old Navy Web Site. It certainly more than sets the scene before you visit the store. Terrific staff make shopping so much less stressful. I usally just give 'my list' to one of the crew, who round up everything for me. Get there early. Animal at weekends and holidays. Check out lines can go on forever.

 Value 10   Range 10   Service 10

O.M.G inc

www.omg.com
476 Broadway
between Broome
and Grand Streets
Ph: 212 343 1164
And at
546 Broadway
between Prince
and Spring Streets
Ph: 212 925 9513
And at
428 Broadway
between Canal and
Howard Streets
Ph: 212 925 5190
Hours
Monday-Saturday
9.30am-9.00pm
Sunday:
10.00am-8.00pm
Credit Cards:
Mastercard, Visa
and American
Express

This mini chain has brilliant value if you are looking for casual clothes. This is a good place to buy discounted jeans, tee shirts and shirts. There is also a quite good line in calvin klone and Donna karan underwear at knock out prices. Stock is constantly changing so don't plan on mulling over your purchases, if you want it, buy it. Clothing for men, ladies and children. Great for sweat shirts and gym clothes too. Expect to see Calvin Klein, DKNY etc. very deeply discounted.

 Value 9   Range 7   Service 7

Pearl River Mart

www.pearlriver.com
477 Broadway,
between Grand St.
and Broom St
Ph: 212 431 4770
Hours 7 days
10.00am 7.20pm
Credit Cards Major
credit cards and
ATM on premises

Since this Chinese superstore went mainstream last year and moved from upstairs on Canal Street, it has lost a lot of it's charm. It used to be like a Hong Kong market, now it's gone all sleek and organized. The stock and prices are still the same and since it's where many of the Chinese Americans shop themselves, you know you're in the right place. Everything from Oriental silk fashions, currently all the rage, silk fabric, flip flops, bags, bed linen, bamboo blinds, paper lanterns, you name it, this is where to find it. They also sell food and the special appliances needed to cook it. There is a Chinese pharmacy where all kinds of potions and weirdo looking things, are pounded and ground by offical looking pharmacists. Even if you are not going through a Chinese phase, it's well worth a visit just for the experience.

They have a wonderful china and pottery section and beautifully glazed plates here were less than half the price I saw them in a midtown homeware chain. If you are planning to purchase here, make sure you have plenty of time. At weekends queues are endless, service is very iffy. Shipping can be arranged.

Value 10   Range 10   Service 4

Pottery Barn

www.potterybarn.com
600, Broadway at
Houston
Ph 212 219 2420
Hours
Monday Saturday
10.00am 9.00pm
Sunday
11.00am 7.00pm
Credit Cards Major
credit cards

Since furniture, furnishings and interiors in general have all become subject to seasonal fashion, this is a great place to get the beat of what's hot for your living room, bedroom, garden etc. It is also where you will find seasonal gift items, Christmas, Thanksgiving, 4th July etc. Time was when this was a "must visit" store but so many newer stores are now doing the same thing and often with better prices. Still, it's always worth a visit!

Value 7   Range 8   Service 7

Raes Interior Fabrics

www.raetrading.com
452 Broadway,
South of Grand
Street
Ph: 212 966 1414
Hours
7 days
11.00am-6.00pm
Credit Cards Major
credit cards(but a
better deal for
cash)

This is yet another Alladin's Cave of wonderful furnishing fabrics. Prices are quite incredible and there are frequent sales. They love the Irish here. Pay cash and you won't pay tax. I love Raes fabrics. The vast selection of all kinds of furnishing fabric covers all the bases: from top designer names to just regular cottons, silks and moirés. The value is terrific even so don't be afraid to bargain. The staff is particularly helpful and knowledgeable here but do bring you window measurements with you. They also make curtains and furniture coverings. They do beautiful work in minimum time and their prices are the most competitive. Also check out the bargain basement, amazing fabrics, many at under $10.00 a yard.

Value 10   Range 8   Service 10

Scoop

www.scoopny.com
532 Broadway at
Spring Street
Ph: 212 925 2886
Hours
Monday-Saturday
11.00am-8.00pm
Sunday:
11.00am-7.00pm
Credit Cards
Major credit cards

This is not a discount store but it is one of the hippest boutiques in the city. This one is far more fun than the very snooty one on 3rd Avenue on the Upper East Side. Prices are quite outrageous outside of sale time but two terrific sales give huge reductions and it's always good to know what's happening in the fashionista's world. It's straight from Sex in the City.

Value 7   Range 8   Service 7

Sephora

www.sephora.com
Location
555, Broadway
Ph: 212 625 1309

This is a branch of the hugely trendy LVMH owned cosmetic store that took Paris by storm when it was launched there a few years ago. There are no counters or pushy sales assistants. All products are arranged on shelves and free

Credit Cards
Major credit cards

standing show cases, by category rather than maker so you will find acres of lipsticks by every cosmetics house, moisturizers, nail enamels, brushes, perfumes etc. It's self service but if you need expert or any advice the sales team are extremely helpful. The price range also runs the whole gamut from extremely inexpensive all the way up to the stratosphere. Look out for Sephora own label, colours are always to die for and bang up to the minute as well as terrific value. Despite all the hype the flagship 5th Avenue store at Rockefeller Center only lasted jig time.

Value 9   **Range 10**   **Service 10**

SOHOME

www.sohome.com
499 Broadway
between Spring and
Broome Streets
and at
70 Mercer Street
Ph: 212 226 5446
Hours:
Everyday except
Thursday
9.30am -7.30pm
Thursday:
10.00am -8.00pm
Credit cards:
Major credit cards

I love this rather quirky home store. It has all sorts of unusual pieces for the home and the value is terrific here. Check out bed linen and towels as well as funky shower curtains and cushions. Amazing prices and quality keeps improving. Lots of fun stuff at seriously discounted prices.

Value 10   **Range 10**   **Service 8**

Stephane Kélian

www.stephane
kélian.fr
158 Mercer Street
Ph: 212-925-3077
Hours:
Mon-Sat.
11.00am -7pm;
Sun.
12.00pm-6pm
Credit Cards: All
major credit cards.

To die for shoes, nightmare prices but fabulous reductions at sale time. Sales held twice a year. Call for info.

Value 8   Range 10   Service 6

Western Spirit

www.westernspirit
2000.com
486 Broadway at
Broome Street
Ph: 212 343 1476
Hours 7 days
11.00am 8.00pm
Credit cards:
Major credit cards

This claims to be the largest Western shop in New York City stocking native American art, crafts, jewellry, pottery, moccasins, western clothing. Hats, belts, buckles, boots, children's clothing and toys. It's not cheap but it is unique. Look out for sale time.

Value 7   Range 10   Service 9

Yellow Rat Bastard

www.yellowrat
bastard.com
478, Broadway
between Broome
and Grand Streets
Ph: 212 334 2150
Hours
Monday Saturday
9.00am 8.30pm
Sunday
10.00am 7.30pm
Credit Cards Major
Credit Cards

As I write this rather cutely named establishment is a wow with cool teens. It's a relative newcomer to this red hot part of Soho and in cavern rather than warehouse surroundings stocks every permutation of jeans, teeshirts, baseball hats, shoes etc. it could be a rappers paradise. The borthers all ooze steet cred. The queues seem to go on forever and the general racket in the store, what with blaring music and shrieking teens, well you need to be in top form for this place.

Value 6   Range 9   Service 6

Zara

www.zara.com
580, Broadway
between Prince
and Houston
Ph: 212 343 1725
Hours:
Monday -Saturday
10.00am -8.00pm
Sunday:
12.00pm-7.00pm
Credit Cards:
Major credit cards

Unless you get here early, it's always busy here. Indifferent staff don't do much to put one in the mood to shop. Personally I think H&M has over taken Zara and now that the label is available all over Europe, it's lost a lot of it's cachet for many of us.

Details as for Zara Midtown

 Value 10   Range 9   Service 6

Chinatown

Chinatown is an experience not to be missed. It is a whole other world in Lower Manhattan. It literally seems like a part of South East Asia has been uprooted and put down in the Lower East Side of New York. The sights, the scenes, the smells, don't miss it. It's a fun place to shop and this being Chinatown, be prepared to haggle over prices; and remember cash is usually the only currency to bargain with here.

The area of Canal Street between Avenue of the Americas and Layfayette Street is a mecca for those in search of knock off (fake) copies of top designer bags, luggage, sunglasses, watches, pens, tee shirts. Tiffany style silver jewellery and some clothing. It is a long block of mini arcades and street stalls and prices and quality vary hugely along the street. For first time shoppers here, I recommend that you do a dry run to see what's there on the day. When you have sourced the best quality and price, then do your deal. Because of the haphazard nature of the stalls which are everywhere, it is almost impossible to give exact addresses for small traders. Check goods very carefully- though everything is usually so inexpensive that it's not really the end of the world if you get caught with the odd dud.

If they ask $35.00 offer $20.00 and walk away, 99% of the time they will follow you and the bargaining begins.

Some stalls are much better than others. Also note, many stalls are deceptive, way at the back of bazaar like warehouses or even in dark basements. You'll find much better deals in the more out of sight scene and the further back they are from the street, the better value you'll find.

Pirated CDs here are dodgy and videos and DVDs are so bad they're hilarious as long as you weren't planning on actually trying to watch a movie.

Canal Street is where you will buy Louis Vuitton style bags that can look so authentic it would take an expert to detect the difference. Chanel, Gucci, Prada, Burberry, Kate Spade, Ralph Lauren and Tommy Hilfiger lookalikes are all to be found in this area. The stalls around the Avenue of the Americas end of Canal Street and just around the corner on Lafayette, have the best quality goods, they are also quite a bit more expensive, relatively speaking, of course. Police sweep the area for counterfeit from time to time and if you are unlucky enough to be shopping on one of those occasions you will find little worth buying. Because all the great knock offs simply disappear until the heat is off. Sometimes it might take as little as an hour or more, at other times the purge can last for the best part of a week. Remember, technically it is an offence to buy knock off merchandise.
The street begins to wake up at around 10.00am on Saturdays and Sundays and trades until about 7.00pm. During the summertime and before Christmas Canal Street is a nightmare. People come from all over the world to stock up on these knock offs. During the week it's much easier to shop here but I have found that early in the week some of the traders don't show up at all and most of the others don't have too much stock.
Beware pickpockets and conmen and why are the tradersd salways eating?

Canal Street

A.W. Kaufman

73 Orchard Street (between Broome and Grand) Don't throw a tantrum if you can't find your favourite thong here. Oy vay, doesn't anyone smile here. This is more your basic meat 'n

Ph: 212 226 1629
Hours: Closed from
noon Friday until
Sunday
Credit Cards:

potatoes underwear. Think longevity not lust!
OK you got it, few frills here. Forget about
trying anything on. Some good labels at great
prices but the family who have ruled this store
with a rod of iron for over seventy years take
their business very seriously. Know your own
size and don't expect a charm assault.
Sometimes the staff are so rude it's funny!

Value 10   Range 6   Service 4

Canal Hi Fi

www.canalhifi.com
319 Canal (bet
Greene and
Mercer)
Ph: 212 925 6575
Hours:Daily
10.00am to 6.00pm
(except major
holidays)
Credit Cards:
Major Credit Cards
but cash is king.

Heaven for boys who love all the latest toys and
when you check out the prices it really is joy
unconfined! While you are definitely not in
luxury land here, you will, eventually find just
about every manufacturer worth having and a
staff who know their onions and are extremely
helpful to boot. I have bought here on several
occasions and got terrific deals for cash.

Value 10   Range 8   Service 9

Danny Lee

Where:
A moveable feast.
Ph: 917 971 6760
Hours Call for
details of hours
and range
Credit Cards:
You must be
joking! **CASH
ONLY**

I single Danny out because he has the best
selection of designer knock offs in the area. He's
not the chattiest young man I've come across
and like so many of the traders in this area,
seems deeply suspicious of anyone who asks too
many questions. Prices range from about
$50.00 to $200.00 but his range of bags and
luggage are virtually indistinguishable from the
originals. By the way the originals would set
you back anywhere from $300.00- $ 3.000.00.
Some times he has most of his merchandise on
display other times you have to ask for the
specific model you are looking for. He's not the
greatest to bargain either. He knows he has the

best stuff in town. His Louis Vuitton style bags confounded a friend who once worked with the company. Likewise Fendi, Dior, Hermès, Gucci and Chanel type bags sell like hot cakes. If you know the exact model bag you want, if he doesn't have it, quite often he can get it for you.

 Value 9   Range 9   Service 3

EZ Enterprises Co

261 Canal Street
between Lafayette
and Broadway
Ph: 212 625 1535
Hours Seven Days
10.30am 7.00pm
Credit Cards Major
credit cards

This is a mini bazaar. They have great prices on Samsonite luggage and also have great discounts on radios, walkmans, batteries, calculators, some toys and especially on large canvas bags. At less than $25.00 you will get a 42 inch bag that is big enough to bring half of Manhattan home. In my experience this store offers the best value in town on these mega canvas bags. Extremely helpful staff. Be prepared to bargain. Best deals for cash.

 Value 9   Range 9   Service 9

Pearl Paint

www.pearlpaint.com
308, Canal Street
between Broadway
and Church Street
Ph: 212 431 7932
Showroom 42
Lispenard Street
(out the back door
of the store)
Ph: 212 431 7932
Ext. 3717
Frame Shop 56
Lispenard Street
(as above)

Recognized as one of the best places not only in the city but possibly in the world to source discounted artists supplies. This store claims to be the biggest artist's supply store in the world. I can't vouch for that but there are six fabulous floors that carry everything under the sun for art of every kind...one floor just specializes in paper. The second floor is where you will find every kind of artist's paints, brushes, pastels, pigments, palettes, pencils, charcoal, tempera paint, varnishs etc. Stationery requisites are displayed on the main floor along with calligraphy instruments, fine writing pens, rubber stamps, lined journals and gift items. All

Ph: 212 431 7932
Ext 6966
Home Decorating
Ph: 212 431 7932
Ext. 4530
Hours Monday
Friday 9.00am
7.00pm
Saturday 9.00am
6.00pm
Sunday 9.30am
6.00pm
International Mail
Order
Ph: 212 431 7932
Ext. 2297
Fax 212 431 5420
Credit Cards Major
credit cards

major brands and all at reductions of from 30% to 70%. There is also a superb framing shop that has a huge variety of ready made frames, a custom framing service, framing supplies, glass cutters, mat cuppers, plexi glass, posters, hanging supplies etc.

You could quite easily spend a day browsing throughout this store and it's three satellite stores nearby and I sometimes do just that. The staff have encyclopedic knowledge about the art supply business and are so enthusiastic and helpful. Even if you are not in the market for art supplies, interesting post cards, stationary etc. if you are in the area, I recommend a visit here. There is an international shipping service available.

 Value 10   Range 10   Service 10

Also worth noting.....

Chinatown is full of herbal remedy shops. Herbal teas and vitamin supplements that are currently all the rage are available here significantly cheaper than in Midtown or in Europe. There are several Chinese 'pharmacies' that sell Chinese remedies for everything from weight loss, baldness, impotence etc. However you need a Chinese doctor's prescription to have the miracle cure dispensed. Staff in these stores are notoriously unhelpful. If you don't know exactly what you want, don't count on getting any help or advice here.

Massage Studios are commonplace all over Chinatown. These are quite bona fide, there is no sexual innuendo. Foot massage is particularly welcome if you have been trekking down town all day. It's usually $11 for 15 minutes, $21 for 30 minutes and $42 for an hour (it's a set fee for body or feet and you can split the time per foot) I love to have my feet pummeled for about half an hour, just long enough to renew the spirits. In some places they keep trying to get you to have a longer treatment. But don't be bullied. The Chinese are extremely good masseurs and masseuses but I don't feel happy having anyone whose background I don't know working on my neck. Also since they do the body massage with your clothes on I don't find it especially effective. Now don't think in terms of luxury, these places are extremely basic but the massage is worth it. The one I use at the moment is:

La Grande

179 Grand Street (corner of Mulberry/Grand Streets) Ph: 212 965 1165

You don't need an appointment.
Hours This place seems to be open from about 11.00am until about 10.00pm
Credit Cards Major credit cards

Restaurants

There are great restaurants all over the area. Remember this is the 2nd largest Chinatown outside of China. (San Francisco boasts the largest one)

My advice is to check the menus outside the doors. Some of these eateries are just too Eastern for Western palates. Also many of the restaurants here are very, very basic: formica tables, papers napkins etc. But you can count on authentic and inexpensive food. Don't plan on fine dining and don't be put off by vast tables of Chinese eating, talking and gesturing all at the same time. At least you know you are not doing the tourist trail!

Joe's Ginger Restaurant

113 Mott St. near Grand St. Ph: 212-966-6613

Crab-and-pork-stuffed steamed buns that will get the juices flowing. Divine dumplings Crazy prices.

Hours : Lunch and dinner daily
Credit Cards: Cash Only   Liquor: Beer and Wine Only
Price Range: Inexpensive to Moderate

Fried Dumpling

**92 Allen Street
between
Delancey/Broome
Ph: 212 941 9975**
Fried dumplings, mini pork rolls and sesame pancake with shredded beef and you still get change out of $10.00. But remember, we're not talking fine dining here.

Daily: Lunch and dinner
Credit Cards: Cash only   Reservations: No   Liquor: No
Inexpensive

Yeah Shanghai Deluxe

**65 Bayard Street at
Mott Street
Ph: 212 566 4884**
Great for brunch, wontons to die for. Very easy on the pocket!

Daily: Lunch and dinner Credit Cards: Cash Only
Liquor: Beer and wine Inexpensive
Reservations: Recommended

Dim Sum Go Go

**5, East Broadway
(between
Catherine St and
Chatham St.)
Ph: 212 732 0797**
Don't miss the Dim Sum Platter $8.95, also the fluffy rice seafood platter and 24 varieties of dumplings.

Daily: Lunch/Dinner
Credit Cards: All major credit cards
Liquor: Beer and Wine   Inexpensive
Reservations: Recommended

(Lower) West Side Story

This is one of the really happening parts of the City. Now dubbed the new West Coast new stores, galleries, restaurants and clubs open almost daily which adds to the downtown buzz. This is cutting edge culture. some people find it too raw and earthy. There are already so many really funky places and cafes down there that were once considered 'underground'. But yesterday's underground is to-days main steam and no doubt in no time the Lower West Side will become less bohemian and a little bit more bluestocking as funky moves on to a new playground.

New York Style

Bed Bath and Beyond

**6th Avenue
between 18th and
19th Streets
Ph 212 255 3550**

**Hours:
Monday-Sunday
9.00am-9.00pm
Credit cards :
Major credit cards**

A vast store packed with every imaginable
brand of towels and bed linen. If you know your
thread counts, you can find 600 thread count
Egyptian, cotton sheets here, they look and feel
like silk. of course they have everything in
between fromcotton/poly mix non iron (ugh!)
right up to the Rolls Royce. You'll find
everything for the well dressed kitchen and they
also stock holiday decorations, general
household goods and small pieces of furniture.
Good value, though not in the same league as
the Outlets. Extremely helpful staff here,
especially the doorman who will hail a cab at
the front door. At weekends and holidays it's a
bit like the Superbowl here.

   **Value 8   Range 10   Service 9**

Burlington Coats

**116, West 23rd
Street at 6th
Avenue**

Details, as before; page 21

Bluefly

**www.bluefly.com
143 W. 24th Street
Ph: 212-929-7070
Hours: Mon.-Fri.
11:30am-7pm
Sat. and Sun.
Noon-6pm
Credit Cards: All
Major Credit Cards**

Bluefly has been one of the best on line sites for
fashion and accessories for yonks. Now this new
clearance store has an ever-revolving stock of
discounted Prada, Gucci, Diane von
Furstenberg, Ralph Lauren and other big-time
names, as well as a divine selection of cashmere
at totally crazy prices. Deep discounts of up to
83%

**BEST BUY: Huge cashmere wrap, I won't even board my G5 without
it! $79.00 instead of the $650 I shelled out about ten years ago at
N. Peal then at 57th Street..**

TJ Maxx

www.tjmaxx.com
620, 6th Avenue
(between W.18th
and W.19th Streets)
Ph: 212. -229-0875
Hours:
Mon- Sat.
9.30am - 9.00pm
Sunday
11.00am-7.00pm
Credit Cards: All
Major Credit Cards

You need plenty of time to rummage here because there are plenty of great bargains to be found. As America's largest off-price retailer, there are always top designer and brand name fashions for you, your family and your home - at savings of up to 60% off department store prices. The home departments has improved hugely in the last year. Personally I find it very claustrophic here. It gets very crowded at weekends and is like a zoo at holiday time. But because there is so much good shopping in the area, it's worth popping in to check it out when you are downtown.

Loehmanns

www.loehmanns.com
7th Avenue and
16th St.
Ph: 212 352-0856
Hours:
Mon - Sat
9:00am - 9:00pm
Sun
11:00am - 7:00pm
Credit Cards: All
major credit cards

Since it began in 1921, Loehmann's has occupied a unique position in the fashion industry; it stands alone as the only national upscale off-price specialty retailer. It is best known for its world-famous Back Room, where fashion-conscious women can find their favorite designers at prices that are always 30% to 65% lower than department or specialty stores. Brilliant for designer evening dresses. Stock changes daily so if you are in the area, it's always worth dropping in. In recent years, it has expanded its range to include shoes and accessories, juniors, fragrances, gifts and intimate apparel. There is also a complete men's departments. The New York store is the East Coast anchor. It still breaks my heart when I remember it in it's heyday as Barneys, perhaps one of the greatest fashion stores ever. Back then I used to blow the best part of a year's salary on two Chanel suits. But that was before it's owners the Pressman family lost the plot and moved uptown to Madison Avenue. That was such a disaster, they ended up losing the store. By the way Loehmann's is anchored on the West Coast by its Beverly Hills store on La Cienega and 3rd Street. If you are ready for your close up at the Oscars or suffer from red carpet fever and your budget doesn't spring to Rodeo Drive or Melrose, this is the only place to shop.

Filenes

620 6th Avenue at 18th Street

Details
As before; page 26

Find Outlet

361, West 17th Street at 9th Avenue

Details:
As before: page 25

Flower Market

West 28th Street between 6th and 7th Avenues
Hours
Monday-Friday From about 4.00am-2.00pm
Saturday Some stores open
Sunday All stores closed
Credit Cards Policies differ from store to store but best value for cash

I just adore the flower district and would be happy to hang out here for hours every morning, if I only had time. When I do, I love to roam from store to store. This is one of the top flower markets in the world with every imaginable, exotic bloom flown in from all over the world. The shops run on both sides of the street for the full block and there are also some shops on 6th avenue. Some specialize in shrubbery, others in plants and potted blooms, others in terrific containers, vases, ribbon etc others in orchids of every kind. There are some great silk flower shops on this street. As weddings and parties become more extravagant everywhere, people from all over the world are increasingly ordering deliveries of special flowers from the New York Flower Market. For Europeans this is a bit ironic when you consider that most New York flower merchants order their flowers from Amsterdam in the first place. All the top florists and decorators buy their blooms here. If the guys are not too hassled they are delighted to share their encyclopedic knowledge of everything floral and I have learned more here than I have at endless classes and from numerous books and magazines and my New York parties always start here.

The street starts humming around 4.30am and begins to wind down around noon. It's more or less closed by 2.30pm. Most of the people who work here are extremely friendly and helpful and while it is a wholesale market they will sell small quantities…. for cash.

 **Value 10**   **Range 10**   **Service 10**

Jacks World

110 West 32nd Street between 6th and 7th Avenues

Details:
As before: page 28

Le Firme

120 W. 23rd Street (1st Floor) between 6th/7th Avenues
Ph: 212 989 3071
Hours
7 days 10.00am-9.30pm
Credit Cards Major credit cards

Great Italian fashion for men and women. 5,000 sq. feet. Now also stocking La Perla underwear and swimwear. Also excellent selection of accessories. You need to keep checking this one.

 **Value 8**   **Range 8**   **Service 6**

LS Mens Clothing

19 W 44th Street, Suite 403
Ph: 212 575 0933
Hours
Monday-Thursday 9.00am-7.00pm
Friday 9.00am-4.30pm
Saturday 10.00am-5.00pm
Credit Cards Major credit cards

Great place for top of the range men's clothing, also a great place to check out Wall Street lawyers who shop here and know where to buy the top designers with 50% reductions or more.

 **Value 8**   **Range 8**   **Service 7**

NY Cake and Baking Company

56 W22nd Street at
6th Avenue
Ph: 212 675 2253
or 646 638 0275
Hours
Monday-Friday
9.30am-6.00pm
Saturday
10.00am-6.00pm
Sunday
11.00am-5.00pm
Credit Cards Major
credit cards

This isn't a discount store and I'm not a baker but I never skip this little gem when I'm downtown. Bakers and confectioners from all over the United States and the rest of the world consider this their Mecca. It is superb for special occasion cakes: weddings, special birthdays, theme cakes etc. Every kind of cake tin and pan, decoration, flowers, candles, numbers etc. It makes it all look so easy. I fantasize about baking amazing birthday cakes for all the gang whenever I drop in here..... but that's as far as it goes for me. I'm afraid. **Remember this store does not sell cakes !** Just the where with all to bake the very best and innovative. I'd guess that there is nothing the staff here don't know about baking and decorating cakes.

Value 9   Range 10   Service 10

Odd Job Trading Company

149 W. 32nd Street
between 6th and
7th Avenues

Details:
As before: page 29

Old Navy

www.oldnavy.com
6th Avenue at 18th
Street
Ph: 212 645 0663
Hours
Monday-Saturday
9.00am-9.30pm
Sunday 11.00am-
8.00pm
Credit cards Major
credit cards

Major fashion bargain alert! This is a must for anyone with kids, teens or indeed people of any age who like cutting edge casual clothes at really relaxed prices. It is a shopping experience made so much more enjoyable by a really friendly, well informed, switched on staff. Owned by The Gap it has been the most successful retail story in the US since it opened about seven years ago.

Anything a street wise guy or gal needs is to be found here. Sizes go up to 18 for ladies and 3xxx for men. Plus there is a really hip baby, kids and little kids section where the prices are unbeatable. This is directional fashion at its best with keenest prices, good quality and terrific value. Again get here as early as possible. In the mid and late afternoon over the weekends, it's nearly impossible and queues are endless. But the staff are very helpful. It is hard to beat for up to the minute jeans, tee-shirts, polo shirts, lounging gear as well as jackets and sweaters.

Prices are about half those at sister stores, The Gap and Banana Republic. When I was shopping here on one occasion, Madonna and her new husband Guy Richie arrived in with their baby Roco in tow and bought up half the store. Good enough for the Material Girl, OK for me too!

Value 10   Range 10   Service 10

S & W

165 West 26th Street at 7th Avenue

Ph: 212 924 6656

Hours
Monday-Wednesday
10.00am-6.30pm
Thursday 10.00am-8.00pm
Friday 10.00am-3.00pm
Saturday Closed
Sunday 10.00am-6.00pm

Credit cards Major credit cards

Not the most attractive store, in fact downright dingy looking, but there are great bargains to be found. I have one friend who swears by this place. Since she lives in NYC she is able to go by there regularly and she has the most stunning wardrobe. The staff are unhelpful and the changing rooms quite appalling. But the deep discounts on serious designers are definitely a carrot for bargain hunters.

Value 7   Range 7   Service 4

The Men's Warehouse

115 Broadway between
Cedar/ Thames Streets
Ph: 212 233 0675
Hours:
Monday Friday
10.00am 8.00pm
Saturday
10.00am 6.00pm
Sunday
12.00pm 6.00pm

A bit like ToDay's Man, this is another safe haven for safe suit'n shirt'n tie dressers. They do informal wear but it's formal informal, if you get my drift. We are not talking Gap or Paul and Shark here. I mean you're not going to be doing 'serious dude strutting' nor will you have Charvet chic either! I guess you could call it meat and potatoes dressing for nine to five guys.

655, 6th Avenue/ 20th
Street
Ph: 212 243 3517
Hours:
Monday Friday
9.30am 9.00pm
Saturday
10.00am 7.00pm
Sunday
10.00am 7.00pm
Credit Cards
Major Credit Cards

Value 8   Range 7   Service 8

To-Days Man

625 6th Avenue at 19th
Street
Ph: 212 924 0200
Hours
Monday Saturday
9.30am 9.00pm
Sunday
11.00am 7.00pm
Credit Cards
Major credit cards

This is a fairly comprehensive men's store carrying a wide range of suits as well as a huge selection for dress down Friday wear. It's not hip or happening just safe clothes at very safe prices. The staff are a bit pushy, once you get the suit they are trying to flog the shirt, tie, socks etc. You will not exactly set the world on fire if you are kitted out here.

Value 8   Range 7   Service 7

Weber

160 W. 32nd Street
between 6th and 7th
Avenue

Details:
As before; page 33

Madison Avenue

The Miracle Mile and a Half

Rick and Elsa might always have Paris but give me Madison Avenue any day especially if the amazing sales are on. These take place at least twice a year - after Christmas and in July but sale or no sale, a ramble up here should be mandatory for anyone with fashion chic aspirations.

Indeed for the serious shopper, Manhattan's Gold Coast, which extends from 59th to 96th streets, makes Paris, Milan and London redundant. I prefer to start at 59th Street at Crate and Barrel and ramble all the way up the avenue to about 89th. The mile and a half walk will give your senses a total work out, not to memtion your black Amex, as you pass some of the most famous art and antique galleries, fabulous stores, the legendary Whitney Museum of American Art, super shoe salons and great restaurants.

You can spend the whole day here and not even feel it until your feet tell you that they need some rest. That's your cue for time out with a serious Vodka Martini in **Bedelmanns Bar** in the **Carlyle Hotel**. *35, East 76th St. at Madison Ph: 1 800 20 69 20 29 (Europe)* And if the legendary Bobby Short is playing, well that's a New York experience not to be missed. A high altar to luxury, this is one of the best hotels in the world and you will definitely be rubbing shoulders with some celeb. or other here. Most of the accommodation is owner owned in this hotel, these little pads start at around $6 million and the sky's the limit , think $25 million plus! It's straight out of Sex in the City. Manoloed gals in the latest Chanel, Gucci and Pucci while most of the men come from matinee idol central casting. How come New York men have impossibly polished shoes that they can and do see their well moisturised faces in? But be aware, you won't feel at home here in your anorak and jeans! And it's one place where you can never be too thin or have too much bling either!

My good friend, Ireland's couturier Jen Kelly just adores Madison Avenue. In early summer, at the crack of dawn, we have run the thirty blocks, strolling back down for breakfast at the famous **Three Guys Diner** on *Madison between 76th and 77th Streets.* The original 'Three Guys' who came from Greece are still there. When I lived around the corner on 74th Street it was my local and I never tired of eating there. **Coco Pazzo** *also at Madison and 74th* is one of the smartest Italian eateries in the city. It was in my building – The Volnay. The paparazzi lurking outside most nights confirm this another celebrity favourite. The food is fine, but not remotely in the same league as **Il Mulino** in the West Village. Woody Allen and Soon Yi would pass by most evenings on their way to **Elaines** , another legendary hangout, over on 1st Ave. Woody then lived in the fab. coop building on 74th and 5th Ave. which he later sold.

By the way there is also a rather cute coffee shop in the **Whitney**, a visit to the Museum is always a must for lovers of American art. I sat next to John Kennedy Jnr at an opening gala there several years ago. It was the first black tie event he and his wife Caroline attended after their marriage. It was one of those bulb popping, New York evenings that was quite unforgettable. Of course John's mother, Jackie O knew every block of Madison intimately. She lived a block west on 5th Avenue and always walked to work down Madison usually stopping at **YSL** at 71st Street and

Valentino, *774 Madison (between 64th and 65th) Ph: 772 6969* (who designed the wedding dress for her marriage to Ari Onassis.) to check all the latest arrivals. Jackie also sold her clothes to **Michaels** *at 81st St.* (check consignment and second hand shops) where the same Valentino, Size 10, could be had for about one tenth of what she had paid for it. I bought a full length cocktail skirt in hand pleated Irish linen which Sybil Connelly had designed for Jackie for $30.00. It had never been worn by Jackie nor have I ever worn it either. It's just nice to have, since Sybil was a good friend.

By the way Michaels has a really brilliant bridal section, Vera Wang gowns, many will have cost in excess of $50,000, will have been worn for a few hours and are now on sale for maybe a grand or two at most. The only problem is many Madison Avenue matrons seem to be about a size 4. Madison Avenue men like their women X ray thin. In some cases a maximum weight again is written into pre nuptial agreement. Marriages have been known to founder when Muffy got puffy and ballooned the whole way up to size 8! And the venerable **Vera Wang Salon** *is at Madison and 76th.* Remember by appointment only!

If the best bed and table linen in the world are on your shopping list then Madison Avenue boasts the top three with another two that I always recommend. **Frette**, *799 Madison Avenue (bet. 67th & 68th streets) Ph: 212 988-5221* is a must. **Pratesi**, *829 Madison at 69th Street Ph: 212 288 2315* is equally beautiful and **D. Porthaud**, *18 East, 69th Street at Madison. Ph: 212 772 38 77* is possibly my own favourite because I no longer need to make that mad dash to the Rue Collange in Paris to order my bespoke linen. You might wonder how some of the most expensive and exclusive stores in the world qualify for inclusion in this book. Well they do have sales and after all, like everything else in life, it's all relative. A set of sheets at $18,000 might just be the biggest bargain ever for you! I hope so. Don't you agree that between the sheets is one of the most important places for down time? So go ahead and seriously indulge yourself here. Having a little identity crisis, peut etre? No worries. You can have your sheets and towels monogrammed, so you will always remember who you are. I have a much married, Manhattan friend who insists each woman he marries has the same first name initial, just so that he doesn't have to keep changing his Porthault! Nothing like having your priorities right! If the price tags at the above stores, which cater to royalty and aristocracy all over the world, and we are not just talking palaces, there's also the G5 and the yacht to remember not to mention the bambini linen section, seems too steep, why not check **Leron**, *750 Madison at 65th Street, (212) 753-6700* or **E. Braun & Co.** *717 Madison near 63rd St. Ph: 212-838-0650*. Dowagers go to Braun for exquisite, hand-embroidered place mats and napkins. You'll go for sheets, throws, towels, and table linens-some of which match famous china patterns, like Jensen's Flora Danica ($4,800 for a linen service for twelve). Both produce exquisite bespoke, if needed, linens at slightly less exotic prices than the top three.

So spare a thought for the guy, who is often forking out for all this bedroom luxury! Lets hope he too gets to enjoy it! But then he can stop off at **Sherry-Lehmann**, *679 Madison Ph: 212 838-7500*, one of the best wine stores in the world and have a case or ten of his favourite Chateau Margaux delivered. And then a gentle stroll down to **Davidoff of Geneva**, *535 Madison Avenue, at 54th St. 212-751-9060*. New York's premium cigar store with over 1,000 different cigars and smoking accessories. It is rather great if you run out of Cubans, ironically still banned in the US.

He might cross the Avenue to stock up on shirts and ties in **Addison on Madison**, *689 Madison at 62nd, Ph; 212 308 2660*. God! does he miss Sulka who went out of business. He felt at home with Revlon supremo Ron Pearlman who got his cashmere there and Henry Kissinger had his sweaters and ties delivered from there too. But truth be told, he is a bit of a Francophile and is really is a Charvet man.

Madison Avenue, synonymous with the advertising industry, much of which has decamped downtown during the last decade, is not only a fashion lovers paradise, it is also home to some of the City's wondrous art galleries,. The famous **Wildensteins** are in 64th Street. They still talk about Jocelyn, who used extreme plastic surgery to look like a pussy cat. But then her husband had taken up with an eighteen year old Russian "actress". What is it about these Russian beauties that has billionaires all over the world smitten? Donatella Versace uses the stunning town house Gianna was working on before he was murdered. It has a medusa on the front door while Ivana Trump has a nice house across the street, though she did have a bit of hassle getting planning permission for her indoor swimming pool.

You will also find the richest concentration of crystal decorative objects and jewellery in the world: the Crystal

District. **Baccarat**, *625 Madison, Ph: 212 826-4100*, **Lalique**, *712 Madison near 63rd St. Ph: 212-355-6550*, **Steuben**, *667 Madison, Ph: 212/752-1441* and **Swarovski** are all located along the five-block stretch of *Madison Avenue between 59th Street and 64th Street.*

Autumn/Winter 2003/2004 was the season when fur made a grand re entry. Fur or fur trimmed garments were in vogue in every fashionable city in the western world. Most of the Madison Avenue designer stores and speciality fur boutiques are having sales on fur coats from the 2003 collections once Spring officially arrives. So it's very likely that you can now afford the coat you've been dreaming about all season. **J. Mendel**, *723 Madison Ave, Ph:212-832-5830*, is one of the most famous New York furriers. You will find every style to choose from. Many carry price tags that could well be the GNP of a small, Third World country. Furs are not on sale here or at **Dennis Baso** *765 (at 65 & 66th) Ph:212 794-4500* who finally opened his own salon last year and in addition to his A list existing clientele already boasts several crowned heads of Europe. He has every kind of fur that you can think of: sable, chinchilla, mink, sheared and shearling. **A.S. Parker**, *1001 Madison, Ph: 212-794-6276* has a great selection of A. S. Parker label furs but not on sale.

Of course you can go downtown to **Peter Duffy** and buy more or less the same coats (made to measure, if you like), Hillary Clinton's new sheared mink came from here, for a fraction of the price, at any time of the year.

Givenchy, *63rd and Madison Ph: 212 688 4338* has had beautiful fur, in addition to the most stunningly beautiful fashion again this season. **Barney's**, *660 Madison at 61 St, Ph:212-826-8900*. At time of press, they had one gorgeous leather and mink coat for $18,000 (+20% off) and a rabbit and leather jacket for $2500. Sale time is the ideal opportunity to add some Givenchy pieces to your wardrobe. They are so stunning, they will be there for decades. **Bottega Veneta**, *635 Madison Ave, Ph:212-371-5511*, I just think their bags are so cool, had one Russian sable coat that is reversible darling with 30% off of $80,000. While that other total Sweetie, **Michael Kors for Celine**, *667 Madison Ave, Ph:212-486-9700* had one short pink fox jacket, really cute -30% off! Don't you just have to have a pink fur in 2004?

Donna Karan, *819 Madison, Ph: 212 223 DKNY*, opened her flagship store here a few years ago. The construction ran late, way over budget and the store was just about to have it's mega, celeb. opening, when Ms Karan remembered she had forgotten to have a Feng Shui expert sweep the building! Ohmigod! A fate worse than death for the lady who invented 'the body.' The Feng Shui practioner was less than happy with the energy and vibes emanating from the store. So the entrance, which had been directly on Madison, was hastily reconfigured to open, at an angle onto the Avenue and the Street, with some symbol placed into the ground outside the door, to keep bad karma at bay. Donna, you go girl! And she now has shearlings 40% off in the Spring 2004 sale. How's that for great karma?

Back to Barneys where there is a focus on fashion that is truly New York in every detail, making this Madison Avenue apparel a true icon. It features top designers like Dries Van Noten, Ann Demeulemeester, Martin Margiela, Donna Karan, Ralph Lauren and Calvin Klein. Enjoy all seven floors of the spacious and airy store interior that features modern furniture and unique architectural elements

Hermès, *691 Madison at 62nd, Ph: 212 751 3181* stands as one of the last truly classic boutiques featuring doormen and top-of-the-line styles for the shopper with truly exquisite taste. Every object in this shop is designed with the finest fabrics and craftsmanship. Accessories include scarves, ties and handbags. This is not a shop for the weak-walleted buyer, but be assured that designs are themselves works-of-art - and for this, the price is definitely right. They do have sales. They are a bit cloak and dagger. I get a call from my vendeuse to alert me to a tie sale... like the following day. My problem is I am as likely to be in Milan, Marbella, Paris or London, not to mention Dublin at that stage. So it's too bad for all my boys who love the cute Hermes snails, birds and puppies. And no the saddles have never been on sale. I have a friend who put a bespoke Hermes saddle on her bridal wish list. What's more she got it... the bones of $10,000. They divorced a year or so later. Her mega wealthy husband did not ride well! At least there was no argument about custody of the saddle.

With fashion on Madison, it's not where to start, it's how to finish that is the biggest dilemma. I can't pass **Carolina Herrera**, *954 Madison , Ph: 212-249-6552.* A stunningly elegant lady, her clothes are just perfect. So is her newish

Madison salon that has a rather stunning chair that alone cost a cool million.

Dolce and Gabbana, *825 Madison between 68th and 69th Sts, Ph: 212-249-4100* boast A a symphony of different styles, textures, looks and designs, the offerings at this sophisticated shop run the gamut from sexy and daring to serene and classic. Expect top-line labels to be featured in an understated, spare environment that simply enhances the beautiful lines of these select garments. And you will seriously score here at sale time, and score even more when you strut your stuff in D&G.

Prada, *841 Madison, at 71st Street, Ph:212-327-4200* serves the trendy shopper in you. And I love it, need it, want it. Right Now! Today's clothing, bags, shoes and more are all available for the stylish man or woman on your shopping list. Well shaped eyebrows were raised when Prada moved all the way up here but before you could say Ciao Bella, most of the other top designers followed suit. Stylewise, where New York goes, the rest of the world will follow. That's one reason why designs from this shop are becoming popular all across the world. **BCBG Max Azria**, *770 Madison, Ph: 212-717-4225* seems a little out of it's depth here. Great knock off cat walk looks, really well priced. Great sales too. But sizes here are small! **Ralph Lauren**, *888 Madison, at 72nd Ph: 212-434-8000* is already well covered elsewhere in this guide. The flip side of RL is the flamboyant **Roberto Cavalli**, *711 Madison , Ph: 212-755-7722*. This can look so brassy, depending on the wearer. It looks great in the Hamptons but still looks best in St. Barts.

I always check out **Ferragamo**, *655 Madison, Ph: 212-759-3822*. Just love these shoes, boots, they appeal to every woman's inner Imelda. And the belts! I met Wanda, the matriarch a few years ago and my was she an impressive lady? Totally dedicated to carrying on the business started by her late husband. And can any gal every have too many pairs of **Tods**, *650 Madison, near 60th St.* Audrey Hepburn really started something when she first wore them. Last season they had fabulous fur boots on sale in the Spring.

Maternity clothes are now at the cutting edge of fashion so it's no surprise to see some of the very best here. **Liz Lange Maternity**, *958 Madison, Ph: 212-879-2191*. Chic styles, luxurious fabrics and flawless fit can all be found in this one stop shop for pregnant princesses. **Mimi Maternity**, *1125 Madison at 84th St. Ph: 212-737-3784* has equally edgy fashion that celebrates that bump with great aplomb while **A Pea in the Pod** *860 Madison at 70th St. Ph: 212-988-8039* has less expensive and more casual wear for the nouvelle mamam. The driver will take Madame a few blocks to **Tartine et Chocolat** *1047 Madison at 80th Street, Ph; 212 717 2112* to get the new baby's layette while further up, on the other side **Zitomer's**, *969, Madison at 76th Ph: 212 737 5560*, is the only drug store/pharmacy for the jet set. And now they have that lovely little doggy boutique next door, Millie and Molly can have their own designer wardrobes too. And if her skin is causing problems she will drop by , **Georgette Klinger**, *978, Madison Ph:212 744 6900* for a treatment. Then to **Fogal**, *988, Madison at Ph; 212 717 7958* for some lacy thigh highs, a snip at $89 but they are so 'belle de jour.'

She might hook up with him for a lettuce leaf at Evi at and Evian at**Café Nosidam**, *768 Madison bet. 65th an 66th. Ph: 212 223 2900* or meet some friends at **Aureole**, *34 East 61st between 5th and Madison, Ph: 212 319 1660*, the birth place of vertical cuisine.

On the way up home to their great coop on 5th where their ballroom is finally finished and George Soros is their neighbour, they pass **Frank E. Campbell's Funeral Home** on *Madison at 81st* There are no sales at this Manhattan landmark. After all Dorothy Parker, rapper Biggie Small and even Judy Garland had their 'going away' parties here. And she knows they have a fab. Web site *www.frankecampbell.com* with a forward slash for really meaningful information on how to handle grief. Madison Avenue, from the cradle to the grave and designer luxury all the way.

Midtown

Baranzelli (Silk Surplus)

942, Third Avenue
bet. 56th and 57th
Streets.
Ph: 212
Hours: Mon - Fri
10.00am - 6.00pm
Sat 10.00 - 5.30pm

This is an outlet for Scalamandre furnishing fabrics. These wonderful silk, brocades, organzas etc would normally set you back a serious four figure sum, here they cost about half price or less. The sales every four months are advertised widely. Then the value is even better.

 Value 10   Range 7   Service 9

Daffys

www.daffys.com
135, East 57th
Street bet. Park
and Lex. Avenues.
Ph: 212 376 4477
Hours: Mon-Fri
10.00am - 8.00pm
Sat
10.00am - 7.00pm
Sun
11.00am -6.00pm
and at
355 Madison
Avenue at 44th

This is yet another store catering mostly for teen and teen wannabees. It has extensive ladies fashion, jeans, shirts, dresses, jackets, casuals etc. The quality is very mixed here. There was a great selection of quite stunning Italian shearlings at unbelievable prices the last time I was here. ankle length coats were selling for about $700. Coats that were not remotely in the same league were going for a few thousand in London. The mens department here can be a bit iffy. Great infant and baby section and great kids italian shoes and boots. But you can't argue with the prices and you could well pick up a nice skirt or shirt. The 57th Street store is

Street
Ph: 212 557 4422
Hours:Mon - Fri
8.00am-8.00pm
sat 10.00am-
6.00pm
Sun 12.00pm-
6.00pm

the flagship and is reasonably well laid out. I
find the madison Avenue store very chaotic and
claustrophobic

Value 8   Range 7   Service 7

Designer and Decorator Building

942 Third Avenue
between 58th and
59th Streets
Ph: 212 759 5408
Hours: Vary with
different
decorators.
Credit cards: Major
Credit Cards.

This is where most of the top American
decorators are based. Anything to do with
interior décor can be found here. People come
from all over the world to access the best in
interior design. Every thing is at wholesale
prices but you need an introduction here. They
also have one sale a year, usually in the
Lexington Avenue Armory down town. Really
great prices on carpets, mirrors, pictures and all
kinds of furniture, especially on the last day of
the sale. During the year individual showrooms
have sales and these are flagged in the New
York newspapers.

Value 9   Range 9   Service *

*Service Very mixed

Forman's Apparel

550 5th Avenue at
46th Street
145 42nd Street
between
Lex Avenue and
3rd Avenue
Ph: 212 777 3600
Hours
Monday - Thursday
8.00am-9.00pm
Friday
8.00am-2.00pm
Saturday Closed
Sunday
10.00am-6.00pm

Details as Orchard Street

Gale Grant

Ph: 212 753 6511
Hours
Monday - Friday
10.00am-6.00pm
Saturday
10.00am-5.00pm
Sunday Closed
Credit Cards
Major credit cards

Huge selection of great costume jewellery from a couple of bucks a piece to a few hundred dollars for the greatest faux baubles. A great favourite with Upper East Side matrons who keep their real rocks in the bank vaults.

Value 9   Range 9   Service 8

Lanciani Travel Jewellery

www.lanciani.com
510 Madison
Avenue bet 52nd
and 53rd Streets
Ph: 212 317 2200
Hours Mon-Sat
10.00am -6.00pm
Closed Sunday
also
826 Lexington
Avenue bet 63rd
and 64th Streets
Hours: Mon-Fri
10.30am-7.00pm
Sat.10.00am-
6.00pm

I just love the name of this store. It's actually really great costume jewellery made in Italy by the family that started the company ten years ago. It has been worn in several Hollywood movies including Analyze That and Town and Country and I know several millionaires wives who shop here and claim they are sporting the real family rocks. Ideal for the woman who travels and leaves her jewellery at home, some of the pieces are quite breathtaking and I have seen a top London jeweller totally taken in by some divine 'sapphires' and 'diamonds' from here. Prices are a dream too. If you want to be taken seriously as 'a bling babe' and your bank balance doesn't add up head staright for Lanciani.

Value 7   Range 10   Service 10

Lexington Luggage

Lexington Avenue
at 58th Street
Ph: 1 800 477
8844(for all
location details)
Hours
Monday - Friday
8.30am - 11.00pm
Sat/Sun 11.00am -
8.00pm
Credit cards Major
credit cards

This is a real little treasure. Very good prices, they will do a deal and they are both pleasant and helpful. It is also very good for fast luggage repairs.

	Value 9	Range 10	Service 10

Odd Job Trading

66, West 48th
Street (between
5th and 6th
Avenues)
Ph: 212 334 7444

Details in Discount Stores Section

Pottery Barn

117, East 59th
Street at Lexington
Avenue
Ph: 917 369 0050
Hours
Monday Saturday
10.00am 8.00pm
Sunday
11.00am 7.00pm
Credit Cards
Major credit cards

This newest store in the Pottery Barn chain is a very welcome addition to the midtown area. Just across from Bloomingdales, it's dead easy to combine your fashion forays with equally fashionable shopping for the home and garden at one go. Other details as before.

Suarez Handbags

Location
450 Park Ave
between 56/57
Ph: 212 753 3758

Legendary for its bags and shoes. The address of this store is sure to be in every savvy socialite's little black book. Superb copies of Hermes, Chanel and Gucci in real alligator.

Hours
Monday - Friday
10.00am-6.00pm
Saturday 10.00am-
5.00pm
Sunday Closed
Credit Cards Major
credit cards

snakeskin, ostrich, leather and suede, pricey but still so much cheaper that the original. They don't sport the labels but often have been made in the same factories in Italy. Suarez also has at least one major sale (usually in July) every year. Mark downs are terrific. Look for advertisements in the New York papers or call or information.

Best Buy. "Kelly Bag" in ostrich $425.00 the real thing would set you back over $4000

Value 8   Range 9   Service 9

SYMS

www.syms.com
Location
400, Park Avenue
at 54th Street
Ph: 212 317 8200

Details as in Discount Stores.

Toto

868, Lexington
Avenue at 65th
Street
Ph: 212 288 7171
Hours
Monday-Saturday
10.00am-7.00pm
Closed Sunday
Credit Cards Visa,
Mastercharge,
American Express

Good Upper East Side neighbourhood store. Off the beaten tourist track. Huge selection of unusual Pashminas, bags, some clothes. Pleasant, helpful staff.

Value 8   Range 6   Service 8

Best Buy Pashmina $69.00

Victoria's Secret

www.victoriassecr
et.com
Location
34 East 57th Street
at Madison Avenue
Ph: 758 5592
Hours
Monday - Saturday
10.00am - 8.00pm
Sunday 12.00pm -
7.00pm
Credit Cards Major
credit cards

A good place to find inexpensive lingerie. Quite a selection, everything from the most mundane cotton undies to some of the more exotic items that are snapped up by high maintenance professional ladies.

	Value 10	Range 6	Service 4

Zara

Locations
750, Lexington
Avenue at 59th
Street
Ph: 212 754 1120
Hours
Monday Saturday
10.00am 8.00pm
Sunday Noon
7.00pm
Credit Cards Major
credit cards

This Spanish chain has been a huge hit in New York. Regular travellers to the Costas have been raving about Zara for years now. Great knock offs of current high fashion but small sizes. Brilliant for fashion victims and as of the beginning of 2001 there is now an equally great men's fashion section. At time of writing the US stores still don't have a preteen or baby section nor do they have a home department yet. But hang in there. This is one of the more successful retailing stores in the US, the darling of the fashionistas and glossy fashion magazines. Now a publicly quoted company, it is literally dancing as fast as it can to open new stores and new sections. The stock changes every couple of days. So if you see something you like, snap it up. There is no guarantee it will be there when you return and they don't reorder. Regulars to Marbella are already big fans of this emporium that has also great bags boots and shoes.

And at
101, 5th Avenue

101, 5th Avenue between 17th/18th Street
Ph: 212 741 0555
Hours: Monday Saturday 10.00am 8.00pm
Sunday Noon 7.00pm

And at
580, Broadway

580, Broadway at Prince Street

Ph: 212 343 1725
Hours: Monday Saturday 10.00am 8.00pm
Sunday Noon 7.00pm

**And at
39, West 34th
Street**

39, West 34th Street (between 5th and 6th
Avenues)
Ph: 212 868 6551
Hours
Seven Days 10.00am 8.30pm

 Value 9   Range 9   Service 9

AMS Shoe Warehouse

**1690 Second
Avenue at 87th
Street
Ph: 212 426 6600
Hours
Tuesday-Saturday
11.00am-8.30pm
Sunday
Noon-7.00pm
Closed Monday
Credit Cards Major
credit cards**

A relatively recent discovery for me, I have had
mixed success on my several visits here. There is
a huge range of men's and ladies shoes at
discounted prices... from 30%-60% off retail.
Some designer labels but there is always a good
supply of basics. In addition there are end of
season sales when discounts are even more
inviting. The men's department has a solid
selection of formal footwear as well as a good
selection of Timberland at very good prices.

 Value 8   Range 7   Service 6

Chuckies

**1073 Third Avenue
between 63rd and
64th Streets
Ph: 212 593 9898
Hours
Monday Friday
10.30am 7.30pm
Saturday
10.30am 6.30pm
Sunday
12.30pm 5.30pm**

This shoe boutique is worth a mention because
it always stocks cutting edge shoes, Jimmy
Choo, Versace, Armani, Dolce & Gabana and
tons of others.Out of sale time prices are right
up there but there is wonderful value at sale
times in both little branches of this extremely
well stocked little store. Helpful staff and knock
out sales after Christmas and in July.

Also at
399 West
Broadway

Credit Cards Most
major credit cards

399 West Broadway between Spring and
Broome in Soho
Ph: 212 752 8009
Hours as above except
Saturday 10.30am 7.30pm
Credit Cards Most major credit cards

Value 8   Range 8   Service 8

(during sale time)

Giordano's Petite Designer Labels Shoes

1150, 2nd Avenue
between 60th and
61st Streets
Ph: 212 688 7195
Hours Monday
Friday 11.00am
7.00pm
Saturday 11.00am
6.00pm
Credit Cards Major
credit Cards

Not a discount store but I include it because it is
a terrific store for ladies with tiny tootsies. In
fact it is the best selection of designer, petite
shoes I have seen in New York City. It's not
hugely expensive and of course there are terrific
mark downs at sale times...main sale the
beginning of July.

Value 9   Range 10   Service 9

at sale time

Jimmy Choo

645 5th Avenue at
51st Street
between 5th and
Madison Avenues
Ph: 212 593 0800
Hours
Monday Saturday
10.00am 6.00pm
Credit Cards
Major credit cards

The shoes here are definitely among the
trendiest and most beautifully made shoes. If
you shop at sale time you won't break the bank.

Value 9   Range 10   Service 10

(during sale time.. January and July)

Manolo Blahnik

31, West 54th
Street between 5th
and 6th Avenues
Ph: 212 582 3007
Hours
Monday Friday
10.30am 6.00pm
Saturday
11.00am 5.00pm
Credit Cards
Major credit cards

This is the mecca of all major shoe lovers. You are talking about the very best with prices to match. But they do have wonderful sales, so that's I how justify including Manolo Blahnik in a discount guide. Get there on the first day and you have a great choice. Service can be snooty and the sales assistants always seem to be hysterical in French or Italian. It feels a bit like a club, if you are not part of it, you don't get the charm switched on

Value 7   Range 10   Service 5
(during sale time)

Pancaldi Shoes

331 East 81st
Street between 1st
and 2nd Avenues
Ph: 212 755 2212
Call for dates
Hours
Monday-Friday
10.00am-600pm
Credit Cards
CASH ONLY

Sales held twice a year. Usually widely advertised, they run for a week. Beautiful Italian shoes, usually on sale for less than a third of their retail price. A good selection of sizes. Naturally the best of the crop disappear very quickly but keep an eye on this sale. They reduce the prices even further on the last day. Expect huge crowds especially during lunch time.(11.30am to 2.30pm)

Value 9   Range 9   Service 7

Manolo Blaniks

The Boroughs

Queens

Shopping at Northern Boulevard

It's just across the East River from Manhattan. You can get there by Car, Cab, Bus or Subway from the City. It will take about 10 minutes from midtown if traffic moves on the 59th Street Bridge and is a great alternative to shopping in the crowded city, especially at holiday time.

Home Depot

www.homedepot.com
50-10 Northern Boulevard @ 50th Street
Ph: 718 278 9031
Hours:
Open 24 hours, seven days a week
Credit Cards: Major Credit Cards

This is a major branch of the hardware hyperstore that remains open 24 hours a day year round. So if you find you need a few bags of compost in the middle of the night, hop out to Home Depot. It has a vast stock of great lighting and mirrors. It has every kind of knob and knocker imaginable and it has a great garden furniture department during late Spring and Summer. You will also find a huge selection of Christmas decorations, tree trimmings and seasonal bric a brac at extremely competitive prices.etc.

Best Buy: Cantilevered Garden Parasol: $99.00

 Value 9   Range 9   Service 7

Old Navy

Northern Boulevard
at 48th Street
Ph: 718 267 8448
Hours Monday
Saturday 9.30am
9.30pm
Sunday 11.00am
7.00pm
Credit Cards Major
Credit Cards

The same as the City but not as crowded. Huge selection of jeans and related fashions for men, women, teens, kids, babies and infants. The baby department is particularly good. Again, as in the City, the staff are terrific and make shopping here fun and stress free.

Value 10   Range 10   Service 9

Marshalls Mega Store

Northern Boulevard
at 48th Street
Ph: 718 626 4700
Hours:
Monday -Saturday
9.30am--9.30pm
Sunday
10.00am-6.00pm
Credit Cards :
Major Credit Cards

This is a branch of a discount, department store chain. It has a full fashion department for men, ladies and kids. It also has a terrific household section. I have often got Ralph Lauren shirts here at less than half Bloomingdales prices. It also has nice gift ideas, jewellry boxes, picture frames, etc. If you are in the area, it's worth a visit. The merchandise changes regularly and I have got beautiful Italian bed linen here at a fraction of the price the same linen was on Madison Avenue.

Value 8   Range 7   Service 6

National Warehouse Company

34-60 48th Street
at Northern
Boulevard

A new mega store. Details as in SOHO section.

Party City

34-60, 48th Street
at Northern
Boulevard
Ph: 718 433 0100

The Party Place is well worth a visit. One of a chain of party shops that carries just about anything you could ever want for any kind of party, Cards, balloons, every kind of paper plates, napkins, tableclothes, disposable cutlery,

Hours:
Mon to Sat
9.30am-9.00pm
Sunday
10.30am-6.00pm
Credit Cards Major
credit cards

bowls and dishes, trays and vases, glassware. Some fancy dress outfits for kids. Great for major holidays like Christmas, Thanksgiving, St. Patrick's Day etc. 4th of July etc. Also great for weddings. Super prices.

Value 10   Range 10   Service 6

ToysR'us

Plaza 48, 35-40
48th Street at
Northern Boulevard
Ph: 718 937 8697
Monday-Saturday
9.30am-9.30pm
Sunday 10.00am-
7.00pm
Credit Cards Major
Credit Cards

This very handy branch of the famous toy store makes shopping much easier than at the Herald Square flagship. Whatever toys are in vogue will be found here at great prices, possibly the best in New York. If you are Santa's helper, the sleigh should definitely stop off here.

Value 10   Range 9   Service 6

Indian Area

Jackson Heights
the streets around
Roosevelt Avenue
and 37th Avenue
from 74th Street
for a few blocks.

Now that everything Indian is a must for the fashion conscious gal, guy and all the best pads, a trip out here by bus, subway or cab is a must. It's totally authentic and prices are so much cheaper than in the city. The area has the biggest Indian population in the United States and this is where most of them shop. Everything from beaded dresses, wraps, shawls, silk dresses and silk fabric to gold jewellry. A real bazaar feeling, the next best thing to being in New Delhi. Wonderful Indian restaurants and food stores: try the Jackson Diner at 37-47 74th Street between Roosevelt & 37th Avenues where you can dine like a maharaja for about $10.00 a head or much less at lunch time. It's a BYOB place. You can buy your beer in the food store next door and there are several liquor stores in the area. Remember cash is king in this area.

Brooklyn

Aarons

627, 5th Ave,
Brooklyn
Ph: 718 768 5400
Hours:
Monday-Saturday
9.30am-6.00pm
Thursday
9.00am-9.00pm
Closed Sunday
Credit Cards Major
credit cards

Terrific selection of current fashion labels with a good range of German and Italian labels too. The prices are always reduced and at sale time you won't know what to do with yourself. This legendary store has a loyal following of savvy Manhattan fashionistas who always look so chic, but don't count on them to tell you that they hotfoot it to Brooklyn for their top labels.

Value 8   Range 9   Service 7

Kleinfelds

8202 5th Avenue,
Brooklyn.
Ph: 718 765 8500
Hours Tuesday and
Thursday 12.30pm-
9.00pm
Wednesday and
Friday 11.00am-
6.00pm
Saturday and
Sunday 10.00am-
6.00pm
Closed Monday.
Credit Cards Major
Credit Cards

People come from all over the world to shop for the bridal party at this legendary store. Remember shopping here is by appointment only. There are literally thousands of bridal dresses in every size and shape and something for every budget. I went with a bride and found it totally overwhelming. However she did get exactly the gown she had dreamed of. The staff was extremely helpful. An army of fitters is available for alterations and every kind of accessory imaginable is in stock. Dresses are a good 30% cheaper than in the bridal salons in the city and range from a few hundred dollars to several thousand.

Value 9   Range 10   Service 8

Furnishing Fabrics

Baranzelli for Scalamandre (Silk Surplus)

www.baranzelli.com
942 3rd Avenue
bet. 56th and 57th
Streets
Ph: 212 753 6511
Hours Monday
Friday 10.00am
6.00pm
Saturday 10.00am
5.30pm
Closed Sundays
Credit Cards: Major
Credit Cards

Scalamandre is one of the most luxurious furnishing fabric labels in the world and this is the Manhattan outlet. Exquisite silks, brocades, organzas, tulles, taffetas and cottons that normally cost several hundred dollars a yard are on sale here for a fraction of the retail price. Keep and eye out for the sales here a few times a year. They are well advertised in the New York newspapers.

Value 9   Range 8   Service 9

Beckenstein Fabrics/Interiors

4, West 20th Street
(bet 5th and 6th)
Ph: 212 366 5142

I still get excited when I remember Beckenstein's sale before they uprooted from Orchard Street. Some of the best bargains I ever got in the Big Apple were dug out of that store. For the past five years the company has done even more business in it's new location. Suffice to say if it's fabric of any kind they have it here. The price is right, the staff is mostly hugely helpful and they are all incredibly knowledgeable. If they don't have it, they'll get it. And you can't beat the prices!

 Value 10   Range 10   Service 10

D&D Building (Decorator and Design)

www.ddbuilding.com
979 3rd Ave
between 58th &
59th Streets
Ph: 212 759 5408
Hours: Vary
according to
individual
showrooms

This is the HQ for the Interior Décor business for most of the United States. Just about anything to do with interior décor is housed in this high rise building. You need an introduction to shop here since everything is wholesale. A designer can give you a letter for the showroom you want to visit. Many of the companies are not averse to doing cash deals. But since just about every Manhattanite either is or has a decorator, it's not difficult to get the green light to shop here. Several times a year there are sales in the building that are open to the public. These sales are well advertised in the New York daily papers and in Sales and Bargains Section of New York Magazine. And once a year they hold a huge, week long sale for the public in one of the Armories in Manhattan. This sale is also well advertised as above.

Harry Zarin

72 Allen Street /
318 Grand Street
Trimmings and
Supplies 105
Elridge Street
Ph 212 925 6112
Hours
Monday-Sunday
9.00am-6.00pm
Credit cards Major
Credit Cards but
cash is king

At first floor level, you will discover a warehouse full of thousands of different furnishing fabrics. "The best source in town or anywhere for over 50 years "according to ABC News. Great prices and feel free to bargain for remnants. Also if you pay cash, bargain to have the tax dropped.There is now a cool trimmings department and of course there is a full curtain and furnishings service.

 **Value 10   Range 10   Service 9**

Jariel Fabrics

Broadway (one
block south of
Canal Street)
Ph: 212 226 7967
Hours:
10.00am-6.30pm
Closed Saturday
Credit Cards: Major
credit cards

Don't judge this store by it's exterior, not that the interior is exactly plush either. But I love the character of this lower Manhattan store. This is one of my favourite fabric stores in the city. Owner Jack has impeccable taste and his prices can't be beaten either. He specialises in end of runs, overruns, cancelled orders etc and the value here is brilliant. Of course it helps to have your window/sofa etc measurments, but even if you don't genius Jack will be able to help you. He supplies stage, TV and movie sets and ships fabric all over the world. He is also a really pleasant and helpful man.

Value 10   Range 7   Service 10

Joe's Fabrics

102 and 110
Orchard Street at
Delancey Street
Ph: 212 674 7089
Hours Sunday-
Thursday 9.00am-
6.00pm
Friday 9.00am-
3.00pm
Closed Saturday
Credit Cards All
major credit cards
but cash is best

This was one of my favourite interior fabric stores. At first floor level, Joe has transformed this little huckster's shop into a trendy interiors depot. Fabric that could set you back up to ten times as much in mid town is available here. Joe loves out of towners and he also loves to bargain for cash. There is a curtain making service here and the end products look stunning. Joe also recently introduced a wonderful selection of braids, tassels and trimmings downstairs at street level.There is also an inhouse design service and while prices are still keen they are not as cute as they used to be.

Value 8   Range 8   Service 9

Mood Fabrics

225, West 37th St.
3rd Floor
Ph: 212 730 5003

One of the best fabric sources in the city. Fab fabrics, fab prices, fab service. Great job!

 Value 10   Range 10   Service 10

Rae's Home Fabrics

452 Broadway
between Howard
and Grand Streets
Ph: 212 966 1414
Hours
Monday Friday
10.00am 6.00pm
Saturday
10.00am -6.00pm
Sunday
11.00M -6.00pm
Credit Cards Major
credit cards but
cash is best if you
want to bargain.

There is a superb selection of all kinds of fabrics at competitive prices here. Curtains made to measure and are beautifully finished usually within two weeks. This store has a large overseas business, the staff of several major airlines get all their curtains made here. When you meet the great staff, you will know why.

Value 10   Range 9   Service 10

Sheila's Decorating

68, Orchard Street
Ph: 212 777 3767
Hours Sunday-
Thursday 9.00am-
5.00pm
Friday 9.00am-
4.00pm
Closed Saturday
Credit cards Major
credit cards

A great selection of decorating fabrics and wallcoverings. Prices are not as competitive as some of the other stores but again there are great sales in this store too. Check the basement for final markdowns.

Value 7   Range 7   Service 5

Electronics

Nota Bene
Always observe these golden rules:

•If you are planning to buy electronic or electrical goods make sure you are dealing with an approved company.

•NEVER buy anything from the myriad stores around Time Square or other tourist areas. Prices, despite the huge sale signs, are exorbitant.

•Always check the warranty and ensure it covers merchandise outside of the United States.

•Don't succumb to hard selling, fast talking salespeople. Ideally know something about the product you want to purchase. I.E. Model number, Voltage etc. It also helps if you know the price in your own country. Sometimes prices are virtually identical. If so, it is always wiser to buy there.

Circuit City

www.circuitcity.com
Where:
232-240 East 86th
Street
Ph: 212 734 1694
Hours Monday
Saturday 10.00am
9.00pm
Sunday 11.00am
6.00pm
And at
52-54 East 14th
Street at Union
Square
Ph: 212 387 0730
Hours As above
Credit Cards Major
credit cards

The usual panoply of electrical big ticket goods.
Computers and accessories, lap top computers,
audio and video departments and a huge
selection of small electrical appliances in
addition to all the major kitchen applainces at
terrific saving.

Value 8   Range 9   Service 8

CompUSA

www.compusa.com
Where:
1775 Broadway at
57th Street
Ph: 212 262 9711
Hours Monday
Friday 8.30am
8.00pm
Saturday 10.00am
7.00pm
Sunday 11.00am
6.00pm
Credit Cards Major
credit cards

A huge selection of PC's, Laptops, Printers,
Hardware, Software and accessories is stocked
in this First Floor location. I always find it quite
manic here and it's also difficult to get a sales
assistant at weekends. They are reasonably
knowledgeable but it's best to know exactly
what you want. They are very pushy about
trying to sell insurance on the machines.

Value 8   Range 9   Service 6

Harvey

www.harveyonline.
com
2, West 45th Street
off 5th Avenue
Ph:212 575 5000
Hours:
Mon, Tues, Wed, Fri.
10.00am- 7.00pm
Thurs
10.00am- 8.00pm
Sat
10.00am -6.00pm
Sunday
12.00pm to 5.00pm
Credit Cards:
Major Credit Cards
Also inside
ABCCarpet and
Home, Broadway at
19th Street.

If you are looking for the high end of the audio/visual market this is the place to come. It's not cheap but you get what you pay for including a design and professional installation service. This store has a very loyal clientele including many from overseas.

Value 8   Range 8   Service 10

J&R

www.jandr.com
23,Park Row
Ph: 212 238 9000
1 800 426 6027
Hours:Mon- Sat
9.00am - 77.30pm
Sunday: 10.30am
to 6.30pm
Credit cards: major
Credit cards

As far as I'm concerned this is the best electronics store in the city, possibly in the country. Across from City Hall, this store has grown from it's original store on Park Row to now occupying virtually the entire Row. Not only does this series of specialized stores stock every imaginable brand of computers, TV's, Stereos, DVDs, cameras, CDs, DVS, etc. the prices are very keen but best of all the sales people actually know their merchandise and can impart real information. There might be better prices in town, but I will stick with J&R who also provide a superb after sales service. The company provides a terrific 'phone order and online service too. Audio, video, cameras, computers, software, office equipment, music, it's all here.

Value 9   Range 10   Service 10

Staples

www.staples.com
425, Park Avenue
at 56th Street Ph:
212 753 9640
1280, Lexington
Avenue at 86th
Street Ph: 212 426
6190
217 Broadway at
Vesey Street Ph:
212 346 9624
769 Broadway at
8th Street Ph: 646
654 6660
488 Broadway at
Broome Street Ph:
212 219 1299
Hours:
Monday Friday
7.00am 7.00pm
Saturday
9.00am 6.00pm
Sunday
11.00am 6.00pm
Credit Cards Major
credit cards

This chain continues to mushroom all over the City with new stores opening all the time. A limited selection of PC's. laptops, printers and accessories. Huge stationery section. Also Palm Pilots, Blackberries, ipods, Filofax etc. Average prices. On repeated visits to Staples, Park Avenue, the service has always been appalling. However at 488, Broadway, they have always been terrific. There are currently sixteen branches in the City.

Value 7   Range 6   Service 3

Sports Equipment

New York Golf Center

www.nygolfcenter.com
131 West 35th Street at
Broadway
Ph: 212 564 2255
Hours Monday Friday
10.00am 7.00pm
Saturday 10.00am
6.00pm
Sunday 11.00am
5.00pm
Credit cards Major
credit cards

7,000 square feet of golf heaven this is one of the top 100 golf stores in the United States. Large selection of all the regulars Callaway, Ping, Wilson, Titleist etc. as well as customized clubs. Great staff. Good discounts of over 30%. Also good clearance sales.

   Value 9   Range 10   Service 9

Paragon Sport

www.paragonsports.com
867 Broadway at 18th
Street
Ph: 212 255 8036
Hours
Monday-Saturday
10.00am-8.00pm
Sunday
11.00am to 6.30pm
Credit Cards
Major credit cards

New York's finest sports specialty store on three floors is also one of the best sports stores in the US catering for just about any sport you have ever heard of. Excellent sales are held twice a year. Good value in golf clubs and tennis racquets.

Value 7   Range 10   Service 10

Masons Tennis Mart

911 7th Avenue
near 57th Street
Ph: 212 757 5374
And at
56 East 53rd Street
between Park and
Madison Avenues
Ph: 212 757 5374
212 755 5805
Hours:
Monday Friday
9.00am 7.00pm
Saturday
10.00am 6.00pm
Closed Sunday
Credit Cards Major
credit cards

This is total paradise for tennis lovers. Acres of racquets, wonderful clothes by a wide range of designer and best of all, competitive prices. A top class racquet stringing service is available. It also stocks all the official US Open merchandise.

 Value 8   Range 10   Service 10

Sports Authority

www.sports
authority.com
Where:
845, 3rd Avenue at
51st Street
Ph: 212 355 9725 (
call for other store
details)
Hours Mon Fri
9.00am 8.00pm
Saturday 10.00am
7.00pm
Sunday 11.00am
6.00pm

One of a chain of extensive sports stores around the City. Great for sneakers, just about every make is in stock. Tennis racquets are also much cheaper than in Europe. Huge selection of golf clubs and attire. All the Major League Football and Baseball team shirts are in stock. Good for gym attire and equipment.

Value 8   Range 9   Service 8

World of Golf

147 East 47th
Street (between
Lexington and
Third Avenues)
2nd Floor
Ph: 212 755 9398
Hours:
Monday Saturday
9.00am 7.00pm
Sunday
11.00am 5.00pm
Credit Cards
Major credit cards

This is one of the most popular golf equipment discounters in the City. Really helpful staff here. I'm not a golfer, but I continually hear good things about this store from my golfing friends who both buy and sell their clubs here.

 Value 9   Range 9   Service 10

Beauty on a Budget

Makeup is notoriously expensiv everywhere but many brands, especially American lables are so much cheaper in new York, even if you are paying full whack!. But you don't have to fork out top dollar for the latest anti aging miracle cream or pink lipstick of the nanosecond. There are wonderful ways you can source your fave brands at a fraction of full price and have a free make over in the process. Here are eleven elegant options guaranteed to save you a bundle!

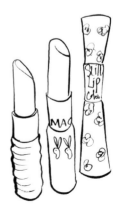

Get painted by the pros at M.A.C.

Multiple Locations

Faced with over 140 lipsticks, 120 eye shadows, and addictive odds and ends like Studio Fix powder, you may drown in this sea of colorful, stageworthy makeup. Fortunately, the professionally trained M.A.C. artists can rescue you. In addition to free makeovers, the store offers makeup lessons ($40 for a 40-minute session; includes complimentary color chart and mascara) in which the pros do half your face and you do the other half. Watch for their big in-store events.

New York International Beauty School,

www.nybaweb.com
312 W. 36th Street
Ph: 212 868 7171

Want a new look? Strapped for cash? Feeling bold? Try a makeover from a student in training. Services range from hair coloring and cutting to facials, and the prices - $3 to $15 - are unbeatable. No appointment necessary.

AVEDA

Multiple Locations

Take a break from shopping and indulge in some of Aveda's complimentary pampering: Sip a cup of "Aveda Comforting Tea", relieve stress with a neck and shoulder massage, take an aromatherapy sensory tour, or replenish with a quick makeup touch-up.

Kiehl's

109 Third Ave., at
13th St.
Ph: 212-677-3171.

A-list celebrities and downtown hipsters alike swear by Kiehl's terrific all-natural products. Try for yourself: The store is famously generous with free trial-sized samples, probably because they know you'll be back to buy more.

Shiseido Studio

155 Spring St.
Ph: 212-625-8820

There are hours of fun to be had at Shiseido's SoHo playhouse, but leave your wallet at home: Nothing's for sale. Instead, mini-facials, makeup lessons, and beauty seminars are given free of charge, and visitors are issued personal information cards to use for further Shiseido services and goodies.

Cosmetic Show

55th Street
between 3rd and
Lexington Avenues
Ph: 212 750 8418
Hours:
Monday-Friday
8.00am 6.45pm
Saturday
10.00am 4.45pm
Closed Sunday
Credit Cards
Major credit cards

A real find and fab for pressies and everyday basics. Huge selections of Elizabeth Arden, YSL, Revlon, l'Oreal, some Lancome, and lots of other brands. Good discounts on perfume. The other bonus here, tax included in the price. Also look out for makeup bags, candles, hair accessories and other things that have been special offer inducements for the major cosmetics companies. I always end up with a very full, heavy bag coming out of this one. Great for Christmas and birthday presents.

 Value 8   Range 10   Service 7

Estee Lauder Employee Store

767, 5th Avenue
between 58th and
59th Street
(lower level)
Ph: 212 572 4200
for details
Hours:
Monday-Friday
1.00am 4.00pm
Credit cards
Major credit cards

You'll find this little beauty tucked away in the basement of the old GM building (now owned by Trump.) It's not a shop and doesn't have a shop front. You'll have to ferret it out. You can get knock out value here in Estee Cosmetics and perfumes. Also Prescriptives, MAC Aveda, Bobbi Brown, and Origins. The selection varies. On some trips I find everything on my shopping list; on another I might be lucky to score three out of ten. From Thanksgiving to Christmas the stock is definitely much better and much more varied and there is amazing value in boxed sets of products. This is an employee store and you need a pass to get in here, but access depends on the doorman. Prices are about half Irish and UK prices.

 Value 10   Range 7   Service 9

Perfumania

www.perfumania.
com
Ph: Call 1 800 676
0004 for nearest
location
1585 Broadway
212 541 8047
Hours:
Monday Friday
10.00am 9.00pm
Saturday and
Sunday 10.00am
11.00pm
Credit Cards
Major credit cards

A huge selection of fragrances discounted by up to 75 % depending on the product. All the major cosmetics companies are featured and it's an ideal place for gift shopping with all kinds of gift boxes, baskets etc. at terrific discounts.

 Value 8   Range 9   Service 8

Revlon Employee Store

767, 5th Avenue
between 58th and
59th Street
(lower level)
Ph: 212 527 4000
(for details)
Hours:
Monday Friday
10.00am 4.00pm
Credit cards
Most major credit
cards

It's right next door to the Estee Lauder employee store as above. Again great value here, less than half already competitive New York Drug Store prices. They are not as fussy about their door policy as they are at the Estee store. In fact the public seems to be welcome here. It's a great place to top up on basics like shampoos, conditioners, bath gels and body moisturizers etc. They do also have an enormous selection of cosmetics.

Value 10   Range 8   Service 8

Ricky's

466 6th Avenue at
11th Street
Ph: 212 924 3401
590 Broadway at
Houston Street
Ph: 212 226 5552
718 Broadway
(Washington Place)
Ph: 212 979 5253
44 East 8th Street
(Broadway/Greene St)
Ph: 212 254 5247
1189 First Avenue
at 64th Street
Ph: 212 879 8361
Hours:
Monday Friday
9.00am-11.00pm
Saturday
9.00am-11.00pm
Sunday
10.00am-11.00pm
Credit cards
Major credit cards

A vast array of cosmetics, hair care products and general toiletries.
Everything is well discounted by over 30%. Heaven for the tweenies and teenies with every up to the nano second, high fashion lip gloss or whatever usually found here first. Well stocked sex toys section. Well worth a visit.

	Value 10	Range 6	Service 4

Sephora

www.sephora.com
Sephora Soho
555 Broadway
Ph: 212 625 1309
M, T, W, Saturday
10.00am - 8.00pm
Thursday & Friday
10.00am - 9.00pm
Sunday
Noon - 7.00 pm
And at:
Sephora Flatiron
119 Fifth Avenue
Ph: 212 674-3570
Monday - Saturday
10.00am - 8.00pm
Sunday

Sephora is the hippest chain to open in New York for ages. Owned by the French luxury giant Louis Vuitton Moet Hennessy it is a total break through in cosmetics sales. It provides the first counterless cosmetics store in New York. Just about every cosmetics/beauty range you've ever heard of is stocked but is arranged not by manufacturer ie Revlon, Dior, Estee Lauder, Kiehls, Nars, MAC, Murad to name just a few, but arranged by category. So all lipsticks from $2 to $60, all fragrances, brushes, skin care, make up etc.are to be found side by side. It makes it so much easier to browse without a high powered sales pitch but if you do need help or advice the staff are well trained and very helpful. This is not a discount chain but I include it because it has such a mind boggling

Noon-7.00pm
And at:
Sephora Times
Square
1500 Broadway
#304
Ph: 212 944-6789
Monday - Tuesday
10.00am - 10.00pm
Wednesday -
Sunday   10.00am -
12midnight
And at:
Sephora 34th Street
130 West 34th Street
Ph: 212 629-9135
Monday-Friday
9.00am - 8:30pm
Saturday
9.00am - 8:30pm
Sunday
11.00am - 7.00pm
Credit cards: All
major credit cards

range of cosmetics and beauty care products and it is such a stressless way to shop, **if** you know exactly what you want. It also has good mark downs from time to time. You can browse for as long as you like. There is a good range of sample products and you don't have the pressure of pushy sales assistants. However if you do need help or advice there are well trained assistants, who are thankfully devoid of the 'attitude' that seems part of the uniform of so many beauty product sales clerks. There are also in store specialists from different companies who do the usual makeovers. Anything your heart desires in every cosmetic label and fragrance from a dollar to thousands. Also check out their own label and less expensive lines. A great range of baby and kids products are great for the infant or kid who has everything. It's also a good place for high fashion products and new season's colours.

Value *   Range 10   Service 10

* Not discounted

Toys

Jacks World.
Details as in Discount Stores Section

K*B Toys

Locations:
Check newspapers
Hours: Check
newspapers
Credit Cards
Major credit cards

These stores appear all over the city like mushrooms at the beginning of December. They are short leases for the Christmas period so I'm unable to list locations. They do advertise extensively in all the New York newspapers. Prices are rock bottom and the selection is quite good.

 Value 9   Range 6   Service 8

Odd Job Trading
Details as in Discount Store Section

National Warehouse Trading
Details as in Discount Store Section

ToysRus

24 32 Union Square
East
Ph: 212 674 8697
Hours:
Monday Saturday
9.00am 9.00pm
Sunday
11.00.am 7.00pm
Credit Cards Major
Credit Cards

Possibly the best value in toys in the City. Vast selection for all age groups. All the best known brands are here at a fraction of what they cost in Ireland. Whatever the hottest toy of the year is, you have a better chance of finding it here because of the companies huge buying power. But once the Christmas holiday season kicks in... immediately after Thanksgiving (the third Thursday in November), make sure to put this store top of your list, first thing in the morning.

As the day progresses it becomes increasingly like a war zone. Also at this time of the year, it's a complete nightmare at weekends: so bad in fact, that if they were giving the stuff away for nothing, I would still skip it.

Value 10   Range 10   Service 5

Weber

Details as in Discount Store section

Jewellery

47th Street between 5th and 6th Avenues

This is the diamond district, one of the biggest retail diamond shopping areas in the world. It is well worth a look even if discount diamonds are not top of your priority list. Any of the ultra orthodox Jewish traders that you see strolling up and down the street, could have $20 million or more worth of loose diamonds in their pockets.

But I wouldn't upset the bank manager unless you know your carats. It is also THE place to buy gold and other precious metals which are sold by weight and charged at the daily rate quoted on the Stock market.

There are some wonderful antique jewellery booths in the different Exchanges that are located on both sides of the Street. Undoubtedly there are terrific deals to be found in this area and I have seen simply beautiful diamond rings and necklaces that have been bought here. But beware the Sharks who swim up and down this block on the look out for tourists. Everyone I know who shops here has their own special jeweller.

Tiffany

www.tiffany.com
Location
Fifth Avenue at
57th Street
Ph: 212 755 8000
Hours:
Monday Friday
10.00am 6.00pm
Saturday
10.00am 6.00pm
Credit Cards
Major credit cards

What is the world famous Tiffany store doing in a bargain guide? I hear you say. Before you think I've lost it, it's here because it is one of the leading diamond dealers and jewellers in the world. The company enjoys icon status globally and many visitors to New York feel they haven't really experienced the City without a visit to this 5th Avenue legend. However you will find a lot more than rocks at this store. They also sell beautiful stationery, perfumes, silk scarves, china, crystal and there is a magnificent silver department. It's possible to have a cute key ring or money clip wrapped up in the instantly recognizable Tiffany blue box and tied with the signature white ribbon bow for upwards of $60.00. Ireland's wonderful designer, the late Sybil Connolly, is still represented here. But whether you buy anything, it's worth a browse. It's fun to watch young couples agonizing over the solitaire for $45,000 or the emerald cut stone for $50,000. And they do this in full public view and yes they do buy the rings too. Coming up to Christmas there are so many people at the diamond counter, one would be forgiven for thinking that they were being sold at bargain basement prices.

Books

Amazon

www.amazon.com

If you don't want the bother of going to the bookstore and carrying those heavy shopping bags back to your hotel, log on to www.amazon.com If you know the titles you want you can order them on line from Amazon and have them delivered to your hotel. They also ship all over the world. The prices are quite competitive and the process is totally effortless.

Argosy Books

www.argosy.com
116 E 59th Street
bet Lexington and
Park Avenues
Ph: 212 753 4455
Hours:
Monday Friday
10.00am 6.00pm
Saturday
10.00am 5.00pm
Credit Cards
Major credit cards

Old books, first editions etc. Very helpful staff will find what you are looking for. It is also a great place to chill out and browse after a session in Bloomingdales.

 Value 8   Range 7   Service 9

Barnes and Noble

www.bn.com

Credit Cards
Major Credit cards

This is one of the biggest bookstore chains in the City. The selection is superb as are the staff. If they don't have what you are looking for the chances are they can order it and have it within 24 hours. The stores, which also sell magazines, are always busy especially throughout lunch time - 11.00am-3.00pm when they tend to be packed. Expect endless queues at holiday times when the crowds make buying books quite an endurance test. The current New York Times Best Seller List is discounted by 25% at all B & N stores and there is always a good clearance section too.

4 Astor Place — 4 Astor Place 420-1322 Mon - Sat 10 am to 11 Between Broadway and Lafayette Sun 10 am to 10 pm

8th Street and 6th Avenue — 8th Street and 6th Avenue 674-8780 Mon - Sat 10 am to 10pm
Sun 12 Noon to 7pm

105 Fifth Ave At 18th Street — 105 Fifth Ave At 18th Street 807-0099 Mon - Fri 9:30am to 7:45pm
Sat 9:00am to 6:15pm
Sun 11:00am to 5:45pm

33 East 17th Street	33 East 17th Street 253-0810 Every Day - 10am to 10pm at Park Avenue
6th Avenue at 22nd Street	6th Avenue at 22nd Street 727-1227 Mon - Sat 9am to 11pm Sun 10am to 10pm
Fifth Ave at 36th Street	Fifth Ave at 36th Street 779-7677 Mon - Sat 8am to 7pm Sun 10am to 6pm
3rd Avenue at 47th Street	3rd Avenue at 47th Street 697-2251 Mon - Fri 8am to 8pm Sat 10am to 7pm Sun Closed
600 Fifth Avenue	600 Fifth Avenue 765-0590 Mon - Fri 8:30am to 9pm at 48th Street Sat 10am to 8pm Sun 10am to 7pm
54 Street & Lexington Avenue	54 Street & Lexington Avenue 750-8033 Mon - Fri 7am to 9pm at Citicorp Building Sat 10am to 9pm Sun 11am to 6pm
1972 Broadway At 66th Street	1972 Broadway At 66th Street 595-6859 Every day - 9am - Midnight Lincoln Triangle
Broadway at 82nd Street	Broadway at 82nd Street 362-8835 Sun - Thurs 9am to 11 pm Fri & Sat 9am to Midnight
Lexington Ave & 86th Street	Lexington Ave & 86th Street 423-9900 Every day 9am to 10pm
Second Avenue & 86th Street	Second Avenue & 86th Street 794-1962 Everyday 9.00amto 11.00pm

Value **7**   Range **9**   Service **9**

Barnes and Noble Sales Annex

105, 5th Avenue at
18th Street
Ph: 212 807 0099
Hours:
Monday Friday
9.30am 7.45pm
Saturday
9.30am 6.15pm
Sunday
11.00am 5.45pm
Credit Cards
Major Credit Cards

This is the B&N Outlet center, a great place to buy very inexpensive books but check your time. You can pop in here for an hour and come out days later. Tempus fugit.

Value 9   Range 10   Service 8

Strand Books

828,Broadway at
12th Street
Ph: 212 473 1452
Hours: Mon.-Sat
9.30am to 10.30pm
Sunday 11.00am to
10.30pm
Credit cards Major
Credit Cards
also at
95, Fulton Street
between William
Street and Wall
Street.

Used, new, rare and out of print, 8 miles of books is the boast at this New York landmark. INisders know this is where to pick up review copies of all the latest best sellers at 50% discount. Books by the foot is another feature here. from 3 feet to 3,00 ft titles come in a vast array of colours and bindings. At least they are real books unlike some of the new millionaires I know who actually have dummy books in the 'libraries'.

Value 10   Range 10   Service 10

Tower Books and Records

A reliable chain of stores throughout the City. Very helpful staff can either find or order just about any title. Huge selection in numerous categories. One of the best places for CDs and DVDs

Value 8   Range 10   Service 10

Furs

If you want to be warm rather than politically correct, NYC is the place to buy your mink. The Fur District is around 7th Avenue and 28th Street. There are endless fur lofts in this district but beware: unless you know something about skins, bring someone with you that does have the necessary info. There are many sharp operators in the fur trade. The Thrift Stores that are listed in their own section are also good places to check little worn fur coats which usually sell for a fraction of their original cost.

Peter Duffy Furriers

231. West 29th Street (between 7th and 8th Avenues)
Ph: 212 255 5144:
9.00am to 4.30pm
Hours By Appointment
Credit Cards
Major credit cards

This is one of the oldest furriers in New York City. It's also one of the best kept secrets because in the 18th Floor showrooms you will find the most luxurious minks, sables, shearlings, mink lined raincoats, wraps hats and other accessories in traditional as well as all the latest styles for less than half department store prices. Peter Duffy and his wife Marge provide a very personal service. Irish American Peter is a legend in the fur trade and is one of the longest established furriers in the United States. Coats and jackets can be either made to measure or bought off the peg. They also stock a wide range of fur accessories. Their clientele reads like a Who's Who on both sides of the Atlantic, indeed clients come here from all over the world. The staff are knowledgeable, very friendly and not at all pushy. The furs are top quality and up to minute designs. Better still they are between 40% and 60% cheaper than in the department stores.

 Value 10   Range 10   Service 10

Birger Christensen

150 West 30th
Street at 7th
Avenue (20th
Floor)
Ph: 212 736 6944
Hours By
Appointment
Credit cards
No credit cards

This is one company highly recommended by friends who know their furs and their prices. It features a full range of furs that are sold in major department stores, at discount prices. Sales assistants are pushy.

	Value 8	Range 8	Service 8

Ritz Furriers

West 57th Street
Ph:
Hours:
Credit Cards:

This is a very high profile second hand fur shop. They certainly carry top of the range designer coats and jackets but on the many times I have dropped in here, I was never impressed ith the prices which in many cases seemed higher than the same coats at Peter Duffys.

Saks, Bloomingdales and Macys all have great fur sales, especially during the late Spring and early Summer... out of season is the trick for best fur bargains. Great mink coats from $1999 up. These sales are always well flagged in the New York Times, New York Post, New York Daily News and also on TV commercials.

Buttons

Gordon Button Company

222, W. 38th Street
between 7th and
8th Avenues
Ph: 212 921 1684
Hours Monday
Saturday 9.30am
5.30pm
Credit Cards No
credit cards

Any kind of button your heart desires at discount prices.

	Value 9	Range 10	Service 9

Great Buttons

231, West 40th Street
Ph 212 869 6811
Credit cards Major credit cards
Hours:
Monday Friday 9.00am 6.00pm
Saturday 10.00am 5.00pm

All kinds of buttons, especially for bridal and evening wear. This store also has a wide range of bridal head pieces, tiaras, veils and trimmings.

| | Value 8 | Range 9 | Service 7 |

Tender Buttons

East 61st Street, between Lexington Avenue and Third Avenues
Ph: 212 758 7004
Hours:
Monday Friday 10.30am 6.00pm
Saturday 10.30am 5.30pm
Credit Cards No credit cards

This is the Rolls Royce of button stores. Designer buttons, Versace etc. real bone buttons, diamante buttons, faux jewel buttons, pearl buttons, it's rather like a library of buttons with endless little drawers housing these little gems. However prices reflect the exclusivity of this store where you could find yourself rubbing shoulders with lots of up and coming young designers.

| | Value 8 | Range 10 | Service 10 |

Dress Fabrics

Garment District:
West 40th Street
between 7th and
8th Avenues is
Fabric Row.

There are endless fabric stores on both sides of this block that carry a huge stock of every imaginable type of fabric. In the heart of the Garment District and around the corner Parsons Fashion College, this is fabric heaven. Everytime I go by here I am almost reduced to tears remembering all those sewing lessons at school I ignored in favour of Latin and Greek. But then I remember Kamil, my trustee Lebanese tailor on 65th Street, who can whip up an outfit in jig time as good as the best tailor in Hong Kong or Bangkok. Prices are quite literally mind boggling bargains. I shopped here once with an Irish fashion designer who paid, for her wholesale fabrics in Paris, twice what the same fabrics were available for on 40th Street. For bridal or beaded laces in every colour under the sun, this is where you will find it. The staff in most stores are all so knowledgeable and eager to ensure that your outfit will be a total knockout. You fill find fabrics from Chanel, Prada, Dior, Valentino, Ralph Lauren, Donna Karan et al. There are also some trimming stores where you will find buttons, zippers etc. If you have a special inquiry go to the Information Booth on 7th Avenue on the north east corner of 39th Street. The girls are so helpful and can provide you with listings of all the specialist fabric merchants, many of whom don't have street level stores. Of course many are wholesale only but believe me there are more than enough that are delighted to trade with all shoppers.

Ayazmoon Fabric

235, West 40th
Street
Ph: 212 869 3315
Hours:
Monday Friday
9.00am 7.00pm
Saturday
10.00am 6.00pm
Sunday noon
5.00pm
Credit Card
Major credit cards

All kinds of fabric, especially the Oriental silks.
Knock out beaded and jewel encrusted sari
lengths.

Value 9	Range 8	Service 10

B& J Fabrics

263 West 40th
Street (near 8th
Avenue)
Ph: 212 354 8150
Hours:
Monday-Friday
8.00am 5.45pm
Saturday
9.00am 4.45pm
Credit Cards
Major credit cards

Beautiful silks, cottons, wollens, laces and other
fabrics imported from France, Italy and
Switzerland. Very well priced.

Value 8	Range 9	Service 8

C.H Bridal

241, West 40th
Street
Ph: 212 944 8477
Hours:
Monday Friday
9.00am 6.00pm
Saturday
10.00am 5.00pm
Credit Cards
Major credit cards

This little store specializes in veils and
headpieces for the bride and her bridesmaids.
They can make any kind of veil, just bring a
picture of what you want and they will copy it.
They also stock tiaras, buttons, gloves etc.

Value 8	Range 8	Service 8

Felsen Fabrics

264 West 40th
Street
Ph: 212 398 9010
Hours Monday
Friday 8.30am
5.45pm
Saturday 9.00am
4.45pm
Credit Cards Major
credit cards

This store specialises in bridal fabrics and is a must stop for all the ladies in the bridal party. The embroidered and beaded silks and laces are breathtaking as is the gossamer like French Chantilly lace.

Value 8   Range 9   Service 8

Lugo's Fabrics

250, West 40th
Floor, 2nd Floor
Ph: 212 354 0555
Hours Monday
Friday 8.30am
6.00pm
Saturday 9.00am
5.00pm
Credit Cards Major
credit cards

A limited range of bridal fabrics but very good quality and some of the best prices on the block. There is also a wide range of general fabrics. There is a limited range of bridal trimmings, silk flowers, pearl beading, buttons, tiaras etc. Staff couldn't have been more helpful

Value 9   Range 7   Service 10

Mountain Fabric

227, West 40th
Street
Ph 212 354 8442
Hours
Credit Cards Major
credit cards

The selection of silk taffeta here was quite breathtaking. It was like a close up of a rainbow. A wide range of all kinds fabrics line the shelves here where the staff are quite superb.

Value 9   Range 8   Service 10

Paron

The stock here changes all the time but there is usually a good selection of designer fabrics according to season. Donna Karan cashmeres, Oscar de la Renta lace, Chloe silks were just some of the superb fabrics at knock down prices that were in stock when I last visited Paron. Really knowledgeable and helpful shops make shopping a joy here.

Value 9   Range 6   Service 9

206, West 40th Street between 7th and 8th Avenues

206, West 40th Street between 7th and 8th Avenues
Ph: 212 768 3266
Hours Monday Friday 9.00am 5.30pm
Saturday 9.00am 5.00pm
Credit Cards Major credit cards

And at

Paron Half Price Outlet Fabric Store 206 A, West 40th Street

Paron Half Price Outlet Fabric Store
206 A, West 40th Street

(midtown)

56 West 57th Street between 5th and 6th Avenues

56 West 57th Street between 5th and 6th Avenues
Ph: 212 247 6451
Hours Monday Saturday 9.00am 5.45pm
Credit Cards Major credit cards

And at

Paron 11 Half Price Outlet 56, West 57th Street, 2nd Floor

Paron 11 Half Price Outlet
56, West 57th Street, 2nd Floor
Ph: 212 247 6451
Hours Monday Saturday 9.00am 5.45pm
Credit Cards Major credit cards

Poli Fabrics

227 West 40th
Street
Ph: 212 768 4555
Hours:
Monday Friday
9.00am 5.45pm
Saturday
9.00am 4.45pm
Credit Cards
Major credit cards

A great source for top international designer fabrics at a fraction of their original cost. Very generous with swatches too. Like most of the stores on the block, prepare to bargain here.

Value 9   Range 8   Service 9

Rosen and Chadick

Ph: 212 869 0142
Hours
Monday Friday
8.30am 5.00pm
Saturday
9.00am 4.00pm
Credit Cards Major
credit cards

One of the best selections of every kind of fabric on the street. One of the more expensive stores on the block but racks of beautiful beaded fabrics, ideal for stunning evening wear are great value.Staff are particularly helpful.

Value 6   Range 9   Service 9

Royal Fabrics

www.royal
fabric.com
251, West 40th
Street
Ph: 212 398 0215
Credit Cards
Major credit cards

In addition to the usual range of silks and stains, this store had a kaleidoscopic range of silk taffeta, wonderful for curtains and for fine upholstery.

Value 10   Range 6   Service 4

Tapicentro

251, West 39th
Street, 15th Floor
Ph: 212 869 5634
Hours
Monday Friday
9.30am 5.30pm
Credit Cards Major
credit cards

Designer fabrics from $3.00 and up a yard. Upholstery and curtain fabric from $6.00 a yard. Curtain voile $1.50 a yard an up. Also large selection of curtain odds and ends and a large remnant section.

Value 9   Range 6   Service 8

Zohra Fabrics Inc.

235, West 40th
Street
Ph: 212 719 9617
Hours:
Monday Friday
9.00am 6.30pm
Saturday
9.30am 5.30pm
Credit Cards
Major credit cards

This store specialises in designer fabrics and also stocks a wide range of bridal fabrics.

Value 8   Range 8   Service 8

Professional Cameras & Camera Equipment

Everybody say Cheese

Adorama

www.adorama.com

Where:
17th St between
5th & 6th Avenues
Ph: 1 800 223 2500
or 212 741-0052

By phone
Monday through
Thursday 9:00 AM
to 9:30 PM EST
Friday 9:00 AM to
1:15 PM EST
Sunday 9:30 AM to
5:45 PM EST

In Person:
Monday through
Thursday 9:00 AM
to 6:30 PM
Friday 9:00 AM to
1:15 PM
Sunday 9:30 AM to
5:30 PM
Credit Cards: Major
Credit Cards

Say Cheap! This business, now the largest camera company in the United States, started as a trickle - a few Leica cameras bought in Germany after World War II, then shipped to New York for resale. Though small, the business prospered and grew. Today it's called Adorama Camera, and it has become a magnet for photographers from all over the world, amateurs and professionals alike, who want to buy new equipment, sell their old stuff or find a bargain on a used camera. In addition to its extensive selection of used equipment, Adorama offers new cameras and underwater cameras, a rental department, a mail-order operation, a complete lab and studios for rent. All used equipment can be returned in 14 days, no questions asked, and it comes with a full 100-day warranty. Extended warranties are also available.

Whatever their preference or their needs, they're sure to find it at Adorama. A basic Canon AE-1 35mm camera with lens, ideal for a novice, is just $150. A more sophisticated Mamiya 645 medium format, with body, prism and lens, is $350. For those hunting a bargain on the latest technology, a demo Nikon Coolpix 2 100 digital camera, still in the box, is available for $99.

International orders processed.

 **Value** 9   **Range** 9   **Service** 10

Alkit Photo

www.alkit.com
222, Park Ave
South corner 18th
Street
Ph: 212 6741515
Hours:
Mon- Fri
7.30am - 7.30pm
Saturday
9.00am-6.00pm
Closed Sunday
Credit Cards
Major credit cards

Alkit is another mega camera pros mecca. With a vast inventory of new and used equipment, it is also possible to rent about anything to do with imaging here. International delivery.

Value 9   **Range** 9   **Service** 9

B & H

www.bhphoto
video.com
420 9th Ave and
34th Street
Ph: 1 800.606.6969
and 212.444.6615
Hours:
Sunday: 10:00 am
to 4:45 p.m
Monday through
Thursday:
9:00 am to 5:30 p.m.
Friday (winter):
9:00 am to 1:00 p.m.
Friday:
9:00 am to 2:00 p.m.
Saturday: Closed
Credit Cards: All
major credit cards.

Known all over the world as the Professionals suppliers, B&H has been serving imaging markets for 30 years. Through all those years the company's goal has been to deserve the trust of its customers. To do this B&H knew they must offer competitive pricing, but also knew low prices alone could not make its business superior. B&H is the world's leading retailer of imaging products, serving professionals and consumers through the New York City retail store and through direct delivery internationally. Imagine a store as large as a football field, and imagine warehouse space much larger! B&H has the world's most extensive inventory of imaging products, all available at discounted prices in the store, all of them almost always ready for rapid delivery to you. A glance at the list of departments only begins to show the variety of stock which caters to a clientele all over the world.

Value 10   **Range** 10   **Service** 10

Pampering at Pauper Prices

Kenneths Salon

Waldorf Astoria Hotel, 300 Park Avenue Ph: 212 355 3000 Closed Sunday Major Credit Cards:

These are not pauper prices but definitely the best pedicure I have ever had anywhwere in the world, by miles. Tania works with the skill and precision of a surgeon. Your leave the salon walking on air and this fab. feeling lasts for at least a month. I try to get there every six weeks, if I don't I begin to dream about Tania and Kenneths. Book well in advance. $50.00 plus tip. Manicures are also excellent as if the totally wonderful hair salon where Kevin Lee is a pure genius and a really nice guy to boot.

Multi-Service

312 W. 36th St., 212-868-7171; www.nyibs.baweb. com

New York International Beauty School Want a new look? Strapped for cash? Feeling bold? Try a makeover from a student in training. Services range from hair coloring and cutting to facials, and the prices — $3 to $15 — are unbeatable. No appointment necessary.

Jade Beauty and Wellness Spa

2493 Broadway, 212-362-5763

You can get it all done — waxing, facials, massages, tinting, manicures, pedicures, and acupuncture — at this Upper West Side spa that stays open until 10pm on Weekdays. Late manicures are unheard of on the UWS. Prices are competitive for individual services: $10 for a manicure or eyebrow wax. But, the packages are great deals. For $98, you can get a 20-minute massage, facial, manicure, and pedicure.

Massage

Graceful Services

1097 Second Ave., near 57th St.; 212-593-9904 190 Third Ave., at 17th St.; 212-420-7242

No doubt about it—as much as we could all use frequent massaging, paying over $100 for each rubdown can be anxiety-producing in itself. At Graceful Services, there may be no impressive lounge, but the strong Qi Gong massage goes straight to the muscle spasm. Flowing white curtains separate you from the next client, and the rooms are spanking clean. For $60, you'll enjoy your hour and feel stress-free for at least a day or two.

Sal Anthony

190 Third Ave., at 17th St.; 212-420-7242

Sal Anthony's empire near Union Square includes, somewhat inexplicably, this fitness studio (two studios, actually) in a landmarked building. Here you can get a $55 one-hour rubdown ($85 for 90 minutes) from therapists versed in Swedish, Shiatsu, and Thai massage.

Sol Jade Lady Spa

4 W. 33rd St., near Fifth Ave.; 212-594-8040

Possibly the city's best-kept secret, this basement-level, women-only spa offers a 90-minute treatment for $100: A steam is followed by a loofah scrub, a sauna, and a cucumber face mask; then come rubdowns with oil, seaweed emollient, and milk. The finale is a fabulous shampoo and scalp massage. Forget modesty, as you'll share a room with at least two others during busy hours.

Tui-Na

222 Lafayette St., between Spring and Kenmare Sts.; 212-941-6038

If you can't get naked in front of other people, don't bother with Tui-Na. If, however, you can deal with lying nude in a darkened basement room with an equally nude stranger (of either gender) on the table next to you, you'll get a true massage bargain here — once the energetic Tui-Na masseuses start working on your muscles, you'll lose any anxiety about where you are, anyway. And at $40 an hour, it's pretty easy to let go.

Waxing

Elite Day Spa

24 W. 39th St., 212-730-2100

The prices are cheap, but the highly skilled and efficient technicians at this fashion district salon will make you feel like you've paid a lot more. Lip, $6; eyebrow, $15; bikini, $13-$19; brazilian, $25; full leg, $31; arm, $24.

Irene and Lucy

223 E. 74th St., 212-772-0720

This small east side spot is known among the Birkenstock-wearing and the Birkin-bag-carrying alike for fabulous, thorough waxes. Eyebrow, $7; half-leg, $17; full leg, $39; bikini, $15 to $25; brazilian, $45; underarm, $10; arm, $20.

Randee Elaine

180 Seventh Ave., 212-229-0399

The menu of services here lists twenty body areas that Randee Elaine will wax (other areas are negotiable), with prices ranging from $7 for chin or eyebrow to $30 for full leg with bikini. No body-hair issue is too embarrassing to be discussed and dealt with, which makes this place exceedingly popular with men.

Manicure & Pedicure

Bloomie Nails

132 Seventh Ave.,
212-366-4545; 170
W. 23rd St.,
212-741-0105;
294 Eighth Ave.,
646-638-2727

The faithful flock to Bloomie Nails for relaxing pedicures in heated, pulsating massage chairs and mini-screens at the drying stations playing VH1. Considering that the manicure-pedicure is $35 ($3 extra for razor-scraping of your soles), it's no wonder the places are often packed.

Jeniette

58 E. 13th St.,
212-529-1616

It might be worth the $21.85 cost of a pedicure at Jeniette just to hang out in one of their extremely comfy chairs for a half-hour. Considered the best pedicure bargain in town by many of the city's snazzier toes, Jeniette has a famously friendly staff, a good, relaxing foot massage, and a comprehensive polish selection.

SoHo Nail

458 W. Broadway,
212-475-6368

A favorite of fashionistas, SoHo Nail boasts possibly the least expensive ($20) quality manicure-pedicure in town. But you'll pay in other ways, namely the time spent air-drying afterward, as this joint owns no drying machines. Ask for Lucy or the owner, Susan Kang. They're favorites of SoHo Nail regulars.

Make-up

M.A.C.

Multiple locations.

Faced with over 140 lipsticks, 120 eye shadows, and addictive odds and ends like Studio Fix powder, you may drown in this sea of colorful, stageworthy makeup. Fortunately, the professionally trained M.A.C. artists can rescue you. In addition to free makeovers, the store offers makeup lessons ($40 for a 40-minute session; includes complimentary color chart and mascara) in which the pros do half your face and you do the other half. Watch for their big in-store events.

Chow Time

When it comes to eats my advice is to buy a copy of the Zagat Survey. Price $11.99. I have found it to be a totally reliable restaurant guide. It's available from most newstands and bookstores and amazon.com It's often on sale from the street booksellers around the City for considerably less than the cover price. Published annually, the Survey gives ordinary diners reactions to just about every eatery in the City. This year over 20,000 people participated in the Survey, eating over 3.2 million meals in the process. They are always volunteers, so there is no fear of compromised integrity here. The Survey works well because it lists restaurants alphabetically and then does sub sections according to area, ethnic cuisine, the most romantic spots, best value, where to eat outdoors etc. I have relied on the Zagat Survey for new places to eat for nearly twenty years and I have never had a major disappointment.

However these are a few of my own favourites dotted around town. There is a mixture of locations, price points and ethnic food. If one had to eat out for every meal, every day of the year, you still wouldn't come near to sampling the mind- boggling variety of cuisine in New York City. Talk about being spoiled for choice !!! The citizens of New York, represent virtually every culture and population group on the planet and they expect high standards when they dine out! The diversity of cuisine is unbelievable and one can choose to sample the wondrous variety at any size or level of eating place, take-outs, tiny dining rooms that seat 15 or 20 people and the full range of serious restaurants serving the finest cuisine in elegant surroundings at seriously high prices!

With a Metro Card and a desire to explore you can satisfy a craving for anything from authentic Mexican tacos at four in the afternoon, near Penn Station, to grilled Italian sandwiches and great espresso at 23h30 in the West Village! The next day you can dine in a French bistro with the feel of old Les Halles in SoHo!

There are great new takes on Mediterranean food, still the most accessible and familiar of cuisines, that has would-be diners standing in line for tables and going back the next night for more of the same!

Lupa

170 Thompson
Street
Ph: 212 982 5080

Owned by Mario Battali whose upscale Babbo is rated as one of Manhattan's top Italian restaurants. Lupa is full of atmosphere and noise. At the simply set wooden tables you can enjoy great ciabbata served with black olives and fruity olive oil before your order of Antipasto of aged Prosciutto, smoked beef and salami served with sliced Provolone or Insalata of Escarole, walnuts, red onion, Pecorino and beetroot carpaccio arrives. Follow that with some Citrus-cured Sardines or a dish of Ricotta Gnocchi with sausage and fennel or Pappardelle Straccotto, Market Fish 'Cartoccio' with preserved lemon and fennel or lamb ravioli in white butter sauce with pea shoots, fresh peas and orange rind could be another option!

Bar Pitti

268 Sixth Avenue
Ph: 212 982 3300
between Bleecker
and Houston
Streets

This is where Florence- born Giovanni serves up daily specials of Rigatoni with turkey sausage, peas, cream and tomato or Osso Buco with ripe red baby tomatoes and rocket on top! Bar Pitti does not take reservations but the locals seem happy to stand in line!!

Gennaro's

665 Amsterdam
Avenue
Ph: 212 665 5348

On the Upper West Side they do take bookings but still one stands in line!! This very popular neighbourhood trattoria, near 92nd Street seems to do endless table turnarounds in an evening! Grilled Calamari with Sicilian Couscous and Salad with walnuts, pear, fresh Pecorino and warm Portabella tart with Goat Cheese are crowd pullers and that's before you get to the entrées of Slowly Braised Lamb Shank in Red Wine Sauce with Israeli Couscous or Grilled Salmon with Honey-Mustard sauce!

Nick & Tonis

100 West 67th
Street
Ph: 212 496 4000

In the Upper Westside, this is small and stylish, between Columbus and Broadway. An inventive Mediterranean menu lures patrons with appetizer and pasta offerings such as Dandelion Salad with anchovy, lemon and shaved parmesan, Fresh Ricotta Ravioli with fava beans, baby spinach and fresh morels or Risotto with lobster and spring peas. Tempting entrees include whole fish from the wood oven with roasted asparagus and fennel or Hanger Steak with cabrales mashed potatoes, French beans and tomatoes.

Capa

189 East Houston
Street

Mediterranean, Latin American and Oriental with a New York twist is on the menu. A tiny dining room where you can order. Yuca and platano with black bean, delicious as a starter while crabcake with mesclun in spicy raspberry vinaigrette vies for attention with salt and pepper fried calamari with arrabiata sauce and steamed mussels in a lemongrass broth with chinese chives!

Homemade gnocchi with chopped walnuts in a light gorgonzola sauce and Fusilli, garden vegetable, extra-virgin olive and roast garlic are pasta choices. Striped Bass baked in ginger scallion sauce served with bok choy, Pork chops grilled in apple marsala sauce served with shitake mushrooms are the creative entrees on offer. Capa is particularly reasonably priced and entrees vary between $10 and $13 each.

Moustache

90 Bedford Street,
West Village
Ph: 212 229 2220
and 265 East 10th
Street(bet 1st Ave
and Ave A)

This is definitely in the cheap and tiny category, a Middle Eastern eating place which has two locations. Now the Metro Card option becomes really worth while!! Extremely popular for its Middle-Eastern Pizzas with toppings of Lamb, onions ,tomato, parsley and spices or lemon-marinated chicken with garlic, red bell peppers,

scallions and parsley. Delicious Spinach and
Chickpea salad and wonderful Hummus and
Tabouleh is delectably fresh and taste-tempting
and a casual meal taken outside in the covered
garden and washed down with a cold Budweiser
or a glass of fresh lemonade is a real treat!

Pico

**349 Greenwich
Street in Tribeca**
Staying in the Mediterranean ambit but moving
up on the elegance and price scale is this
Iberian restaurant. This is fine dining in the
chic New York City style. A Pico Prix Fixe Menu
of three courses at $52 dollars could give you
Seared Rare Tuna with Goan red masala,
mango and fenugreek sprouts or Crisped
Bacalhau Cake with Blood Orange and Radish
salad, roasted beets, cilantro and parsley as a
first course, followed by Organic Suckling Pig,
roasted 'Bairrada' style with crisp potato and
wild flower honey or Grilled Sargo, walnut
puree, roasted shallot, fingerling potato, green
olive and lemon confit as the second choice.
Dessert could be a Double Chocolate Timbale,
cinnamon-scented chocolate cake and chocolate
sauce or Chilled Praline flan with Pralette
cookies!
The impeccably prepared food is served on
exquisite Portuguese porcelain with silver
service and salvers, while attentive and
knowledgeable waiters fill your glass with
choices from the wine lists great selection of
Portugal's fine wines!!

*New York's neighborhoods have totally unique and
different characters and moving north from trendy
Tribeca and its high-priced lofts is the West Village
with its endless choice of places to stop and places to
shop!!*

*In the Meat-Packing districts cobbled streets, where
old warehouses with faded paint signs and brick-
faced buildings make the area look like a movie set
about to happen- is*

Pastis

9th Ave at W. 12th
Street
Ph: 212 929 4844

This is a replica of a Parisian brasserie where you can play 'spot the movie star' while you sample the Omelette Fines-Herbes, the French-toast with Fresh Fruit or the Irish Oatmeal with sautéed bananas!

Balthazar

80 Spring Street off
Broadway in Soho
Ph: 212 965 1414

Complete with Art-Deco interior and a zinc-topped bar offers and an authentic brasserie menu, the beautiful people who jostle for tables keep coming back for the superb raw seafood tower with its variety of oysters. The pommes-frites that accompany the burger and steak are pretty good too! It's one of my favourites and is open from breakfast through to dinner. It also has a terrific bakery where you can buy all kinds of freshly baked bread. Or you can just sit at the bar and enjoy a glass of champagne and oysters.

Fitzers

687 Lexington
Avenue between
56th and 57th
Streets
Ph: 212 355 0100

A little bit of Irish heaven, definitely the best Irish food in New York.All that wonderful comfort food, Irish Stew, Shepards Pie, just what you need after a hard night out or a long day shopping. But food is not exclusively irish. Great pizzas and pasta and a really good chicken curry.I love the BLT with fries and the fish and chips are nearly as good as Burdocks. It also has the best Irish breakfast/brunch in New York. Moderately expensive.

21 Club

21 East 52nd
Street between 5th
and 6th Avenues
Ph: 212 582 7200

My own all time favourite. Simply the best of everything. It's not a club but it might as well be. Much loved by Wall Street and washington DC powerhouses. Bill Clinton is a regular here too. Ask for Bruce. He is a total sweetie. if they are not too busy you might be lucky enough to get a tour of the legendary cellar which dates back to 'speak easy' days. Wine belonging to the rich and famous is stored here, half of Hollywood have their favourite cuvees laid down at 21. Reservations a must.

Les Halles

411, Park Ave
South bet 28th and
29th Streets
Ph: 212 679 4111

Good Bistro food, great steak and frites. Also good butchery department.Tres Francais. Great atmosphere and good value. Reservations recommended

Park Bistro

414 Park Ave South
bet 28th and 29th
Streets. Ph: 212
689 1360

The same owners as Les Halles. Very Parisian, great buzz. The food is really good hearty, peasant fare.

La Goulue

746 Madison
Avenue bet 64th
and 65 Streets Ph:
212 988 8169

Great atmosphere. Look out for movie stars and moguls. Gabriel Byrne lunches here. Long wait for tables. Very good food.

Gino

780, Lexington Ave
bet 60th and 61st
Streets
Ph:212 758 4466

No reservations. No credit cards. This Italian is an institution. Great food. Lively atmosphere. Used to be a big Sinatra hangout. Look out for Tony Bennett at the front table.

Giambelli

46, East 50th Street
bet Mad and Park
Aves.
Ph: 212 688 2760

Great midtown location for this very popular family owned Italian. Great food.

Gallagher's Steak House

288,West 52nd
Street bet B'way
and 8th Ave Ph:
212 245 5336

Carnivore heaven. Steaks look more like roasts, very macho. Very expensive.

Les Sans Culottes

2nd Avenue at 57th
Street

Very inexpensive: Great value French brasserie food. Three courses for under $25.00

Café Un, Deux, Trois

123,West 44th
Street bet B'way
and 6th Ave Ph:
212 354 4148

Big noisy brasserie. Good buzz. Good basic food. Moderately expensive. Res. recommended.

The United Nations Delegates Dining Room

First Avenue and
46th Street

Open to visitors for early lunch on weekdays.
Great value: Fabulous cuisine: You need to
bring your passport: Call for details.

Our Place

1444 3rd Avenue at
82nd Street
Ph:212 288 4888

Res not always necessary. Busy at
weekends.Very inexpensive lunch. Dinner
moderately expensive. Great Chinese. Fab.
Peking Duck And at 141 East 55th Street
between Lexington and 3rd Avenues

Metropolitan Café

959,1st Ave bet
52nd and 53rd Sts
Ph: 212 759 5600

Great outdoor garden during the summer. Good
food. Great weekend brunch
Reservations a good idea for brunch and
weekends. Moderately expensive

Mary Ann's Chuala Vista

1503 2nd Ave bet
77th and 78th Sts
Ph: 212 249 6165
80 2nd Ave at 5th
Ph: 212 475 5939
2452 B'way bet
90th and 91st Sts
Ph: 212 877 0132
116 8th Ave at 16th
Ph: 212 633 0877

Great Mexican, knock out margaritas, fabulous
home made guacamole.Inexpensive, great value
at lunchtime. Very child friendly.

Mediterraneo

1260 Avenue at
66th Street
Ph: 212 734 7407

My favourite informal Italian on the Upper East
Side. Great food. Sit outside during the summer.
Moderately expensive. Good value.

Water Club

500 East 30th
Street at the East
River,
Ph: 212 683 3333

Stunning setting just about justifies the very
expensive menu. So romantic. Good American
cuisine.

Willow

1022 Lexington Ave
at 73rd St
Ph: 212 717 0703

French American, popular East Side spot much loved by the captains and kings of Wall Street.

Orsay

1057-59 Lexington
Avenue at 75th
Ph: 212 517 6400

Great food, great buzz, very good value French Brasserie. Moderately expensive

Nello

696 Madison
Avenue bet 62nd
and 63rd St
Ph: 212 980 9099

Too expensive, but it's a celebie hangout for Eurotrash, lots of air kissing. OK Italian fare and pretty cool cocktails

Katz's Deli

205 East Houston
Street at Ludlow
Street Ph:212 254
2246

This was featured in When Harry Met Sally. The pastrami sandwiches here are legendary about enough meat to feed a family. Inexpensive Great value and extremely rude waiters make this place memorable.

Jackson Diner

at 37-47 74th
Street bet
Roosevelt & 37th
Aves Ph: 718 672
1232

This Queens Diner is a really great Indian, though I think it has lost some of its atmosphere since it moved a couple of years ago. Bring Your Own Bottle. Indifferent service and what a din You could find it very difficult to spend $10.00 a head for lunch here.

Nearys

358, 1st Avenue at
East 57th Street
Ph: 212 751 1434

Another celeb hang out as they walk around from their Sutton Place pads. It boasts solid American/Irish fare at great prices. Say hello to Jimmy, the owner.

City Hall

131 Duane Street
bet Church and
West B'way
Ph: 212 227 7777

Very good American food, great shellfish and seafood. And as for cosmopolitans!

Le Colonial

149, 57th Street at
Lexington Avenue
Ph: 212 757 0808.

Interesting Vietnamese. Very fashionable crowd.
Great for drinks upstairs.

Smith & Wollensky

East 49th Street at
Third Avenue
Ph: 212 753 1530

This is one of the top steak places, carnivore
heaven. Possibly the rudest staff in the City. But
it's still always full.

Il Mulino

86 W. 3rd St bet
Sullivan and
Thompson Sts Ph:
212 673 3783

The best Italian outside of Italy, possibly the
best Italian I have had anywhere. Owned and
run by a totally charming family. Very, very
expensive but worth every dollar. Tables are like
gold dust.

Jo Jo

160 E 64th Street
bet Lexington and
3rd Aves Ph: 212
223 5656

This is where Jean George Vongerichten started
in New York and look at his empire now! Still
very good French food.

Il Cantinori

32 East 10th Street
bet B'way & Univ.
Place
Ph: 212 673 6044.

Very good Italian. Very popular with the movie
stars and fashion crowd who live in the Village.
Expensive.

Quatro Gatti

205 E. 81st St bet
2nd and 3rd Aves
Ph: 212 570 1073

A moderately expensive Upper East Side
neighbourhood Italian.

King's Carriage House

251, E. 82nd St bet
2nd and 3rd Aves
Ph: 212 734 5490

A cutsey mews house, the cuisine is very good
American even though one of the owners is
Irish.

Caffe Buon Gusto

East 77th St bet
2nd and 3rd Aves
Ph: 212 535 6884

Basic Italian and great value. Cash only

Coconut Grill

1481 2nd Ave at
77th St
Ph: 212 772 6262

Moderately expensive: a bit of everything, salads, pastas, burgers, sandwiches and rather good cocktails. Good value brunch.

Swiftys

1007 Lexington Ave
72nd and 73rd
Streets
Ph: 212 535 6000

Much loved by the ladies who lunch from the Upper East Side. Very good French/American. Very Expensive and reservations necessary well in advance.

Sant Ambroeus

1000 Madison Ave
bet 77th and 78th
Streets Ph: 212
570 2211

One of the best bakeries in the City. Trustfund kid heaven. To die for desserts, ice creams, sorbets etc

Patsy's

236 West 56th St
bet B'way and 8th
Ave Ph: 212 247
3491 and at
Second Ave at 69th
Ph: 212 639 1000

Pizza and pasta, huge portions family style service. Excellent food and great value.

Il Nido

251, East 53rd St
bet 2nd and 3rd
Aves
Ph: 212 753 8450

A first class mid town Italian, Northern Italian cuisine at it's best.

Rain

1059, Third Avenue
Ph: 212 223 3669

Pan Asian, great food, great ambience. Hugely popular bar, great cocktails.

China Fun

1223 2nd Avenue
at 64th Street,
Ph: 212 752 0810
Also at
246 Columbus
Avenue between
71st and 72nd
Streets. Ph: 212
580 1516
and 1653Broadway
at 51st Street
Ph: 212 333 2622

Authentic Chinese food, best value on the Upper East Side.

Morrell Wine Bar

One Rockefeller
Plaza
Ph: 212 688 9370

Light food with a great wine list. Wonderful wine available by the glass. Great place to watch the world go by from the outdoor tables.

Isabellas

359 Columbus
Avenue at West
77th Street
Ph: 212 724 2100

Terrific brunch. Very stylish, owned by Isabella Rosellini and her movie director husband. Very good value.

Ruby Foo's

2182 Broadway at
77th Street;
Ph: 212 724 6700
Also at 1626 B'way
bet 49th and 50th
Ph: 212 489 5600

Nouveau Chinese/American. Great buzz and interesting décor. Moderately expensive.

Chez Josephine

414 West 42nd St
bet 9th and 10th
Avenues
Ph: 212 594 1925

Franco/American. V. popular with the theater district crowd. Owned by Josephine Bakers adopted son and packed with La Baker memorabilia.

Joe Allen

326 W.46th Street
bet 8th and 9th
Aves
Ph: 212 581 6464

Inexpensive, good basic American food. Good pre theatre is you are in a hurry.

Carmines

2450 B'way bet
90th and 91st Sts.
Ph: 212 362 2200
And also 200 West
44th Street bet
B'way and 8th
Aves; Ph: 212 221
3800.

Carmines now has two very good, basic Italian eateries. Vast portions served family style, you need about a half dozen people to make any in road on the food.

Mr Chow

324 East 57th St
bet 1st and 2nd
Aves
Ph: 212 751 9030

Sophisticated Chinese. Still great food and still attracts a celeb. crowd.

Jane's

100 Houston Street
Ph:212 254 7000

This gem offers a variety of Eggs Benedict. Jane has crab and crawfish cakes with spinach and tarragon hollandaise and Johnny gives you house made maple sausage with corn pancakes and roasted tomato hollandaise. New York is also big on the egg white omelette for those who eschew cholesterol rich egg yolks. That's fine if they don't order blueberry pancakes with lemon crème fraiche or Vanilla Bean French Toast after!!

Blue Ribbon Bakery

33 Downing Street
at Bedford Street
Ph: 212 337 0404

B.R.B. has a wonderful downstairs bakery and the Walnut and Raisin Bread with Berries served alongside a great Caffe Latte is a wonderful way to ease into Sunday!

@SQC

270 Columbus
Avenue near 72nd
Street

Crowds stand in line for up to an hour on a Sunday waiting to enjoy chef Scott Campbell's scrambled eggs with scallions and Montrachet or sunnyside eggs with avocado salsa. A Mimosa is the perfect accompaniment to liven up the morning and a side order of the most perfect pommes frites served in a cone- shaped container are a must!! Finish with an apple cinnamon pancake soufflé and a glorious cappuccino.

Sunday's pace is a little more leisurely but on Monday the pulsating energy levels are revived and Manhattan's seemingly tireless residents begin a new week of high activity- challenging each other and those who provide them with services to reach new heights of excellence! No wonder then that the next week could offer an entirely different set of fabulous places to dine each with its particular character and dimension designed to

Dean & De Luca

at 560 Broadway at Prince Street

Is another gourmet piece of heaven and after you have walked through the fruit and vegetable section and marvelled at the white peaches, golden cactus peaches, red frying peppers and red grilling peppers, huge purple eggplants, fava beans, Idaho potatoes and orange tomatoes on the vine you begin to realise why eating in New York has become so ambrosial - the effort to provide produce in variety and excellence is overwhelming!

The Chelsea Market

on 75 Ninth Avenue between 15th and 16th Streets

This the best example of the freshness and quality available to restauranteurs and serious home cooks. The flower hall with its chilled temperatures is a mass of blooms in colour and profusion, the bakery where you can watch the ciabattas being kneaded through huge glass windows, the vegetable department where peppers of every size, colour and 'heat', freshly picked herbs, baby corn cobs, baby okra and baby cactus leaves- all indicate how serious New Yorkers are about cuisine!

Luxury Food/Delis

Citerella

Third Avenue between 75th Street
Ph: 212 874 0383
Hours
Monday Saturday 7.00am 9.00pm
Sunday 9.00am 7.00pm
And at Broadway at 75th Street
Ph: 212 874 0383
Hours As above
Credit Cards
Major credit cards

Another huge foodmarket with a great fresh meat and fish section. Endless salad department and excellent fruit and vegetable section too. Good cheese, OK patesserie and regular grocery section. Delivering and catering services available.

Value 7   Range 7   Service 7

Dean and Deluca

560 Broadway
Phone: (212) 226-6800
Hours:
Mon-Sat

One of New York's landmark, specialist grocery stores. Just about everything from a\anywhere in the world. Exceptional staff are a mine of information and extremely helpful. Great sandwiches and coffee to go. A real New York

9am-8pm;
Sun
10am-7pm
Credit Cards:
Major Credit cards

experience.

Value 9   Range 10   Service 9

Dean and Deluca Café

235 W 46th Street
Ph: (212) 869-6890
Hours: Sun-Mon
7am-8pm
Tue-Fri 7am-12am
Sat 8am-12am
Also at:
9 Rockefeller Plaza

These are great pit stops during the day for a
coffee or a light lunch. The food is consistently
good even if it is a tad expensive for what it is.
Surroundings wouldn't exactly knock you out.
~try the smoothies. Do they do the trick or
what?

9 Rockefeller Plaza across from The Today
Show NBC Studio.
Ph: (212) 664-1363

Also at:
75 University Place

75 University Place
Ph: (212) 473-1908
Hours: Mon-Thu 8:00am-10:00pm
Fri-Sat 8:00am-11:00pm
Sun 9:00am- 8:00pm

Fauchon

442 Park Avenue at
56th Street
Ph: 212 308 5919
Hours Monday
Saturday 10.00am
7.0pm
Sunday 12.00pm
6.00pm

You no longer need to fly to Paris for your
Truffles. These smallish stores are packed with
all the Fauchon specialties. The Park Avenue
store also has a little café which serves very
good light meals from 11.00am and it's also a
great celeb. spotting place.

And also at:
1383 3rd Ave

1383 3rd Ave, b/w 78th and 79th
Ph: 212-517-9600
Hours: 9am to 8pm (7 days)Credit cards

Value 9   Range 6   Service 10

Graces Market Place

1237, Third Avenue between 71st and 72nd Streets Ph: 212 737 0600 Hours Monday Saturday 7.00am 8.30pm Sunday 8.00am 7.00pm Credit Cards: Major credit cards

My local and I just love this place. We always get all our picnic and dinner party food here. Wonderful salads and prepared foods, superb fresh fish, shellfish and meat departments, great bakery and patisserie and Godiva chocs to die for. I adore the cheese section too and the fresh veggie section looks like an impressionist painting. Regular grocery section. Spotlessly clean. Delivery and catering service available. Also excellent Trattoria. The motto here is "Remember Taste is a matter of choice, quality is a matter of fact."

 Value 9   Range 9   Service 10

Marche Madison

1237 Third Avenue at 71st Street Ph: 212 737 0600 Hours:Mon -Sat 7.00am-8.30pm Sunday 8.00am - 7.00pm Credit Cards: Major credit card

Super Upper East Side deli. Great food, freshly prepared. Limited grocery section. Delivery available

931, Madison Avenue at 74th Street. Ph: 212 794 3360 Hours: Mon - Sat 8.00am - 8.30pm Sunday 8.00am - 8.00pm Credit Cards: Major Credit Cards

Zabars Food and Housewares

www.zabars.com

2245 Broadway at
80th Street

Ph: 212 787 2000

Hours

Monday Friday
8.00am 7.30pm

Saturday
8.00am 8.00pm

Sunday
9.00am 6.00pm

Credit Cards Major
credit cards

I never tire of a visit to the West side to inhale
all the wonderful aromas that permeate the air
in Zabars. It reminds me of Harrods Food Hall
and at weekends it is always packed. The
produce here is as fresh as you will get
anywhere. The food is beautifully displayed and
tastes as good as it looks. However, it's not
cheap.

Value 9   Range 10   Service 9

Really Happy Hours

A $4 lycheetini? Now we're talking! Check out the following for some great happy hours

Acme Bar & Grill

9 Great Jones St., 212-420-1934

Chic NoHo scene? Try Rehab across the street. Cheap, daily-rotating happy hour? Acme's back bar, which offers half-price appetizers from 4pm to 7pm. Tuesdays feature $2 "Acme Brew;" Wednesdays ladies get two for one; and Thursdays are all about $4 Hurricanes. And on Sundays cheap apps are offered all day long -- perfect to sop up all that booze you'll be swilling.

Blind Tiger Ale House

518 Hudson St., 212-675-3848

It's not so much the discounted prices ($1 off all drafts, domestic bottles and well drinks), as it is the sheer length of Blind Tiger's happy hour, which runs from noon to 8pm, Monday through Friday. That means you can practically get started on your cheap cocktail immediately upon downing your morning coffee.

Boxcar Lounge

168 Avenue B, 212-473-2830

This tiny bar specializes in creative cocktails made with champagne and sake — just $5 each, they're two-for-one until 10pm (till 8pm on Friday and Saturday).

Fitzers Bar

620 Lexington
Avenue bet 56th
and 57th Streets
212 355 0100

If you want a decent pint and some pretty nifty canapes this is the place to come. Miller on tap $3.00 a pint. Always a great atmosphere, plenty of craic in this irish oasis in the middle of Manhattan

Guastavino's

409 E. 59th St.,
212-980-2455

There's nothing more satisfying than visiting one of the city's spectacular spaces, imbibing an assortment of delectable wine, and coming away with barely a dent in your wallet. That's what Guastavino's is starting up in August, with Tuesday-night wine-tastings and Sunday-night sherry tastings, featuring three flights for $25, from 5pm to 8pm. Plus, all the cheese and crackers, olives and finger food you can eat.

Landmark Tavern

626 Eleventh Ave.,
212-757-8595

With three-for-two buybacks, "Single-Malt Mondays" offer the best opportunity for cash-strapped connoisseurs to sample the Tavern's 70 fine scotches.

La Linea

15 First Ave.,
212-777-1571

Soulful, dive-y lounge for the romantically sleazy, with $2 discounts on all drinks 3pm till 9pm, seven days a week. The currently running summer special includes $3 margaritas and $4 apple martinis during those same hours.

Magnetic Field

97 Atlantic Ave.,
718-834-0069

At this welcome addition to the Brooklyn Heights/Cobble Hill bar scene, tap beers and well drinks are $3 for several hours, six days a week. Tuesday is happy hour all day -- all day -- and on Sundays the bar gives a BK shout-out with all Brooklyn beers $1 off.

Mars 2112

1633 Broadway, 212-582-2112

Once you get over the sight of mute aliens in rubber-and-spandex costumes, the fake red-rock terrain of Mars 2112 can be silly fun. And gimmicky theme bars are much more appealing when they offer drinks and appetizers for half off from 5pm to 9pm seven days a week, with a DJ adding to the vibe several nights as well.

Parkside Lounge

317 E. Houston St., 212-673-6270

This once-sordid dive has gotten a second wind, with raucous parties and $3 beer and well drinks from 1pm until 8pm.

Patio Bar

31 Second Ave., 212-460-9171

Patio's happy hour runs from just 5pm to 7pm, but that's plenty of time to pound an array of two-for-one cocktails, including the Sparkling Vodka Lemonade, the Citrus Margarita, the Tart Me Up (blackberry liqueur, grapefruit juice and vodka), or the Spicy Pomegranate Margarita. And for sustenance, Patio Dining, the bar's adjoining restaurant, will send over that day's special appetizers. House liquors and wine are also two for one; shelf drinks and beers are $1 off.

The Slide

356 Bowery, 212-475-7621

This gay bar next to Marion's Continental (same owners) takes happy hour to the next level with 30 minutes of open bar nightly. Happy hour officially runs from 5pm to 9pm, during which time beers are $2 and well drinks $3. But from

5:30pm to 6pm, the cash register shuts down
entirely and patrons drink for free.

Welcome to the Johnsons

**123 Rivington St.,
212-420-9911**

Seventies throwback with recession-ready drink
deals: $2 for Buds and well drinks until 8pm.
Free snacks, too — of the Doritos variety.

Wheeptapper

**141 East 44th
Street bet. 3rd and
Lex Avenues
Ph: 212 351 6800**

Full of the charm of an authentic Irish 'pub'
this Fitzpatrick owned bar really packs a punch
at happy hour. Located across from Grand
central it's the ideal place to grab a cocktail or a
pint as you wait for your date... or even your
train.Great snacks.

Rudy's Bar

**627 Ninth Ave.,
212-974-9169**

All drinks here are cheap, but the best deal — if
you've got strong tastebuds — is Rudy's Red,
the house's own somewhat swill-ish brew served
in plastic "buckets" for $7.75. Bonus: Free hot
dogs!

Corner Bistro

**331 W. 4th St.,
212-242-9502**

$2 mugs of McSorley's and some of the best
burgers in town ensure that there's always a line
at this West Village classic.

Holiday Cocktail Lounge

**75 St. Marks Pl.,
212-777-9637**

W. H. Auden once lived next door, and Trotsky
across the street. Both knew a little something
about the low life, and so does the clientele of
this East Village landmark. In fact, we voted it
New York's best bar if you're unemployed!

International Bar

120 1/2 First Ave.,
212-777-9244

Whether you're drinking whiskey on the rocks or beer in a can, you'll get change back from a $5 at this friendly dive known for its great jukebox.

Jeremy's Ale House

254 Front St.,
212-964-3537

Starting at 8am, an unlikely mix of construction workers, fishmongers coming off their shifts, and Wall Street suits down 32-ounce Styrofoam cups of Bud ($1.75) at this one-of-a-kind waterfront dive.

O'Connor's

39 Fifth Ave.,
Brooklyn,
718-783-9721

The biggest change this place has seen in the past twenty years came in 2000, when drink prices went up by 50 cents (leaving most still under $3).

Mug's Ale House

125 Bedford Ave.,
Brooklyn,
718-486-8232

Archetypal old-school tavern with $2-pint specials for both waterfront workers and starving artists.

Gowanus Yacht Club

323 Smith St.,
Brooklyn, no phone

Most Smith Street hangouts charge Manhattan prices. Not so this outdoor-only glorified hot dog stand, where the Carroll Gardens hipoisie enjoys $2 PBRs.

A Sole Reason for being in the Big Apple

Think you know New York? Free walking tours dish the dirt on neighborhoods, landmarks, parks, and celebrities. Rediscover City classics or set out for the road less travelled.

Surveillance Camera Outdoor Walking Tours

Sundays at 2pm (check website as locations vary); tour lasts about an hour and a half 212-561-0106; www.notbored.org/scowt.html

Let the Surveillance Camera Players expose you to Manhattan's Orwellian underside. Alarmed by the extensive and little-known presence of surveillance cameras, the group leads free tours of "heavily surveilled neighborhoods." Pick out cameras installed on poles, building exteriors, and other public places. Try not to look too suspicious....

"Discover Places, Tidbits, and Gossip That Even New York's Cognoscenti Don't Know" 8th Street Walking Tour

Selected Saturdays from June through September at 11:30am; tour lasts an hour and a half Meet at the northwest corner of St. Marks Pl. and Second Ave.; 212-777-2173; www.villageallianc e.org

And what exactly will you discover? You'll see the site of Jimi Hendrix's Electric Lady recording studio, Jack Kerouac's local haunts, and Edward Hopper's home. Gossip dished by guide Arthur Marks.

Something Old, Something New Orchard Street Walking Tour

Sundays at 11am, April through December; tour lasts about an hour and a half Meet at Katz's Delicatessen, 205 East Houston St. at Ludlow St.; 212-226-9010; www.lowereastsid eny.com

Get a taste of the bustling Lower East Side, from past to present. Hit the former Municipal Public Bath House; the First Roumanian-American Congregation; Salwen Umbrella, the City's only remaining umbrella shop (you know you want to see it); and the fishy Russ and Daughters where I always buy my caviar.

The Federal Reserve Bank

Monday through Friday, 9:30am, 10:30am, 11:30am, 1:30pm, 2:30pm; tour lasts one hour 33 Liberty St.; 212-720-6130; www.newyorkfed.org

Itching for an insider's peek at the world's richest bank? The Fed's free tour will take you five stories underground into their gold vaults, demystify how the Bank functions, and let you test your new knowledge at Fedworks, an interactive, multimedia center. You'll even pocket some (shredded) money at the tour's end. Call to make a reservation at least a week in advance and don't be late as security procedures are lengthy.

Brooklyn Brewery

Saturdays from noon to 5pm; tour lasts 30 minutes 79 North 11 St. (between Berry and Wythe Streets); 718-486-7422; brooklynbrewery.com

For an in-depth look at the science of beer mixing, take a free tour of this stylish Williamsburg brewhouse. Two fresh beer samples finish off the day!

34th Street Historic Walking Tour

Thursdays at 12:30pm; tour lasts an hour and a half Meet at the Fifth Ave. entrance to the Empire State Building; 212-719-3434; 34thstreet.org

Why is the Empire State Building the perfect symbol for New York architecture? Which famous store owner drowned on the Titanic? What's the link between Andy Warhol and a Con Edison substation? You probably know already, don't you? But hear it all again on a tour by architectural historian Francis Morrone or architect Alan Neumann.

John J. Harvey Fireboat

reservations e-mail: trips@fireboat.org. Pier 63 Maritime, The Hudson River at West 23rd St.; fireboat.org

Spend the afternoon cruising New York Harbor for free on board the historic Harvey. Ooh, ahh, and get soaked as the historic boat's brass cannons shoot water into majestic 200-foot arcs at the rate of 18,000 gallons a minute. Launched in 1931, the swift and powerful boat was brought out of retirement in the aftermath of 9/11.
Check their website for "irregular but frequent" tour offerings; tour length varies.

Battery Park City Walking Tours

2 South End Ave. at West Thames Street; 212-267-9700; bpcparks.org

Want to hear about the birds and the bees and the flowers and the trees? Let a Battery Park City Parks Conservancy horticulturist take you for a garden stroll or join one of their fall bird walks -over eighty types of birds spotted to date. Free tours devoted to nature, art, and history sponsored from March through October. For tour dates visit their website; tour length varies

Grand Central Station

Wednesdays at 12:30pm; tour lasts about one hour
Meet in front of the information booth, main level of Grand Central Station; 212-935-3960; mas.org (website includes listings of other tours priced between $10 to $15)

You've gazed at Grand Central's celestial ceiling, now take note of symbolic mythological figures, sculptures, and other architectural details lurking throughout the Beaux Arts landmark. The Municipal Art Society's long-running tour is light on gossip, heavy on design, urban planning, and historical preservation. Donation requested.

Trinity Church Walking Tour

Thursdays and Saturdays at noon; tour lasts 15 to 20 minutes
Broadway and Wall Sts; 212-602-0800; www.trinitywallstreet.org

Visit the graves of Alexander Hamilton, William Bradford, and other historical figures as you roam through Trinity Churchyard. The tour also stops by the Church Museum where you can view art and artifacts dating back to the 1600s.

Central Park

212-360-2726 (tour hotline); centralparknyc.org

The free tours are eight more reasons to be thankful for Manhattan's 843-acre backyard. Explore the nooks and crannies of the North Woods, designed to replicate the Adirondack Mountains; learn about the innovative architecture of the Dakota and Bethesda Terrace; tour the Harlem Meer, high ground crucial to the City's defense during the American Revolution; or pick from five other options.
For tour schedules visit their website; tours last about one hour

A Real Steal That's the Ticket!

TKTS isn't the only place in town to score inexpensive tickets to theater and performance events.

Discounted Theatre Tickets

Location
TKTS Booth Broadway and 47th Street
Cost Tickets, reduced by from 35% to 50%from box office prices and (are available ONLY on the day of the performance, matinees or evening
Hours
Matinee Tickets: Daily
10.00am-2.00pm
Matinee and evening tickets   Daily
5.00pm-8.00pm
Credit Cards   Cash only
Comment
The TKTS Booth on Broadway is a holy grail for theater lovers who don't want to lash out anywhere from $60.00 to $100 a seat to see a Broadway show and who don't mind standing on line for half price tickets

Classical Music

Carnegie Hall Partial-View Seats

57th St. and 7th Ave.; 212-247-7800; www.carnegiehall.org

How do you go to a concert at Carnegie for next to nothing? A limited number of $10 partial-view tickets are available for performances in Carnegie Hall's Isaac Stern Auditorium (excluding Carnegie Hall Family Concerts and galas). Same-day tickets go on sale at the box office beginning at 12pm, with a limit of two per person. Student/senior rush tickets for concerts at Isaac Stern, also priced at $10, are sold two hours before the concert for a half hour period. Rush tickets for Weill Recital Hall performances are sold at the box office one hour before the concert. Present valid ID. Cash only.

Carnegie Hall/Citigroup Neighborhood Concert Series

212-903-9670; www.carnegiehall.org

For more than twenty-five years Carnegie Hall has ventured out to the five boroughs, providing free concerts in libraries, shelters, community, cultural, and religious centers. Performances cover a variety of musical styles such as classical, jazz, popular, and folk.
o locations throughout NYC;

The Juilliard School

60 Lincoln Center Plaza; 212-769-7406;

Juilliard's exemplary Music, Drama, Opera, and Dance divisions all put on student performances at little or no cost to the public. Music: All performances free with the exception of those at Carnegie Hall. Drama: fall productions are free; spring productions are priced at $15 general admission, $7 students and seniors. Opera: $20 general admission; $10 students and seniors. Dance: $15 general admission, $7 students and seniors. Tickets are required for all performances and can be obtained at the box office beginning two weeks before the show. A standby line forms outside the theater an hour prior to showtime. You may request to be placed on the mailing list for information on a division and its performances.

Lincoln Center

65th St. and Broadway; 212-875-5050 or www.lincolncenter.org

Students can purchase up to four $20 tickets for the following Lincoln Center programs: Great Performers, Mostly Mozart, Lincoln Center Festival, and American Songbook. Present valid ID at the box office.

BAM Student/Senior Rush Tickets

718-636-4100, ext. 1; www.bam.org

The Brooklyn Academy of Music offers $10 tickets to students (full- and part-time) and seniors with valid ID. Tickets for unsold seats may be purchased at the box office two hours prior to showtime. There is a two ticket per person limit. No checks.
o For shows at Harvey Theater, visit the box office at 651 Fulton St.; for shows at BAM Howard Gilman Opera House, visit 30 Lafayette Avenue; for ticket availability, call 718-636-4100, ext. 1.

New York Philharmonic

65th St. and Broadway; 212-875-5656 or www.newyorkphilharmonic.org

Students, senior citizens (62 and over), and disabled persons are eligible to purchase $10 tickets on the day of the performance. Two tickets per person; sold at the Avery Fisher Hall Box Office.

Trinity Church - Concerts at One

Trinity Church, 74 Trinity Place (Broadway at Wall St.); 212-602-0747; www.trinitywallstreet.org

Sponsors a free, year-round concert series with performances on Mondays and Thursdays at Trinity Church at 1 p.m. (During the summer, concerts are held only on Thursdays.) The church alone is worth a visit — it qualifies as a National Historic Landmark.

Dance

Joyce Theater

175 8th Avenue; 212-242-0800 or www.joyce.org

The Joyce Theater hosts performances by a variety of dance companies such as Hubbard Street Dance Chicago, Aspen Santa Fe Ballet, and Flamenco Vivo Carlota Santana. Full-time college students and seniors with current ID can purchase $12 rush tickets at the box office one hour before showtime. Limit of one ticket per person. Cash only.

New York City Ballet

63rd St. and Broadway; 212-870-7766 or www.nycballet.com

Full-time students under 30 with valid ID are eligible for $10 Student Rush Tickets to select same-day performances. Purchase tickets online or at the box office.

Opera

Metropolitan Opera

64th St. and Columbus Ave.; 212-362-6000 or www.metopera.org

Standing room tickets for the following week's performances go on sale Saturday mornings at 10am. To vie with in-the-know standing room regulars, line up outside the Lincoln Center Box Office at least an hour in advance. Orchestra standing room tickets sell for $16 and Family Circle for $12, with a limit of one ticket per person for each performance. Extra tickets are sold at the box office until show time. Cash only.

Students (29 and under) may purchase discounted tickets to select Metropolitan Opera performances. Weekday shows are priced at $25 while Friday and Saturday shows go for $35. Tickets must be purchased at the box office with a current student ID and there is a two ticket per student limit.

New York City Opera

63rd St. and Columbus Ave.; 212-870-7766 Student Rush hotline; www.nycopera.com

Students can purchase half-price tickets up to a week in advance at the New York State Theater Box Office. Last-minute Student Rush tickets are also available for same-day performances at $10 with a one ticket per student limit. Call the hotline for availability.

Theater

New Dramatists

424 West 44th St.;
212-757-6960;
www.newdramatist
s.org

Committed to developing playwrights, New Dramatists holds readings and workshops of new plays, musicals, and screenplays. Performances often feature top New York actors and directors. Readings are free and the majority are open to the public. Call for a schedule of events and make a reservation to secure your spot.

Shakespeare in Central Park

Delacorte Theater,
midpark at West
81st St. or East
79th St.; Public
Theater, 425
Lafayette St.;
212-539-8750;
www.publictheater.
org

Each summer The Public Theater presents a free production of a Shakespeare play at the outdoor Delacorte Theater, attracting big-name actors and a diverse crowd. Tickets are handed out daily at 1 pm at the Delacorte in Central Park, from 1 pm to 3 pm at the Public Theater, and from 1 pm to 3 pm on select dates at locations in all five boroughs (call for details). Bring a blanket, book, and friend as lines begin forming early in the morning. Despite the long wait, the atmosphere tends to be lively and the people-watching fabulous. Limit of two tickets per person.

HERE Performance Space

Here Performance
Art Café, 145 Sixth
Avenue;
212-647-0202;
www.here.org

HERE strives to support emerging artists in a variety of disciplines, playing host to often edgy performances in theater, dance, music and the visual arts. Tickets cost no more than $15 and some shows are free. Check their online calendar for a weekly schedule. Students and seniors receive a 25% discount. Purchase tickets online, over the phone or at the box office.

TKTS

www.tdf.org

The famous red-and-white booth sells tickets to select Broadway and Off-Broadway shows for 25 or 50 percent off the original price, with a $3 service charge per ticket. The same tickets are sold at both TKTS locations, so no need to hit both. Show up in the early evening — lines are shorter, and additional tickets often go on sale just prior to curtain time. Cash or traveler's checks only.

47th St. at Broadway

47th St. at Broadway: Mon-Sat, 3pm-8pm for evening tickets; Wed, Sat, 10am-2pm for matinee tickets; Sun, 11am-7pm.

South Street Seaport

South Street Seaport, 186 Front St., the rear of the Resnick/Prudential Building at 199 Water St.: Mon-Sat, 11am-6pm; Sun, 11am-3:30pm. At this location, matinee tickets must be bought the day before.

Theater Development Fund

212-221-0885 or www.tdf.org

TDF vouchers offer steep discounts to Off- and Off-Off-Broadway productions as well as other events sponsored by small, independent production companies. To qualify for their mailing list, you must be a student, teacher, performing arts professional, senior citizen (62 and over), union or armed forces member, or clergyman.

High Five Tickets to the Arts

212-HI5-TKTS or www.high5tix.org (Web site includes event calendar).

Kids between 13 and 18 years old (or anyone in middle or high school) can buy tickets to participating arts events or museums for $5 per ticket for weekends or $5 for two tickets for Monday through Thursday events. Tickets can be bought through Ticketmaster and through the High Five website.

Student Rush Tickets

www.telecharge.com 212-239-6200; www.ticketmaster.com 212-307-4100.

Many Broadway and Off-Broadway theaters reserve their front orchestra rows for student rush tickets. Tickets for same-day performances must be purchased at the theater box office and generally go on sale at 10am, with lines often forming in the wee hours. Typical prices are $20 or $25, but check with Tele-charge or TicketMaster as policies vary depending on the show. Cash only.

DISCOUNT CLUB MEMBERSHIPS

Audience Extras

61 Lexington Ave.; 212-686-1966; www.audienceextras.com

Offers subscribers $3.50 tickets when theaters need to fill an audience, particuarly when a show is in previews or expecting a reviewer or celebrity to attend. Expect tickets for Off and Off-Off Broadway shows, movie previews, comedy clubs, cabarets, dance, concerts, and an occasional Broadway show. Yearly membership will cost you $85 plus a $15 refundable deposit on the membership card, and a $30 "personal revenue fund" from which a $3.50 per ticket service charge is taken. Check the Web for event listings.

Play by Play

270 West 36th St., 3rd fl.; 212-868-7052; www.play-by-play.com

Provides the same service as Audience Extras, but with a slightly greater number of tickets to Broadway shows. Yearly membership is $99 with an additional $3.00 per ticket service charge. Participating events are listed online and members can reserve up to two tickets per event.

TheaterMania

www.theatermania.com

Sign up for a free membership with this online

club and save up to 50% on occasional tickets
to Broadway and Off-Broadway shows.
Discounts are available for a small selection of
Off-Off Broadway shows as well. The site's free
newsletter, TMInsider, offers the latest
information on shows, discounts and ticket
sales.

The Playbill Club

www.playbill.com   Playbill offers its online members discounts of
up to 50% on Broadway and Off-Broadway
shows. Subscribers also get restaurant discounts
and an occasional hotel or opera deal.
Membership is free, and you may request
mailings about new discounts and exclusive
theater-related merchandise.

NY Theatre

www.playbill.com   New York Theatre Experience offers online
coupons for a very limited number of off-
Broadway shows. Bring a printout of the coupon
to the box office or mention the coupon code
when calling Tele-charge. Savings range from a
mere $2 off the ticket price to a 30% discount.
No membership necessary.

STANDING ROOM

Many Broadway theaters sell tickets for
standing room, located directly behind the
orchestra seating. The catch: tickets are only
available on the day of the performance and the
show must be completely sold out. Tickets
usually cost between $15 and $25. Check with
specific box offices for details.

VOLUNTEER USHERING

A handful of Broadway theaters and most Off-

Broadway theaters rely on volunteer ushers to work during performances and it's easy to lend a hand in exchange for a chance to see the show. Make a reservation in advance and then arrive about an hour and a half before the performance for a debriefing from the house manager. After you show paying theatergoers to their seats, settle down to enjoy the performance for free. You might be asked to stick around for a bit afterwards to scan for stray playbills or lost-and-found items. Call the box office as procedures (and dress codes!) vary.

Bargain Hunting for Culture Vultures

It is nothing short of a crime to spend a few days in New York without visiting some of the superb museums that are an intrinsic part of the City's legendary cultural fabric. Even some of the best museums in the world afford bargain viewing opportunities. Many museums operate 'pay what you want policies' on Friday evenings and often offer entertainment and food as well. But if you are hell bent on a shopping only holiday, then take note that most of these famous museums have superb shops that offer wonderful art books, jewellery, posters etc, AND they also have great sales. These stores are particularly worth visiting in the run up to Christmas.

I always do a major part of my Christmas shopping in the Metropolitan Museum Shop at Rockefeller Center. If you travel to New York a few times a year it is worth looking into to becoming an Overseas Member/Friend of these Museums. They all offer different deals but for a small layout (usually less than $50.00) you get discounts of up to 20% as well as free admission to the museums at any time. And of course, in the process, you are also making your own philanthropic gesture to the museum . Most of the museums also have very attractive coffee shops.

Most museums are closed on Mondays and
Federal holidays.

The Metropolitan Museum

Location
5th Avenue at 82nd Street
Ph: 212 535 7710
Admission
$10.00. Students with ID $5.00
Hours
Open: Sunday 9.30am-5.30pm.
Tuesday/Wednesday/Thursday 9.30am to
5.30pm
Friday/Saturday 9.30am-9.00pm
Closed: Monday

No strollers/pushchairs allowed on Sundays.

The Frick Collection

Location
1, East 70th Street at 5th Avenue
Ph: 212 288 0700

Admission
$7.00: OAPs and students with ID $5.00

Hours
Open Tuesday to Saturday 10.00am-6.00pm
Sunday 1.00pm - 6.00pm
Children under 10 not admitted

Whitney Museum of American Art

Location
945 Madison Avenue between 74th and 75th
Streets
Ph: 212 570 3676

Hours

Open:
Tuesday/Wednesday/Thursday/Saturday/Sunday
11.00am to 6.00pm
Friday: 1.00pm-9.00pm. (from 6.00pm to
9.00pm it's Fab Friday at the museum and
admission is pay what you wish. Enjoy food,
drink and fun on Friday evening)

Admission:

Adults $10.00. OAPs/Students with ID $8.00.
Children under 12 free

The Guggenheim Museum

Location

1071, 5th Avenue at 89th Street
Ph: 212 423 3500

Hours

Open Sunday-Wednesday 9.00am-6.00pm
Friday/Saturday 9.00am-8.00pm Friday
6.00pm-8.00pm pay what you wish
Closed Thursday

Admission

Adults $12.00. OAPs and Students with ID:
$8.00. Under 12's free.

Guggenheim Museum Soho

Location

575 Broadway at Prince Street
Ph: 212 423 3500

Hours

Open Thursday-Monday: 11.00am-6.00pm
Closed Tuesday and Wednesday

Admission

There is no charge for this Museum

The Museum of Modern Art (MOMA)

Location
11,West 53rd Street between 5th and 6th
Avenues
Ph: 212 708 9400

Hours
Open:
Saturday/Sunday/Monday/Tuesday/Thursday:
10.30am -5.30pm
Friday: 10.30am-8.15pm
Closed Wednesday

Admission
Adults: $10.00. OAP's and Students with ID
$6.50
Under 16's free. Friday from 4.30pm to 8.15pm
pay what you want

Museum of Television and Radio

Location
25 West 52 Street
Ph: 212 621 6800

Hours
Open Tuesday/Wednesday/Sunday: 12.00 noon-
6.00pm
Thursday: 12.00 noon-8.00pm
Friday: 12 noon - 9.00pm
Closed Monday

Admission
Adults: $6.00. OAP's and Students $4.00.
Under 13's $3.00

Children's Museum of Manhattan

Location
212 West 83rd Street
Ph: 212 721 1234

Hours
Open Wednesday-Sunday: 10.00am-5.00pm

Admission
$6.00. Children under 1 year are free.

Children's Museum of the Arts

Location
182 Lafayette Street
Ph: 212 941 9198

Hours
Open Wednesday 12 noon -7.00pm
Thursday-Sunday 12 noon - 5.00pm
Closed Monday and Tuesday

Admission
$5.00 for all ages

Cooper-Hewett National Design Museum

Location
2, East 91st Street
Ph: 212 849 8400

Hours
Open: Tuesday 10.00am-9.00pm
Wednesday-Saturday 10.00-5.00pm
Sunday 12 noon - 5.00pm
Closed Monday and Federal holidays

Admission
Adults $3.00. OAP's and Students $1.50. Under 12's free

Museum at the Fashion Institute of Technology

Location
7th Avenue at 27th Street
Ph: 212 217 5800

Hours
Open Tuesday-Friday 12.00 noon- 8.00pm
Saturday 10.00am to 5.00pm
Closed Sunday and Monday

Admission
Free

Lower East Side Tenement Museum

Location
90 Orchard Street at Broome Street
Ph: 212 431 0233

Hours
Tours of the historic area tenements leave from
90 Orchard Street at the following times:
Tuesday-Friday: Every half an hour from
1.00pm-4.00pm
Saturday and Sunday: from 11.00am to 4.30pm
From April to October there are additional tours
at 6.00pm and 7.00pm
From June-August there are Monday tours at
1.00pm, 2.00pm, 3.00pm, 4.00pm.

Admission
$9.00 OAP's and students $7.00pm

Intrepid Sea-Air- Space Museum Pier

Location
86 W.46th St at Hudson River
Ph: 212 245 0072

Hours

Open Tuesday-Sunday 10-00am-5.00pm
(last tour admission at 4.00pm)
Closed: Monday

Admission

Adults: $12.00: OAP's Students $9.00: 6-11yrs
$6.00
Children 2-5yrs: $2.00. Wheelchair bound
visitors pay half price: Under 2 yrs free
Museum store open seven days

Statue of Liberty Museum
and Ellis Island

Location

Liberty Island via ferry at Battery Park
Ph: 212 363 3200

Hours

Open 7 days a week 9.00am to 5.30pm
The islands stay open later during the summer
season
Closed July 4th and December 25th

Admission

Ferry ticket includes island entrance.
Adults: $8.00. Children: $3.00

Second Hand Designer Clothes, Shoes and Bags

The better the neighbourhood the more likely you are to find designer clothes often unworn with the labels still on at a tiny fraction of the original price.

Or else these Chanel, Fendi, Valentino, Celine etc is deemed to be, as they like to put it, "gently worn".

For this reason there is nowhere like the Upper East Side. The Park Avenue Princesses might all be trustafarians but they still like to get a few shekels for their last seasons collection or better still their msny fashion faux pas!

Bis

1134 Madison
Avenue (between
84th and 85th
Street) 2nd Floor
Ph: 212 396 2760
Hours
Monday Thursday
10.00am 7.00pm
Friday/Saturday
10.00am 6.00pm
Sunday
Noon 5.00pm

Really top quality never and gently worn top designer labels. Now here's my dilemma. Why are all the most expensive designer fashion only available in tiny sizes? Are there no average sized, wealthy women or do wealthy men only bank roll shopping sprees for tiny tottys ? You will find a good selection of Chanel here, usually not more than a season old but you will rarely winder anything larger than a Size 10.

Value 8   Range 9   Service 9

Children's Resale

303, East 81st
Street(between 1st
and 2nd Avenues)
Ph: 212 734 8897
Hours
Monday-Friday
11.00am-7.00pm
Saturday
10.00am-6.00pm
Sunday
Noon-5.00pm
Credit Cards
Major Credit cards

The same owners here as the other two resale stores on the same block. The selection changes from season to season. You can be lucky and find great designer labels here, unworn, for tots at a fraction of their original price. You can also find nursery furniture, pushchairs/ buggies/strollers and car seats in excellent condition, all at knock down prices.

Value 9   Range 7   Service 9

Designer Resale Ladies Fashions

324 E 81st between
1st and 2nd
Avenues
Ph: 212 734 3639
Hours:
Monday Friday
11.00am-7.00pm
Thursday
11.00am-8.00pm

This is a terrific store, full of Chanel, Versace, Donna Karan Couture and other labels. Clothes are worn maybe once or twice and frequently have never been worn and still have the labels attached. Current season's fashions are here at a fraction of the RRP. Particularly good shoes and bags. In fact this little terrace of Resale Shops caters for women, men and children providing

Saturday
10.00am-6.00pm
Sunday
Noon- 5.00pm
Credit Cards Major
Credit Cards

something for everyone at the same general location.

 Value 10   Range 9   Service 10

Encore

1131 Madison
Avenue at 84th
Street
Ph: 212 879 2850
Hours:
Monday-Friday
10.30am-6.00pm
Thursday
10.30am-7.30pm
Saturday
10.30am-6.00pm
Sunday
Noon-6.00pm
Credit Cards Visa
and Mastercharge:
No American
Express

With all these stores you can be extremely lucky and hit the jackpot with a huge selection of Chanel, Armani, Valentino, Prada, Gucci etc on one visit and on the next visit the cupboard is totally bare. This store often has very good, little used, designer handbags and shoes as well as ladies clothes.

Value 9   Range 7   Service 9

GentleMen's Resale

322, East 81st
St(bet 1st and 2nd
Aves)
Ph: 212 734 2739
Hours Mon to Fri
11.00am-7.00pm
Sat 10.00am-
6.00pm
Sun Noon- 5.00pm
Credit Cards: Major
Credit Cards

Right next door to the Designer Ladies Resale, the quality here is top class. So are the designer labels. The store is well laid out and clothes are either new or nearly news. Prices are the best as is the service. Unworn Hermes and Charvet shirts at $60.00. Colorful, high fashion Versace, if you like that gear and beautiful Brioni cruise wear.

Value 8   Range 8   Service 10

Good Byes *(Great for kids)*

230 E. 78th Street
bet 2nd and
3rd Aves
Ph: 212 794 2301
Hours Mon- Fri
11.30 5.15pm
Sat
11.00am 5.00pm
Credit Cards Visa,
Mastercharge: No
American Express

An interesting Upper East Side children's resale. It tends to cater mostly for smaller tykes from newborn to about 5 years. You can be very lucky here as I once was. I found a silk organza dress, unworn with the store label still on for $30.00. In a Madison Avenue boutique, the same dress, that very day, was in the window for $620.00. Quite an investment for a 2 year old who wore it once to a wedding and then refused to have it put on again. There is also a good selection of toys and nursery furniture and accessories here. The owner is an extremely pleasant and helpful lady. If she doesn't have what you are looking for, you can leave your number and she will call if it comes in. Clothes and equipment either new or nearly new.

 Value 9   Range 6   Service 10

INA

10, Thompson St.
Ph: 212 941 4757
Hours 7 days
Noon 7.00pm
Credit Cards: Major
Credit Cards
And at:
21 Prince Street
Ph: 212 334 9048
Hours
Sunday Thursday
noon 7.00pm
Friday/Saturday
noon 8.00pm
Credit Cards Major
credit cards

Very good condition, little or unworn top designers. These stores have the top hot labels and receive much of their merchandise from fashion sources.

 Value 8   Range 10   Service 9

La Boutique Resale

1045, Madison
Avenue, near
80th Street
Ph: 212 517 8099
Hours
Monday Saturday
11.00am 7.00pm
Thursday
11.00am 8.00pm
Sunday
noon 6.00pm
Credit Cards
Major Credit Cards

They're all here. The Chanel, YSL, Escada, Prada, Valentino and Versace to name just a few, impulse purchases or mistakes of the Platinum Princess Credit Card Set who cut their losses by selling them here. On a good day the selection is knock out but why are we stuck between Size 4 and Size 6 again. Talk about rock and a hard place?

Value 8   Range 8   Service 9

Leyla

227 E 50th Street
bet 2nd and
3rd Aves
Ph: 212 421 8138
Hours: Mon Sat:
Noon 6.00pm
Credit Cards
Credit Cards

This little midtown hideaway houses some great designer fashions, shoes, bags and accessories at extremely keen prices. I find a good selection of new and almost new Chanel at extremely manageable prices whenever I drop by there. However, here again, the sizes tend to be on the small size. The store is tiny but the merchandise is in superb condition. Well worth a visit if you are size 10 or smaller.

Value 9   Range 6   Service 10

Michaels

1041 Madison
Avenue at 79th
Street
Ph: 212 737 7273
Hours
Monday-Saturday
9.30am-6.00pm
Thursday
9.30am-8.00pm
Closed Sunday

Recognized as a fave place for the ladies who lunch to lose their mistakes. Jackie O often unloaded her closet here. Given that she was frequently given her couture gratis, this was a complete win win situation for Mrs O who knew the value of a greenback better than most! Again it's a case of being lucky on the day, though this store also has a terrific bridal department which always seems to have to die for gowns that were literally worn for a few hours. Their original price tags could easily have been well in excess of $8,000 and they are on sale here, having been dry cleaned and looking in pristine condition, for less than $500. Staff seem to vary from being extremely helpful to being brusque. But it's well worth a visit. My best buy here: a Sybil Connolly hand pleated, long, linen evening skirt $35.00

Value 10   Range 8   Service 9

New and Almost New

65 Mercer Street at
Broome Street
Ph: 212 226 6677
Hours:
Sept-May:
Wed-Sun
noon-6.30pm
June-August
Tues-Sat
noon-6.30pm
Credit Cards
Major Credit Cards

The good news is that there is a great range of Miu Miu, Commes des Garcons etc here as well as some superb vintage fashions. The bad news is the largest size stocked in Size 10. If you are a Size 4 or Size 6, this should be heaven for you especially if you enjoy Italian or Japanese inspired fashion.

Value 8   Range 8   Service 10

Repeat Performance

220 East 23rd St
bet 2nd and
3rd Aves
Ph: 212 643 5344
Hours:
Mon-Sat
10.00am-5.45pm
Sun
Noon-5.00pm
Credit Cards:
Major credit cards

I wouldn't go all the way down town to check this one, but if you are in the area it's worth a look. From late summer through spring they tend to have a good selection of furs at amazing prices. I bought a huge mink coat here for $100.00 and had a sweat shirt, a wrap and a tote bag made from it. Everyone thought I had been to Mendels on Madison where I would have had little change from $7,000. However the store is not the most attractive and I'm not too sure that I would queue up for the clothes.

Value 10   Range 5   Service 8

Tatiana Resale Boutique

www.tatianas.com
860, Lexington
Avenue between
64th and 65th
Streets (First Floor)
Ph: 212 717 7684
Hours
Monday Friday
11.00am 7.00pm
Saturday
11.00am 6.00pm
Credit Cards Major
Credit Cards

This store claims to be the biggest resale in New York City... I wonder ? Anyway it does have a good selection of top couture labels as well as another larger section that carries a wide variety of general fashions in a good range of sizes. There is a quite good shoe, bag and accessory section here too as well as jewellry and furs. But, as in all resale stores, stock varies from one visit to the next. The clothes are well displayed and easy to check through. The owner is extremely helpful. You have to keep checking before that ultimate bargain falls into your lap. I got a great, unworn, basic black Chanel jacket here with the label still on. $2,800 was the price, I paid $500.00, though it was priced at $750.00. I bargained. Quite a difference !!! But that was my one and only purchase here. This store has a very informative, well designed web site where you can view some of the better bargain, high profile designer creations.

 Value 8   Range 8   Service 9

Transfer International

594 Broadway
between
Prince/Houston,
Suite 1002
Ph: 212 941 5472
Hours
Tuesday Sunday
10.00am 8.00pm
Credit Cards:
Major Credit Cards

I have never been lucky here myself but I have friends who swear that this place is the real mc coy. Slightly used or unused, very funky fashion with that edgy downtown feel is all the rage here. Not surprising since it's slap in the middle of SoHo

Value 7   Range 7   Service 8

Yu

151, Ludlow Street
between Stanton
and Rivington
Streets
Ph: 212 979 9370
Hours:
Monday Saturday
Noon 7.00pm
Sunday
Noon 6.00pm
Credit Cards Major
credit cards

Commes des Garcons, Prada and Yojhi are some of the labels you will regularly find here. Prices are about one third of retail. Clothes are new or little worn.

 **Value 8**   **Range 8**   **Service 10**

Kavanagh's Inc

146, E.49th St.
bet.3rd and Lex
Aves.
PH: 212-702-0152
Hours:
Tues - Fri
11.00am - 6.00pm
Sat.
11.am - 4.00pm
Closed Sunday
and Monday
Credit Cards:
Major Credit Cards.

The owner of this rather smart resale worked in bergdorfs, so not only does she know her couture she also knows that display must be dynamite too. This makes shopping at Kavanaghs a rather leisurely experience and there is plenty of space to try on the Chanel, D&G, Dior, YSL, Roberto Cavalli etc, most of which have never been anywhere near the bodies of the original purchaser. Knock bargains on Manolos and jimmy Choos and some serious bags here too. Prices a little bit more serious than the other stores, but I wouldn't quibble about that.

Value 8   **Range 9**   **Service 10**

A Second Chance Designer

1109 Lex Ave,bet.
77th and 78 Sts
2nd Floor
Ph: 212-744-6041
Hours:Mon - Fri
11.00am - 7.00pm
Sat
11.00am - 6.00pm

Beauty, thy name is barely-worn Chanel. At the designer consignment boutique Second Chance, the staff takes great pains in showcasing the best of the bounty: racks of wool boucle suits, mint-condition pumps and jewelry, all bearing those lovely interlocking gold C's. Also worth noting: an extensive collection of fur coats and funky (though somewhat overpriced) vintage purses and clutches. You should sweep the racks for finds on more recent designer fare -- try a burgundy satin sexy shift from Dolce & Gabbana for $150, or strappy, nearly-new Yves St. Laurent heels. In true Upper East Side form, the staff tends to consort only with matrons -- those who've likely come to beg back half their wardrobe.

Value 9   Range 7   Service 9

Thrift Stores

This is, in my mind, the most fun shopping in Manhattan.
People who have lived in the City all their lives remain
blissfully unaware of these Alladin's Caves of real treasures.

The better the neighbourhood the more likely one is to
find good merchandise at extremely attractive prices. The
stores all aid some charity or another. People donate
unwanted clothes, shoes,furniture, pictures etc. In some
cases entire estates are bequeathed to these charities. The
donors can claim the value of the goods they donate
against their taxes. The charity sells on the goods, usually
at a fraction of their retail and/or original value and the
buyers gets a great bargain. So it's a win, win, win
situation.

It's also a great way to meet people since the same group
treks from one Thrift store to another on the Upper East
Side most mornings. The grape vine is terrific. " There's
a piece of silver on 77th Street that I know you'd love "
one shopper confides to another. On one occasion I saw a
period four poster bed in bits in the back room at
Memorial Sloan Kettering on Third Avenue in the
eighties. A very big piece, it languished there for weeks.
It was finally marked down to $750. An antique dealer
spotted it, identified it as original Louis XVI. Bought it
and sold it on to a downtown antique store, over the
'phone, for $15,000. A nice thirty minutes work!! A
Dublin friend of mine bought two beautiful table lamps
for $10 each. Back in the D.4 drawing room, these lamps
look as if they cost several hundred pounds a piece.

Obviously bargains like this don't jump out at you
everyday and I must stress that you need time to
constantly check out these stores. But if you have time,
and you like to collect just about anything, thrifting
really is a lot of fun.

Cancer Care Thrift Store

**1480 3rd Avenue
between 83rd and
84th Avenues
Ph: 212 879 9868
Hours: Monday,
Tuesday, Friday
11.00am-6.00pm
Wed, Thurs
11.00am-7.00pm
Saturday
10.00am-4.30pm
Sunday
12.30pm-5.00pm
Closed Sunday
during the summer
Credit Cards:
Major Credit Cards**

Selection and quality varies hugely here. But you can be lucky with good furniture, lamps, paintings, mirrors, some costume jewellery, handbags and ladies fashions and shoes, very often unworn. Some of the ladies who volunteer here are a delight, courteous and extremely helpful, others are like little Hitlers controlling their little empire. They hold major clearance sales several times a year when the value is sheer dynamite. Magnificent Scalamandre curtains, lined and inter lined, never used $100 a pair instead of the minimum $1,000 they would set you back at the D and D Building. You might be lucky to get a matching tailored bed cover and valance for $50. hey presto, you have a designer bedroom for buttons.

Value 8   Range 6   Service 6

City Opera House

**222 East 23rd
Street between 3rd
and Lexington
Avenues
Ph: 212 684 5344
Hours: Mon Tues
Wed Fri Sat
10.00am 6.00pm
Thursday
10.00am 7.00pm
Sunday
Noon 5.00pm
Credit Cards Major
credit cards**

You can be very lucky here. I have seen some great art deco furniture here. I have also seen some great fur coats for little or nothing. it's a great place for books, old records and CDs, mostly opera of course. Spend, spend, spend here it supports a great cause.

Value 9   Range 6   Service 9

Council Thrift Store

246, 84th St. bet
2nd and 3rd Aves
Ph: 212 439 8373
Hours: Mon-Fri
10.00am - 6.00pm
Sat
11.00am -5.00pm
Credit Cards:
Major Credit Cards

The selection and quality varies here. Like all the Thrift stores you have to keep checking. But you can be lucky with nice pieces of furniture, paintings and bric a brac. I don't rate the clothes here but they often have great furs here during the winter.

 Value 8   Range 6   Service 7

Godmother League

1459 3rd Ave. bet.
82nd and 83rd Sts
Ph: 212 988 2858
Hours: Mon-Sat
10.00am-6.00pm
Sun noon - 5.00pm
Credit Cards: Major
Credit Cards

This used to be a great fave of mine but it changed owners a few years ago and seems rather tatty since. You can be lucky here with furniture and table lamps. You will sometimes find some interesting costume jewellry here. Forget about the clothes

 Value 8   Range 6   Service 7

Housing Works Thrift Store

202 E.77th Street
between 2nd and
3rd Avenues
Ph: 212 772 8461
Hours
Monday Saturday
10.00am 6.00pm
202 E.77th Street
between 2nd and
3rd Avenues
Ph: 212 772 8461
Hours
Monday Saturday
10.00am 6.00pm

Nice costume jewellery, paintings and general bric a brac. I always check the window as I pass by this store. You can be lucky with furs, furniture and fashions, though recently the clothes have been very tacky indeed. The menswear seems much better than the ladies. A good place for second hand books.

 Value 9   Range 6   Service 8

And also at

157, East 23rd Street between 3rd and
Lexington Avenues

Ph: 212 529 5955
Hours Mon Tues Wed Fri Sat 10.00am 6.00pm
Thursday 10.00am 8.00pm
Sunday 10.00am 5.00pm

And at

Housing Works Used Book Cafe
126,Crosby Street off Broadway in Soho
Ph: 212 334 3324
Hours Monday 10.00am 8.00pm
Friday 10.00am 9.00pm
Saturday Noon 9.00pm
Sunday Noon 7.00pm
Credit Cards Major credit cards

And at

143 West 17th Street, between 6th and 7th
Avenues
Ph: 212 366 0820
Hours Monday Saturday 10.00am 6.00pm
Sunday Noon 5.00pm
Credit Cards: Major credit cards

Memorial Sloan Kettering Thrift Store

**1440, Third Ave
bet. 82nd and 83rd
Sts .
Ph: 212 535 1250
Hours:Mon/Wed/Fri
10.00am-5.30pm
Thurs: 10.00am -
8.00pm
Sat 10.00am-
5.00pm
Credit Cards: Major
Credit Cards.**

I rate this one of the best of the Upper East Side
Thrift stores. There is usually a good selection
of furniture and very often there is a good
selection of beautiful drapes (curtains) also.
Sometimes you will find great unworn shoes
and top international ladies,designer fashion in
the designer room. Often a huge selection of
seemingly unworn Charvet and Turnbull and
Asser Sea Island and Egyptian Cotton shirts at
$30.00 a pop are snapped up by smart guys
and savvy gals who use them as nightshirts.

 **Value 9   Range 9   Service 8**

Salvation Army

212 E. 23rd St.
Ph: 212 532 8115
Hours: Mon - Fri
10.00am - 7.15 pm
Sat 10.00am-
5.00pm
Closed Sunday

If you are downtown on the East Side it's worth checking out this one but not worth the trip otherwise. Variety and quality ranges from quite good to grotty. But prices are very keen. Usually a good selection of toys and nursery items.

Value 9   Range 6   Service 5

Outlet Centers

Outlet shopping has become a phenomenon all over the United States, especially over the past ten years. And it is now spreading to Europe, though none of the Outlets I've visited in Ireland, the UK or Italy are evenly remotely in the same league as Woodbury Common.

These special shopping centers are to be found wherever there is a major tourist destination or on the outskirts of the largest cities. Outlets started about twenty years ago as a way of using old factories and warehouses that were no longer in use and also to sell off excess stock. Fashion companies combined their previous season's stock, with samples, overruns, irregulars, slightly damaged, and remaindered stock for these centers.

Because the surroundings were not the most attractive and they were out of the way, a distance from major city centers, prices were much lower than the city department stores. The stores not only didn't object to them, they now regard outlets as a major profit generating base and most major department stores have their own outlet stores in the bigger centers. Huge crowds flocked to the centers and they became so popular that most of them are now purpose built, state of the art retailing centers with multi lingual staff to cater for the millions that fly in from overseas, specifically to outlet shop. In some states, like Virginia, outlet centers are now the biggest tourist attraction.

The stock varies hugely from store to store in these centers. But if you know what you want and are prepared to take time to wade through racks and rails of every kind of fashion, you can score savings of up to 80%. And while the general idea is that stock is a season old, this principle too seems to be biting the bullet. Certainly in Woodbury Common, the center I

visit most frequently, the range of current
season stock just grows each time I visit,
especially in the more upscale designers. Just
before Christmas 2003 I bought a suit, several
cashmere sweaters and two pairs of shoes in the
Donna Karan store in Woodbury Common that
were discounted by up to 75%. I saw the same
items the following day in both Bloomingdales
and the Donna Karan Store on Madison Avenue,
all at full price.

To get the most value from your visit to an Outlet Center remember:

• You have to be informed, know what you want.

• You have to know the merchandise, that's why
I advise checking out the season's look in the
City first.

• It helps to know the retail prices, then you
know just how much you are saving.

I can't stress enough how important it is to have
your shopping list prepared in advance,
particularly for the first time visitor to a major
outlet center. On arrival this will help you to
focus on the stores that stock your
requirements. So often I have gone shopping
with people who wander from store to store for
hours, eventually becoming virtually glazed
over. Then with an hour or so to go, they start
running hither and yon looking for the sweater,
coat or dress that they came to buy in the first
place. By the time they find something that
looks like what they wanted, they are so
physically and mentally done in, they can't
make a decision.

Honestly if I had a dollar for everyone who has
said to me "if only I bought the shoes/boots/bag
or whatever, when I first saw it." The other
chronic problem with some shoppers,
overwhelmed by the huge variety, is
indecisiveness. I have seen people agonize over
an outfit for hours and then decide "no, it's not

really what I need."

Within 24 hours I will get a phone call asking
me to pick up the outfit.... if it's still there,
when I next visit to center. "I don't know what
got into me. I don't know what I was thinking. I
have been kicking myself every second since
I've been home thinking about that fabulous
evening dress for half nothing. I must have been
temporarily mad but honestly I was numb. I
just couldn't make the simplest decision at that
stage". Again and again I hear these sentiments
from men and women who are normally the
most decisive people in their own everyday
lives.

That's just one reason why it is so important to
get to the outlet center early in the morning.
Then you have a much better chance of finding
what you want. You are fresh and full of energy
and you need all your stamina. Believe me
shopping is an incredibly exhausting exercise. I
always suggest you make your most important
purchases early in the day. You will be feeling
sharper and more decisive yourself and your
brain won't be like scrambled eggs, as it is
almost sure to be at the end of a long and
wearying shopping day.

Also be aware that during the major US
holidays especially Thanksgiving, Christmas,
Valentines Day and Easter: all the outlet centers
are mobbed. Opening and closing times are
usually extended during these periods so it is
advisable to check trading times in advance.

I am listing four major outlets in this guide.
They are all an hour or so from Manhattan.
They are all very different in character and in
the stores they feature.

1. Woodbury Common,
Central Valley, New York is the Rolls Royce of
Outlet Centers in the entire United States. It's
an outdoor mall and it's a good hour north of
Manhattan by car. It features just about every

top international designer. Obviously these fashions are far more expensive than less high profile names. So if you don't want to shop for Chanel, Versace, Prada etc. you will probably do better at the other Outlets, though Woodbury Common has lables at every price point.

2. Tanger,

Riverhead, New York is an outdoor Mall, ninety minutes from Manhattan. Out in the middle of Long Island, there is a terrific selection of stores with just about all of the American designers featured. It also has a good Saks Off Fifth Avenue, Waterford Crystal, Ralph Lauren, Donna Karan, Barneys etc, both department stores outlets feature international designers. If you are out at the Hamptons during the summer, it's well worth the 40 minute drive across the Island to Tanger.

3. Jersey Gardens Mall,

Elizabeth, New Jersey is unbeatable for choice and for prices and it's only about half an hour or less from Manhattan by car. It is a very comfortable indoor mall. Heated in Winter and air conditioned in Summer It does not, however, feature the European designers unless they are in Saks Off Fifth or Neiman Marcus Last Call. Most American designers are widely available. For value this Mall is unbeatable and as so many friends who have gone there tell me, they feel they get the best value of all at this Outlet Mall.

4. Secaucus,

New Jersey is closest to Manhattan, I have got there in 15 minutes when traffic through the Lincoln Tunnel was light. It is a combination of an indoor mall but most of the stores are located over an area of several acres. Some could be a mile or more away from others. It is not nearly as well organized nor does it have the same vast selection of stores as Jersey Gardens but is has improved hugely over the past year.

So your best bet is to figure out exactly what you want to buy and choose an outlet center that best suits your shopping needs.

Woodbury Common

Central Valley, Harriman, New York

www.chelseagca.com
Location
Exit 16 off New York Interstate 87
Ph: 914 928 4000
Hours Monday-Saturday 10.00am to 9.00pm
Sunday 10am to 8.00pm
Check for extended holiday hours

Woodbury Common Opening Hours:
"Monday to Saturday 10am to 9.00pm
"Sunday, 10am to 8.00pm
"Closed from 3.00pm on July 4, Christmas Eve and New Year's Eve.
"Closed all day on Easter, Thanksgiving, Christmas and New Year's Day.

Located one hour north of NYC and with 250 Premium Stores, the largest outlet center in the US, this is the Rolls Royce of outlets. Is it any wonder that 10 million shoppers flocked here last year from all over the world ?

How to get there

Coach

Shortline Bus Service
Ph: 212 736 4700
Departs Port Authority, 42nd Street between 8th and 9th Avenue
2nd Level North Wing
Service Almost hourly
Fare $33.00 return
Trip time One hour
Credit Cards No Credit Cards

And also

Gray Line Bus service to Woodbury Common
Ph: Gray Line at 1 800 669 0051 or 212 695 0001
Departs 42nd Street and 8th Avenue Main Level
Service Frequent Departures
Fare $34.00 available at Gray Line office at the Port Authority
Credit Cards Major credit cards
Trip time Just over an hour
All passengers get a discount coupon booklet

Car

See car hire section
By far the best bet is to hire a car. Don't be intimidated by the prospect of driving in New

York. It is a straight run up the New York
Thruway Interstate 87 to exit 16, Harriman.
You can see the outlet center as you exit. In the
Autumn, the foliage is amazingly dramatic in
this part of upstate New York.
Trip Duration: About an hour or less depending
on traffic

Limousine Service
(see limo section)
This makes sense if there are a few people
traveling together. You can bargain with most
limo companies for an out of town day trip.
Check to see if they are including gratuity in the
price. If it is included you don't need to tip the
driver. If it isn't count on at least 15% of the
total cost for the tip.
Average Limo Cost for a day trip to Wood bury
Common: $350.00

Value 10   Range 10   Service 10

After Americans, Japanese and South
Americans, Irish shoppers have been tracked as
the biggest group to make the pilgrimage here.
Just about any designer you have ever heard of
is represented here. This is retail therapy at it's
very best, it literally is as good as it gets when it
comes to shopping.
And just when you thought it couldn't get any
better, it does. Chanel has opened it's first outlet
anywhere here. Oh lead me not into too much
temptation, I pray. Then I check it out before
hopping over to Frette, one of the top bed and
table linen stores in the world that has also
opened here.

Where to start?
The first time visitor to Woodbury Common will
find it really quite overwhelming. I suggest you
start at the very beginning: with a map that is

242

available in any store there or at the extremely helpful information center or better still log on before you leave home and check out the set up. Make sure you have your shopping list. You are not going to be able to check out all the stores in one day so if you have an idea of what your are looking for, it helps to focus your day.

Value:

Where would you find Master Cutter pieces (with certificate of authenticity signed by the Cutter)of Waterford Crystal at about half the price in the Waterford factory in Ireland? How about a Zegna suit for $299.00, the same one is over a thousand pounds in Dublin or London. Need Ralph Lauren jeans for men or women? Expect to pay about $35.00 a pair. Also look out for great baby RL and RL kids stuff. Fancy to die for frillies? Treat your self to some of the finest in the world at La Perla at less than half the Italian price. On my most recent visit La Perla in this Outlet was as well stocked as the exclusive Madison Avenue boutique.

On recent visits to the Chanel store, prices seemed to be about half or less than the Manhattan (57th Street between 5th and Madison) store. Shoes were especially good value, most were less than $100 a pair, the normal price tag-$400-$600. Handbags and costume jewellry were also very well discounted. Handbags were either last season's high fashion range or odd colours in the traditional quilted designs. They had fab. Wellies in pastel candy colours with the Chanel logo for $28.00.Clothes seemed to me to be a season old but then much of Chanel fashion is classic. They did have stunning evening gowns but the sizes were tiny. Gowns that had original prices tags of up to $10,000 were on sale for $500.

The cashmere in both TSE and Malo is definitely an investment at bargain prices and during special sales the value is quite unbelievable. Barneys outlet is worth a trip too, Check out the shoe department. I often buy my

Manolos there for under $100 a pair.
Timberland is another must. Deck shoes, for
men and women that cost well over E 150 in
Ireland are there for $30 or $40 a pair.. I never
miss Givency, Prada, Lancome, Louis Feraud or
Saks Off Fifth. You can be lucky with fashion in
Saks but I usually find nice gifts in the home
department there. Don't miss Mikasa.
Wonderful china, glassware, and general
household bits and bobs for a pittance. Always
check the CLEARANCE section first.

One of my favourite stores:
WestPoint Stevens-Bed, Bath & Linens This
store doesn't look anything special and the
name doesn't ring any bells but it is actually the
cotton mill that makes all Ralph Lauren's bed
linen, towels and table clothes. This store is
even cheaper than Ralph's own outlet around
the corner. If towels or bed linen are on your
shopping list, don't miss this one. On my most
recent visit I bought a King size set of Ralph
Lauren gingham bed linen with matching
comforter... all for less than the price of one
sheet in Dublin. And there wasn't even a special
sale on.

• Relax over lunch or a coffee at one of a
number of acceptable places to eat in the Center
but remember Americans eat lunch very early
and long queues form from about 11.00am
onwards.

Shipping:
If you are worried about breaking your new
bargains or if your purchases are too bulky, ship
them home:
•Contact Liffey Allied in New York. Phone 212
410 3500. Ask for Danny or Mike and this
extremely friendly and professional company
will have your arrangements made at the most
competitive price. Import duty is very little. If
you plan a major shop in New York, this is the
easiest and the best way to go about it and
shipping is much faster than it used to be. 14-
21 days is the maximum time it takes for a

consignment to cross the Atlantic. Woodbury Common does have its own shipping department.

N.B

• The down side of shopping at Woodbury is it can be, and usually is, quite exhausting.

• The center does not supply shopping trolleys. I consider this a major faux pas on the part of management.

• You can rent large shopping bags if needed but you have to carry them.

• A trolley car links up the different areas of the vast complex.

• Life is so much easier if you travel there by car because you can pile it up with your shopping during the day.

• If you take the coach you either have to lug your shopping bags around all day or ferry them to and fro to the left luggage area.

• There is a left luggage service.

• You can also rent pushchairs, wheelchairs and walkie talkies that help you communicate with the others in your group.

I can't recommend a day at Woodbury enough. It's a lot of fun and for a serious shopper it's about as close to heaven as one can get.

For further details about shopping at Woodbury Common either call 914 928 4000 or visit www.chelseagca.com.

By the way ask for a 10% discount voucher. This discount card can be used at most stores in this outlet center and in the companies other centers throughout the US.

Once Thanksgiving is over (the second last Thursday in November) all weekends until Christmas are totally manic in Woodbury Common. If you have to go at the weekend, arrive as early as possible. For the Thanksgiving Sales the crowds begin to arrive shortly after 3.30am to line up for the mega bargains. The car parks can become virtual war zones.There are huge queues for all the big name stores and both shoppers and sales assistants can become very tired and emotional as a result, though the staff at Woodbury are normally especially helpful and pleasant. Weekdays are much less stressful.

Wear comfortable shoes and clothes. Woodbury Common is an outdoor mall: In the winter it gets very cold in Central Valley, the Bear Mountain Ski resort isn't too far away. In the summer it almost sizzles, I remember one summer day when the car park surface was amost too hot to walk on. A trolley car will ferry you around the center and there is a left luggage area where you can check in your purchases, if you don't have your own car. There is an excellent information center where the staff are all remarkably helpful. There is also a hotel just across the street and if you plan a major shopping expedition, it would make sense to overnight there. This is a full day out, so pace yourself !!!!.

Store listings

Designer & SportswearApparel

A
A Pea In Pod Outlet
Adidas
Andrew Marc
Anne Klein Factory Store
Ann Taylor Factory Store
Arden B.
A/X Armani Exchange
Banana Republic Factory Store

B
Barneys New York Outlet
BCBG Max Azria
Benetton
Betsey Johnson
Big Dog Sportswear
Bottega Veneta
Brooks Brothers Factory Store
Bugle Boy
Burberry

C
CalvinKlein
Casual Corner
Chanel
Christian Dior
Claiborne
Club Monaco

D
Dana Buchman
Danskin
DKNY Jeans
Delia's
Dolce & Gabbana
Donna Karan
Dress Barn/Dress Barn Woman

E
Eddie Bauer
Eileen Fisher
Elisabeth
Ellen Tracy
Escada
Esprit
Etro

F
Fendi
Fila
French Connection
Fubu

G
Gap Outlet
Geoffrey Beene

G.H. Bass
Giorgio Armani General Store
Gucci
Guess?

H
Harve Benard
Hugo Boss

I
Iceberg
Izod

J
J. Crew
Jones New York
Jones New York Country
Jones New York - Men & Women
Suit Store
Jones New York Sport
Jones New York Woman
Joseph Abboud

K
Kasper A.S.L.

L
Lacoste
Laundry by Shelli Segal
Levi's Outlet by Design
Liz Claiborne
London Fog
Louis Feraud

M
Malo
Marina Rinaldi
Max Mara

N
Nautica
Nautica Jeans
Neiman Marcus Last Call
Nike
The North Face

O
Off 5th - Saks Fifth Avenue Outlet

P
Pacific Sunwear
Perry Ellis
Petite Sophisticate Outlet
Polo Jeans Co. Factory Store
Polo Ralph Lauren Factory Store

Q
Quiksilver

R
Reebok

S
Salvatore Ferragamo
Space (Prada, Miu Miu)
St. John Knits
Studio 7 (Marc Jacobs, Celine,Loewe, Kenzo)

T
TSE Cashmere
Theory
Tommy Hilfiger

V
Van Heusen
Varizioni
Ventilo Paris
Versace

W
Wilsons Leather
Woolrich

X
XOXO

Z
Zegna

Intimate Apparel

The Jockey Store
L'eggs, Hanes, Bali, Playtex
Maidenform
Natori
Olga Warner's
Wolford
La Perla

Shoes

Aldo Shoes
Bally
Banister Easy Spirit
Bostonian/Clarks
Cole Haan
Donald J Pliner
Dr. Martens
Etienne Aigner
Factory Brand Shoes
Florsheim
G.H. Bass
Hush Puppies
Johnston & Murphy
Kenneth Cole
Liz Claiborne Shoes
Ninewest
Rockport
Skechers
Steve Madden
Timberland
Tod's
Unisa
Vans Shoes
Via Spiga

Accessories/Jewellery

Claire's Accessories
Designer Brand Accessories
Fossil
Judith Leiber
Lids for Less
Movado
Seiko

Socks Galore
Sunglass Outfitters
Sunglass Station
Sunglass World
Ultra Diamond and Gold

Children

Carter's Childrenswear
Gap Outlet
J.M. Originals
K*B Toy Liquidators
Little Me
Oilily
OshKosh B'Gosh
The Children's Place
Warner Bros. Studio Outlet
World of Fun

Home Furnishings & Housewares

Le Gourmet Chef "Mikasa
Off 5th - Saks Fifth Avenue Outlet "Oneida
Silver
Polo Ralph Lauren Home Collection "Royal
Doulton
Sheridan Australia "Villeroy & Boch
Waterford Wedgwood "WestPoint Stevens
Williams Sonoma Co. Outlet "Frette
Corning Revere
Dansk "Farberware
Frette Outlet "Le Creuset

Luggage & Leather Goods

Coach "Dooney & Bourke
Furla "Ghurka
Hartmann Luggage "Hunting World
Kipling "Leather Loft
Samsonite/American Tourister "Samsonite
Travel Expo
Tumi "

Gifts & Specialty Items

Bear Mountain Books
Book Warehouse
Bose
The Company Outlet - Lancome
The Cosmetics Company Store
Designer Fragrances
Fuzziwig's Candy Factory Store
Godiva
Harry & David
Le Gourmet Chef
Mom's Cigar Factory Outlet
Music 4 Less
The Paper Outlet
Perfumania
Sony
Studio 7 (Givenchy & Guerlain Perfume)
Time Factory
Totes
Vitamin World
Warner Bros. Studio Store
World of Fun
Zales The Diamond Store Outlet

Food

Applebees "Au Bon Pain
Blue Chip Cookies & More "Bristol Café
China Taste "Haagen Dazs
The International Eatery "McDonald's
McSnacks "Posa Posa Too
Rocky Mountain Chocolate Factory "Starbucks
The Great American "Thyme to Eat

Secaucus,
New Jersey

www.SecaucusOutlets.com or www.hartzmountain.com
For a free coupon book call Maria at
1 877 OUTLET 2
Shopping Hours
Monday/Tuesday/Wednesday
10.00am 6.00pm
Thursday 10.00am 8.00pm
Friday/Saturday 10.00am 7.00pm
Sunday 11.00am 6.00pm

How to get there

Bus

129 from New York Port Authority, 42nd Street at 8th Avenue
Ph: 1 800 626 RIDE
Fare $1.90 one way
Departs Every twenty minutes

Or

Secaucus Shopping Tours
Ph: 1 800 248 9868 for reservations
Fare $31
Departs 10.00am Tuesday, Thursday and Saturday from Milford Plaza Hotel, 8th Avenue between 44th and 45th Streets. Departs Secaucus for the city at 3.00pm

Limousine Service
(see Limo Service section)

Or

Car
(see Car Hire details)

Trip
Duration: About 20 minutes by car from midtown Manhattan depending on traffic through the Lincoln Tunnel

Directions
Take the Lincoln Tunnel to 1 95. Take Route 3 West to Meadowlands Parkway: **NB:**Do not take the turn off for Secaucus. On Meadowlands Parkway Outlets at the Cove will be on your right. For Harmon Cove and the rest of the outlets continue on Meadowlands Parkway to the 5th traffic light, then turn left onto American Way. There are several car park areas. Many stores have their own car parks.
Now in it's 16th year, this was one of the

original outlet centers in the US and even though it doesn't remotely boast as many stores, especially high quality ones, as Woodbury Common, I still have a very soft spot for Secaucus. It's just across the Hudson River, via the Lincoln Tunnel from Manhattan. In fact you can see the Empire State in the distance as you shop. In the not too distant past Secaucus was one of the major warehouse centers for shipping clothes all over the United States. Fashions were trucked and trained out to cities all over the US when fashion was a major New York/New Jersey based industry. But with so much now flooding in from the Far East and Europe, the warehouses are now longer used as storage HQs and a major outlet area was born. Ironically, on my most recent visit I noticed that both H&M and Century 21 have located huge warehouses out there. Plus ca change, I guess.

New Jersey does not have any tax on clothes of any price so if you are buying something in excess of $110.00, you automatically clock up an 8.25% saving over prices in NYC.

A car is a must for Secaucus, not so much to get there and back but to get around the place. It really is a series of industrial estates and unlike Woodbury Common, Jersey Gardens and Tanger, which are purpose built malls, at Secaucus one store could be up to a mile away from another one you want to visit. The main areas are Harmon Cove, Castle Road, American Way, Enterprise Drive and Industrial Road. At your first stop pick up a free copy of the guide to the area that has all the latest news of sales and special offers. You will find a map on the center pages that provides an easy to find location for each store.

If traffic in the Lincoln Tunnel isn't too heavy you can get to Secaucus in less than 20 minutes from midtown Manhattan, so it's not the major outing that Woodbury is. You can nip over for a few hours in the morning or afternoon. You don't have to devote a full day here.

Facilities

Restrooms
ATMS
Phones
Food Court

 Value 10   Range 6   Service 7

Alphabetized List of Outlets

A
A Real N.Y. Bargain
Adolfo II
Aeropostale
Aldo Shoe Outle
Andrew Marc Outlet Store
Anne Klein Factory Stores
Athlete's Outlet
August Silk

B
Bally
Bannister Shoe Studio
Barbizon Lingerie
Bed, Bath & Beyond
Burlington Coat Factory

C
Calvin Klein Outlet Store
Carter's
Catalog Fashion Outlet
Champion Factory Store
Chaus
Children's Place Outlet
Christian Bernard Outlet
Corning Factory Store
Crystal-Kobe

D
Damon Factory Outlet

Damon
Designer Leather Outlet
Designer Warehouse Clearance Center
Donna Karan Company Store
Door Store
Dress Barn
Duty Free

E
Easy Spirit Outlet
Eileen Fisher
Emanuel Ungaro
Enterprise Golf
Episode
Escada
European Designer Outlet
Evan-Picone
Executive Suite by Jones New York

F
Fragrance & Accessory Outlet
Fur Vault Outlet, The
Futon Corner

G
G.H. Bass Company Store
Gant
Geoffrey Beene
Gloria Vanderbilt
Group USA
Group USA Fur Salon
Gucci

H
Harmon Cove Outlet Center
Harve Bernard Outlet

I
Innovation Luggage
International Cosmetic Outlet
Izod

J
Jones New York Country
Jones New York Dress
Jones New York Sport

Jones New York

K
Kasper A.S.L.
Kenneth Cole

L
La Chine
Leather Express
Leather Outlet Too!, The
Leather Outlet, The
Leggs, Hanes Bali Playtex
Lenox Factory Outlet
Levi's by Design
Liz Claiborne Outlet Store
London Fog Outlet Store

M
Maidenform
Maison Emanuelle
Male Ego Fashion Outlet
Manufacturer's Factory Outlet
Marty's Wholesale Shoe Outlet
Maternity Works
Mikasa
Mothertime...The Maternity Outlet
Music for a Song

N
Nahree Company Store
National Luggage
Natori
Nine West & Co.
Noritake Outlet Store
Northeast Wholesale

O
Olga/Warner's
Oneida Factory Store
Oriental Rugs Outlet

P
Panasonic/Technics Factory Outlet
Perfect Time
Perry Ellis
Prato Menswear Outlet

R

R&M Richards Dress Outlet
Reebok Outlet Store
Renfrew
Rug Importer Outlet

S

Samsonite Company Store
Searle/Steve
Sunglass Outlet
Suzelle Stephanie
Syms

T

TCS Direct
Thrapp Optical
Tommy Hilfiger

V

Van Heusen Factory
Vintage Wear

W

Walter Davoucci
Wanna Play

My Secaucus Favourites:

Gucci

50 Hartz Way
Ph: 201 392 2670
Credit Cards Major
credit cards

Always my second stop in Secaucus (after Calvin Klein at Outlets at the Cove). This store has recently had a huge refurbishment bringing it into line with it's 5th Avenue store. No longer is there that warehouse feeling to the place. The good news is that the store is now bigger and carries and displays much more stock. Fashion here fluctuates from being amazing to rather ordinaire but the value is always fantastic, especially in ladies and gents shoesshoes. But I have also bought beautiful luggage and handbags here for a fraction of what I would pay in their stores in Bond Street or 5th Avenue. Good accessories, ties, bags, scarves, watches and small leater goods make great gifts. And what about those Gucci loafers for new borns !!!! Talk about being born with a silver spoon, the hip kid is now born with Gucci loafers. And by the way all your purchases come wrapped in grey Gucci tissue popped in signature Gucci shopping bags.

Value 10   Range 7   Service 9

YSL rive gauche

50 Hartz Way
Ph: 201 770 2899
Credit Cards Major
credit cards

The great news for Secaucus lovers is that YSL chose this location to open it's first outlet store in the United States. And did they do it in style? The store is so elegant that you would think you are on Madison Avenue or Sloane Street. The fashions for men and women are barely a season old and the prices are historic. I bought a stunning black chiffon dress for $239.00. The original price tag a whopping $2890.00. Shoes here are super value too. Black suede boots originally $900.00 make so much more sense at $109.00 here. Service is superb

here too but then the manager Una Huges told
me her parents were both from Kerry !!!

 Value 10   Range 9   Service 10

Escada

55 Hartz Way
Ph: 201 865 5200
Credit Cards Major
credit cards

This is a recent arrival in Secaucus and a very
welcome one. The store is well laid out with up
to the minute merchandise, all at least 40%
below department store prices. In addition
previous seasons clothes and shoes are marked
down by up to 80%. There are usually some
stunning evening dresses from the couture range
reduced from several thousand dollars to a few
hundred. Accessories include bags, belts, wraps
and shoes. I have also bought beautiful shoes
here for as little as $30.00 a pair.

 Value 10   Range 10   Service 10

Group USA

Enterprise Avenue
at American Way
Ph: 201 867 4455
Credit Cards Major
credit cards

This is group of several American designers.
They seem to specialise in evening wear,
especially great beaded gowns at crazy prices.
There is also a terrific fur outlet here as well as
a little coffee shop if you need a little R & R.

 Value 9   Range 10   Service 7

Charles Jourdan

20, Enterprise
Avenue
Ph: 201 319 1300
Credit Cards Major
credit cards

Value here was so good on one visit that a
girlfriend was worried that everything was
above board. On that occasion most shoes were
$25 a pair or less. The regular price would have

been up to $300. Lovely sunglasses and some
bags and hats are also very well priced.

Value 9   Range 8   Service 9

DKNY

56 Hartz Way
Credit Cards
Major Credit cards

This isn't the best DKNY company store I've
shopped at but there are great bargains and
they seem to constantly seem to have sales.

Value ?   Range ?   Service ?

Mikasa

www.mikasa.com
Location
25 Enterprise
Avenue
Ph:1 800 TO SAVE
BIG
Credit Cards Major
credit cards

This store is a great place to buy all kinds of
glass and china gift items, as well as stocking
up for home. It's a vast china and glassware
warehouse and the prices are something else.
Over 70% off retail prices. I always head
straight for the CLEARANCE section at the
back of the store. I recently bought eight mugs
here recently for $16.00. The identical mugs
were €15.00 each in Dublin.

Value 10   Range 10   Service 8

Nine West

Outlets at the Cove,
45 Meadowlands
Parkway
Ph: 201 319 6824
Credit Cards
Major credit cards

Huge discounts, up to 80%, on a terrific
selection of shoes, boots and bags

Value 9   Range 9   Service 10

Liz Claiborne

2, Emerson Lane
Ph: 201 319 8411
Credit Cards Major
credit cards

This is a vast warehouse with an endless selection of fashion for every occasion for women of all sizes. There is also a limited men's section here as well as shoes, handbags, scarfs etc.

Value 9   Range 10   Service 8

Kenneth Cole

25, Enterprise
Avenue
Ph: 201 319 0140
Credit Cards Major
credit cards

Originally a shoe designer and known for his trendy advetising, Kenneth Cole now designs fashion for men and women as well as a wide range of accessories. At this outlet there is a terrific selection of men's shoes: the women's section is not as good as it used to be. Also some luggage, briefcases, belts and small clothes section.

Value 9   Range 8   Service 10

Enterprise Golf and Sportswear Outlet

600 Secaucus
Road
Ph: 201 348 6544
Hours Monday-
Wednesday-Sat
10.00am 6.00pm
Thursday- Friday
10.00am 9.00pm
Sunday 11.30am
5.00pm
Credit Cards Major
credit cards

Over 14,000 sq feet of the best names in golf all at discounted prices. It also claims to be New Jersey's finest in-house custom club and repair center. It has been voted one of America's 100 best golf shops and has a vast warehouse full of Callaway, Ping, Titleist, Cobra, Yonex, Spalding, Daiwa, Maxifly to name just a few. There is an equally well stocked clothing area and it also boasts golf instruction (by appointment), computer swing analysis and indoor hitting facilities. Their motto is "where you buy your equipement is as important as the equipment you buy."

Value 8   Range 10   Service 9

Burlington Coats

www.bcfdirect.com
275 Hartz Way
Ph: 201 866 1665
Credit Cards Major
credit cards

Famous label fashions for the entire family at unbeatable prices. Even more frenetic than in the City. I have really mega bargains here in Ralph Lauren, Chaps, Gant. But be prepared to pick through all those racks.

 **Value 8**   **Range 8**   **Service 6**

Jersey Gardens

Elizabeth, New Jersey

Where:
Exit 13 A on the
New Jersey
Turnpike
www.jerseygardens.com
Ph: 1 904 354 5900
Hours Monday-
Saturday 10.00am-
9.00pm
Sunday:
11.00am-7.00pm
Holiday hours may
vary

How to Get There

Directions
From Manhattan take to the Lincoln Tunnel to
the New Jersey Turnpike. Exit 13A to Jersey
Gardens Boulevard.

Car
(See Car Hire details)

Limousine
(See Limo details)

Bus
Ph: 1-973 762 5100 for information
Depart New Jersey Transit Bus 111 from Port
Authority, 42nd Street between 8th hand 9th
Avenue
Frequency About every 90 minutes
Trip time About 30 minutes
Cost $3.95
Credit Cards Major credit cards

There is also a free shuttle daily from Newark
International airport at Monorail Station E to
Jersey Gardens, Entrance A

This purpose built indoor mall, 1.3 million
square feet of discount shopping with a 22
screen cinema, opened a few years ago. It's just
across from Newark International airport and
shoppers fly in here from all over the world.
What a difference a year makes! When I first
shopped there the giant mall was only open a
few months and was quite unfinished. It then
appeared to be a combination of regular price
stores and factory outlets and when I departed I
was rather under whelmed by the experience.

What a difference a year makes. I drove out

there on a Saturday morning and got there from mid town Manhattan in just over twenty minutes and I was blown away by just about everything at Jersey Gardens on my most recent visit. However a word of caution: The Mall shares the Turnpike exit with Newark Airport and this part of the Turnpike can, and frequently is, a total nightmare. Traffic can back up for miles near these exits, leaving you plenty of time to mull over the meaning of Bruce Springsteen's song, inspired by the same Turnpike.

The Mall is totally weather proofed being indoors. It's extremely comfortable, good air-conditioning in hot weather and well heated in the winter. It's also well carpeted so it doesn't take a huge toll on your feet. We shopped from 10.30am to 6.00pm with a stop for a very good lunch at Asian Islands and we were still not dropping when we returned to the Jeep.

The fact that shopping trolleys are permitted and supplied free of charge here is a huge plus. You don't have that awful pulling and dragging of packages that you endure at the other outlets listed here. There is also a storage area if you want to store your packages while you shop for more.

Jersey Gardens is right next to the giant IKEA, the Swedish hyper furniture and home store, so if you wanted to visit IKEA it is an added reason to visit the town of Elizabeth. There is also a hyper Toys R Us near by. So renting a car for a day to come out here could be a very sound investment.

The car park at Jersey Gardens looks bigger than that of Newark airport just across the turnpike. But, even though it appeared to be totally full, in fact we found plenty of parking spots close to the stores.

I can't emphasize just how vast this Mall is and it's really quite easy to get lost there, especially on a first trip.

Remember the rules: as for other outlets:

• First stop by the information desk and pick up a Mall Directory. Bring your passport /drivers license as ID and ask for a discount coupon book. These are free to out of state residents and most of the stores in the Mall provide discounts of up to 30%

The Center boasts a huge Food Pavilion with several varieties of ethnic food as well as Johnny Rockets, Sbarro, Wendys etc. We had a late lunch at Asian Islands. The food was very good, the service excellent. The manager even took care of our overloaded trolleys for us. And there was a 10% discount coupon in the coupon book. It was just the reviving R and R we needed to rev us up to take off for another few hours.

I found the usual reliable, great value buys in Saks, Off Fifth Avenue and Neiman Marcus' Last Call. Both stores have super ladies shoe departments with Prada, Miu, Miu, Manolo Blahnik, Yves St Laurent, Todds, Robert Clergerie, Christian Louboutain etc at less than a quarter of the retail price. Both of these stores also have great value in home furnishings and in children's wear. They both sport vast fashion departments for ladies and men and most garments seemed to have been marked down two or three times, making the most incredible value. My best buy here was a great beaded evening dress that I found in Cohoes for $69.00. I wore it to the Oscars. In basic black with a little pearl sparkle and a tiny train it looked like an Armani that would cost a few thousand dollars, everyone thought it was Armani and if they read this they will now learn that it wasn't. I also got great knee high boots for $9.99. Almost identical ones in Marks and Spencers cost E70.00. My other special favourites include Brooks Brothers who have a great outlet here as does H & M where the price of the already well priced clothes, is literally unbelievable. Bed Bath and Beyond, Nautica, Nike all have huge stores as do Vans, Aerosoles and Reebok. Victoria's Secret, Ann Taylor, Banana Republic, Old Navy, Gap and Benetton. Filene's basement and Bebe have also opened. I could fill a book about the stores at this center. The staff are so pleasant, in stark contrast to Manhattan.

• Remember there is no tax on clothes and shoes in New Jersey.

I can hardly find words to describe the value at the H&M Outlet. The retail prices at the 5th Avenue Store seem incredible anyway but they are virtually giving away the goods at Jersey Gardens. The styles are right up to the minute, great copies of the season's cat walk favourites. Indeed your dry cleaning bill will propably be more than the price of some outfits.

• Check out my shopping cart from H&M:

3 white men's polo shirts
2 black men's polo shirts
2 silk ties
1 black beaded mid length halter dress
1 silk jersey dress
I men's black hip length coat

All for $97.00

Guest Amenities

Valet parking

Two Concierge Desks (located near COHOES Fashions & Marshalls MegaStore)

Complimentary Strollers & Wheelchairs

Copies and Faxes

Foreign Currency Exchange

Jersey Gardens Gift Certificates

Multi-lingual Information

Transit Information

Tax-free Shopping on Clothes and Shoes

Automatic Teller Machines

Children's Play Area

Deluxe Food Court and Themed Sit-down

Restaurants

Storage Lockers

Tourism Department

 **Value 10   Range 9   Service 10**

Alphabetized List of Outlets

Anchors and Major Stores

Bed, Bath & Beyond
Burlington Coat Factory
Cohoes
Daffy's
Filene's Basement
Marshalls Megastore
Neiman Marcus Last Call
Off 5th - Saks Fifth Avenue Outlet
Old Navy

Apparel

A
Aerokids
Aeropostale

Against All Odds
Alex & Alex Leather
Altrom
Ann Taylor Loft

B
Bambini Italiani
Banana Republic Factory Store
BCBG Max Azria
Benetton
Brooks Brothers Factory Store

C
Carter's
Casual Corner Annex
Charlotte Russe
Childrens Place Outlet
Club Monaco
Collezione

D
Danskin
Deb
Dress Barn

E
Eye Candy

G
Gap Outlet
Geoffrey Beene
Group USA
Guess Company Store

H
H&M
Haggar Clothing Co.
Hot Topic

I
Izod

J
Jhane Barnes Xtras
Jockey

K
Kids Outlet
Kidstown
Kiziwoo
Knot A Tie

L
L'eggs, Hanes, Bali, Playtex
Levi's/Dockers Outlet by Designs
Lids for Less
Loutie

M
Maidenform
Mandee
Mickey Sportswear
Motherhood Maternity Outlet

N
Nautica Factory Store
Nautica Jeans Company
Norma Reed

P
Pacific Sunwear
Papaya
Perry Ellis
Perry Ellis Clearance Center
Polo Jeans Co.
Prato Fine Men's Wear

Q
Quiksilver

R
Rue 21 Company Store

S
Skechers
Square One
Steve and Barry's University Sportswear
Stylz
Tommy Jeans

T
Triple Five Soul

V

Van Heusen
Victoria's Secret

W

Wilsons Leather Outlet
Windsor

Z

Zan Boutique

Books, Cards, Gifts and Toys

American Greetings
Atlantic Book Warehouse
Bow Wow
Inspired by Nature
KB Toys
Lulu

Electronic Specialty

Executive Cellular
Keep in Touch Cellular
Let's Talk Cellular
Software Etc.
Stop 'N Save Software

Food
Asian Islands
Auntie Anne's
Auntie Anne's
Burger King
Chili's Too
Cindy's Cinnamon Rolls
Cinnabon
Great Steak & Potato Co.
Greenleaf Grille
Haagen Dazs
Harry & David
Jersey Ice
Johnny Rockets

Kelly's Cajun Grill
Nathan's Famous
Ranch 1
Rocky Mountain Chocolate Factory
Sbarro
Yeung's Lotus Express

General Merchandise

As Seen on TV
Corning Revere
Gateway Newstand
Remington

Health and Beauty

Bath & Body Works
Beauty Express
General Nutrition Centers
La Perfumerie
Mastercuts
Perfumania
Victoria's Beauty
Vitamin World

Home Furnishings

Kirkland's
Mikasa
Pfaltzgraff
Rockaway Bedding

Jewelry and Accessories

Afaze
Afterthoughts
Claire's
CR Jewelers Diamond Outlet
Her Highness Fine Jewelry
Jewelers on Fifth
Piercing Pagoda
Sunglass Hut International
Sunglass Hut/Watch Station
Ultra Diamond and Gold Jewelers
Watch Station

Zales The Diamond Store Outlet

Luggage

National Luggage Outlet
Samsonite Company Store
Travel 2000

Music, Video and Entertainment

Cinema Ride
FYE - For Your Entertainment
Jeepers! America's indoor theme park
Loews Theatres

Services

Aquamassage
Cohen's Fashion Optical
Lens Lab Express
Nail Pro
Siso Shoe Repair

Shoes

Aerosoles
Aldo Shoes
Bass Outlet
Bostonian/Clarks
Bruno Magli
Burlington Shoes
Candie's
Etienne Aigner
Factory Brand Shoes
Feet First
Journeys
Kenneth Cole
Naturalizer
Nike Factory Store
Nine West
Payless Shoe Source
Stride Rite
Vans Shoes

Sports and Fitness
Fila

Just Sports
Reebok
Shoot 'N Score

Tanger Outlets

Where:
Riverhead, Long
Island, New York
www.tangeroutlet.
com
Ph: 631 369 3687

How to get there

Car
See car rental

Directions
Take the Mid Town Tunnel at 2nd Avenue and
36th Street to the LIE (Long Island
Expressway (I 495) Stay on it right out to the
very last exit(Exit 72). You will see the Outlet
center from the exit, just a few hundred yards
away.

Coach
Sunrise Express Bus service is available from
Manhattan
The schedule changes according to season
Ph: For up to date information call: 1 800 527
7709.
• Reservation and confirmation necessary
• Bring your bus ticket/receipt stub to the Mall
office upon arrival and you will receive a
$10.00 Tanger Gift Certificate
Cost   All fares One Way
$16.00
Round Trip: $31.00
Credit Cards
Manhattan pick up center: Lexington Avenue
and Third Avenue on 44th Street near 3rd
Avenue, Southwest Corner
Schedule (subject to change)
From October to Memorial Day

To Tanger Outlet Center from New York City
Monday-Friday
11.00am   Leave New York City
1.00pm   Arrive at Tanger, Riverhead
Return To New York City
3.00pm   Leave Tanger Riverhead
5.00pm   Arrive New York City

Saturday
8.30am   Leave New York City
10.30am   Arrive at Tanger Riverhead
11.00am   Leave NY City
1.00pm   Arrive Tanger Outlet Center
Return to New York City
7.30pm   Leave Tanger, Riverhead
9.30pm   Arrive New York City

Sunday
11.00am   Leave New York City
1.00pm   Arrive at Tanger
Return to New York City
7.30pm   Leave Tanger, Riverhead
9.30pm   Arrive in New York City
Additional bus scheduled to leave New York
City at 9.30am from Memorial Day to Labor
Day only

The Jitney Bus is scheduled to provide an
additional service from New York City to
Tanger in mid 2001.
Ph: For information call 1 800 936 0440

Train
The Long Island Rail Road Service
Ph: 718 217 5477 for information
Departs: Penn Station: 34th Street
between7th and 8th Avenues to Riverhead
Station and then by taxi to the Outlet Center.

Regular Hours (April-December)
Monday-Saturday   9.00am-9.00pm
Sunday   10.00am-7.00pm

Winter Hours January-March
Sunday-Thursday   10.00am-7.00pm
Friday-Saturday   9.00am-9.00pm
Cost $15.25 (peak times) One Way
$10.25(off peak)   One Way
Credit Cards   Major credit cards
Trip time   2 hours 10 minutes

Tanger Outlet Center comprises two purpose
built malls and is situated about fifty miles east
of Manhattan, on Long Island. It boasts over

165 outlets and has hugely improved over the past few years. Just how much it has improved was impressed on me when I visited in last June. Several terrific new stores have opened and the standard of the stores has made a giant leap forward. A huge Ralph Lauren store has opened in Tanger One. It stocks a wide range of mens, ladies and children's wear as well as a well stocked home furnishings department. There is also a Polo Ralph Lauren and a Polo Jeans Store. Banana Republic has opened a fashion store as well as a show store. Club Monaco, one of the hottest fashion stores at the moment, has a well stocked store and Bombay Furniture and Home Store has also opened. There is a good Saks Off Fifth and a good Barneys Outlet: both stores great for ladies shoes and also good for evening wear. Both stores have good men's departments. Timberland, Nike, Old Navy, Bose, Jones New York, Waterford Crystal, Royal Doulton and Mikasa are all packed with great bargains

The Following is a listing of the stores at Tanger

Accessories

Bostonian-Clark Shoe Outlet
Claire's Accessories
Club Monaco
Coach Factory Store
Dana Buchman
Fossil
Leather Loft
Lids
Liz Claiborne Outlet
Nine West
Off Saks Fifth Avenue
Polo Ralph Lauren Factory Store
Sunglass World
Time Factory Watch Co.
Totes
 Sunglass

Apparel

Aeropostale
Ann Taylor Loft
Banana Republic
Barney's New York
Bass Clothing & Shoe Outlet
BCBG
Benetton
Big Dog Sportswear
Britches
Brooks Brothers
California Sunshine Swimwear
Calvin Klein
Casual Corner
Casual Corner Woman
Casual Male Big & Tall
Claiborne Men's
Clothestime
Club Monaco
Dana Buchman
Danskin
DKNY Jeans
Donna Karan
Dress Barn
Dress Barn Woman
Eddie Bauer
Elisabeth
Gap Outlet
Geoffrey Beene
Greg Norman Golf
Guess?
Haggar Clothing Co.
Izod
J. Crew
Jockey
Jones New York
Jones New York Men
Jones New York Sport
Joseph Abboud
Kasper
L'eggs Hanes Bali Playtex
L'eggs Hanes Bali Playtex Express
Laundry
Levi's Outlet by Designs
Liz Claiborne Outlet

London Fog
Maidenform
Maternity Works
Natori
Nautica
Nike
Off Saks Fifth Avenue
Old Navy Outlet
Olga Warner
Pacific Sunwear
Perry Ellis
Petite Sophisticate
Polo Jeans Co.
Polo Ralph Lauren Factory Store
Reebok Factory Direct
Rena Rowan
Renfrew
Rue 21
Socks Galore by Hanes
Tommy Hilfiger
Van Heusen
Woolrich

Children's Apparel

Bass Clothing & Shoe Outlet
Big Dog Sportswear
Carter's Childrenswear
Children's Place
Club Monaco
Delia's
Gap Outlet
Guess?
Levi's Outlet by Designs
London Fog
Nike
Old Navy Outlet
Osh Kosh B'Gosh
Polo Ralph Lauren Factory Store
So Fun Kids
Tommy Hilfiger
Woolrich

Footwear

adidas
Aerosoles
Aldo Shoes
Banana Republic Shoe
Banister Shoe Studio
Bass Clothing & Shoe Outlet
Bostonian-Clark Shoe Outlet
Candie's
Cole Haan
Dexter Shoe
Easy Spirit
Etienne Aigner
Factory Brand Shoes
Fila
Florsheim
Greg Norman Golf
Kenneth Cole
Liz Claiborne Shoes
Nike
Nine West
 Off Saks Fifth Avenue
Reebok Factory Direct
Rockport Factory Direct
SAS Shoes
Skechers
Steve Madden
Stride Rite
Timberland
Vans Shoes

Housewares and Home Furnishings

Corning Revere
Craftworks
Kitchen Collection
Lenox
Mikasa
Noritake
Oneida
Pfaltzgraff
Polo Ralph Lauren Factory Store
Royal Doulton
Springmaid-Wamsutta

Waterford/Wedgwood
Welcome Home
Westpoint Stevens

Specialty

Bath & Body Works
Bose Factory Store
Camp Coleman
Chelsea Watch
Class Perfumes & Cosmetics
Cosmetics Company
Country Clutter
Fuzziwigs
Greg Norman Golf
Harry & David
Hoover
KB Toy Outlet
Le Gourmet Chef
Lillian Vernon
Lindt Chocolate
Music 4 Less
New York Jewelry
Office Max
Paper Factory
Pepperidge Farm
Perfumania
Remington Outlet
Samsonite
Scents for Less
The Wiz
Tools & More
Ultra Jewelry
Ultra Watch Co.
Vitamin World
Wilson's Leather
Zales, The Diamond Outlet

Food Court

Great Steak & Potato Co.
Harry & David
McDonald's
Ragin Cajun

Rocky Mountain Chocolate Factory
Villa Pizza
Wok & Roll

Street Fair Calendar

Six months of fairs, fests, carnivals, bazaars, expos, and spectaculars -- more browsing than even a bargain-hungry New Yorker could hope to enjoy.

July

Hermanos Fraternos de Loiza Aldea Carnival
East 109th Street from Second to Third Avenues

NYC Unfolds Street Fair
West 3rd Street from Broadway to Laguardia Place and on Laguardia from West 3rd Street to Washington Square

Village Reform Democratic Club Festival
University Place from Waverly Place to 14th Street

Dutch Kills Civic Association Street Festival
36th Avenue from 29th to 35th Streets, Queens

East Side Summer Festival
Third Avenue from 42nd to 57th Streets

The Motion Picture Club Festival
Seventh Avenue from 47th to 57th Streets

Hellenic Orthodox Traditionalist Church Festival
26th Street from 23rd Avenue to Ditmars Boulevard, Queens

Female Softball League Carnival
East 109th Street from Second to Third Avenues

August

Washington Square Summer Festival
6th Avenue from 8th to 14th Streets

Holy Apostles Soup Kitchen Street Festival
23rd Street between Eighth and Ninth Avenues

Jamaica Arts and Music Summer (JAMS) Festival
Jamaica Avenue from Parsons Boulevard to 169th Street, Queens

Festival Dominicano
Amsterdam Avenue from 190th Street to 193rd Street

Festival of the Americas
Avenue of the Americas from 42nd to 56th
Streets

Lincoln Square Neighborhood Center Festival
Columbus Avenue from 66th to 72nd Streets

Junction Boulevard Festival
Junction Boulevard from Roosevelt Avenue to
37th Avenue, Queens

Family Unity Day
122nd Street and Riverside Drive

Fort Hamilton Board of Trade Street Festival
Fort Hamilton Parkway from 65th to 70th
Streets, Brooklyn

Saint Irene Chrysovalantou Church Festival
23rd Avenue from 36th Street to the Amtrak
Overpass

Manhattan Youth Street Fair
Fulton Avenue from Broadway to Gold Street

Seaport Community Coalition Street Fair
Water Street from Fulton to Broad Streets

The Times Square Expo
Seventh Avenue from 47th to 57th Streets

The Workman's Circle, Inc. Festival
Madison Avenue from 42nd to 57th Streets

Myrtle Avenue SummerFest
Myrtle Avenue from Fresh Pond Road Wyckoff
Avenue, Queens

Borgett Cultural Festival
Steinway Street from 25th Avenue 28th Avenue

The Retired Boxers of PuertRicCarnival
East 109th Street from Second Third Avenues

Wall Street Community Day Festival
Wall Street from Water South Streets

Village Visiting Neighbors Street Fair
University Place from Waverly Place 14th Street

Young Republican Club Festival
Seventh Avenue from 47th 57th Streets

Harlem Week "Uptown Saturday Night"
135th Street from St. Nicholas Avenue Lenox
Avenue

Sixth Avenue Summerfest
Sixth Avenue from 14th 23rd Streets

East 55th Street Conservative
Synagogue Festival
Lexington Avenue from 45th 57th Streets

Harlem Week "Harlem Day 2003"
Street Festival
135th Street from St. Nicholas Avenue Fifth
Avenue

Washington Avenue Merchants Street Festival
Washington Avenue from Eastern Parkway St. Marks Avenue, Brooklyn

Nostrand Avenue Merchants Street Festival
Nostrand Avenue from Empire Boulevard Clarkson Avenue, Brooklyn

Pakistani-American Merchants Independence Celebration
Coney Island Avenue from Newkirk Avenue Avenue H, Brooklyn

Steinway Street Fair
Steinway Street from 28th t34th Avenue, Queens

Feast of Santa Rosalia Society
18th Avenue from 67th Street Bay Ridge Parkway, Brooklyn

Third Avenue Merchandise Fair
Third Avenue from 23rd 34th Streets

Our Lady of Pompei Church Festival
Bleecker Street from 6th 7th Avenues and Carmine Street from 6th Avenue Varick Street

The Fleetwood Neighborhood Association Festival
Gramaton Avenue from Center Cedar Streets

Church of the Good Shepherd Street Fair
Third Avenue from 23rd Street 34th Street

Gramercy Park Neighborhood Festival
Third Avenue from 14th 23rd Streets

Daytop Madison Avenue Festival
Madison Avenue from 42nd 57th Streets

Pakistani Independence Day Festival
Madison Avenue from 23rd Street 26th Street

Brighton Beach 26th Annual Jubilee
Brighton Beach and Coney Island Avenues from Corbin Place tBrightwater Court, Brooklyn

Carnaval AguadillanTeatrModernPuertoriqueno
East 116th Street from Second Third Avenues

Lesbian, Gay, Bisexual and Transgender Community Center Festival
Greenwich Avenue from Sixth Avenue West 12th Street

Katharine Hepburn Garden Fair
Second Avenue from 43rd 53rd Streets

Central Park/Plaza Festival
60th Street from Fifth Park Avenues

Chinese Promise Baptist Church Summer Street Fair
Eighth Avenue from 47th Street 54th Streets, Brooklyn
August 30; 10am-5:30pm

Sunnyside Festival
Greenpoint Avenue from 44th 48th Streets, Queens

Washington Square Outdoor Art Exhibit
Periphery of Washington Square Park

19th Annual Brazilian Day Festival
Avenue of the Americas from 42nd 56th Streets

Americana Jazz Festival
52nd Street from Madison Seventh Avenues

St. Lucia USA Carnival
Webster Avenue from East Gun Hill Road East
233rd Street, Bronx

Forest Hills Austin Street Festival
Austin Street from Ascan Yellowstone, Queens

September

M.E.C.H.A. Family Festival
Third Avenue from 34th t42nd Streets
September 1 (Labor Day); 11am-6pm West
Indian Day Carnival
Eastern Parkway from Howard Avenue
Flatbush Avenue, Brooklyn

**30th Avenue Business Association
Street Festival**
30th Avenue from 29th Street t42nd Street,
Queens

**Federazione Italo-Americana Fresh
Pond Road Festival**

Fresh Pond Road from Woodbine tManahan
Streets

Fulton Street Follies
Fulton Street from Broadway Gold Street

Village Center for Care Street Festival
Bleecker Street from Seventh Avenue Bank
Street

Big Apple Performing Arts Festival
Seventh Avenue from 47th 57th Streets

Forest Hills/RegPark Lions Club Festival
63rd Drive from Queens Boulevard Alderton
Street, Queens

Washington Square Outdoor Art Exhibit
Periphery of Washington Square Park

Ninth Avenue Fall Festival
Ninth Avenue from 23rd 31st Streets

Third Avenue Festival
Third Avenue from 66th 86th Streets

Fifth Avenue Mile
Fifth Avenue from 60th 80th Streets

Washington Heights Children's Health Festival
St. Nicholas Avenue from 181st Street 191st
Street
September 7; 11am-6pm

Tomchei Torah Chaim Birnbaum Church Avenue Spectacular

Church Avenue from McDonald Avenue Ocean
Parkway, Brooklyn

The Bronx Council for Economic Development
East Fordham Road from Morris Avenue tEast
Kingsbridge Road; Valentine Avenue from
188th Street 192nd Street

Figli di San GennarFeast
Mulberry Street from Canal Houston Streets

Congress of Racial Equality Street Fair
University Place from Waverly Place 14th Street

Chelsea Midtown Democrats Street Festival
Eighth Avenue from 14th Street 23rd Street

Vanderbilt Avenue Merchants Association Festival
Vanderbilt Avenue from Park Place Atlantic
Avenue, Brooklyn

West Kiwanis/Kiwanis Club of Jackson Heights Festival
37th Avenue from 83rd Street 90th Street,
Queens

Gracie Square Art Show
East End Avenue from 84th 86th Streets

Staten Island Historical Society's County Fair
Richmond Road from Arthur Kill Road St.
Patrick's Place

Second Avenue - Autumn Jubilee
Second Avenue from 23rd 34th Streets

92nd Street Y Festival
Lexington Avenue from 79th Street 96th Streets

Sunset Park Fifth Avenue Street Festival
Fifth Avenue from 44th Street 59th Street, Brooklyn

Flatbush Development Corporation Street Festival
Cortelyou Road from Ocean Coney Island Avenues, Brooklyn

Boy Scouts of America/Maspeth Lions Club Festival
Grand Avenue from Remsen Place 72nd Street

Wall Street Community Day Festival Series
Wall Street from Water South Streets

Far West 10th Street Block Association Street Fair
West 10th Street from Bleecker Street West 4th Street

The Great Irish Festival
Avenue of the Americas from 42nd 56th Streets

Interfaith Assembly on Homelessness and Housing Fest
E/S Broadway from 110th Street t118th Street

United Community Centers Street Festival
New Lots Avenue from Hendrix Street tJerome Street, Brooklyn

Flatbush Empire Parkside Merchants Street Festival
Flatbush Avenue from Empire Boulevard Parkside Avenue, Brooklyn

Jerome/Gunhill Street Festival
Jerome Avenue from 208th Street tGunhill Road; sidewalks of Gun Hill Road from Jerome Avenue Wayne Avenue, Bronx

Rockaway Music and Art Council Stret Festival
Rockaway Beach Boulevard west of Beach 144th Street/Riis Park

Tudor City Festival
Second Avenue from 43rd 53rd Streets

New York is Book Country - Fifth Avenue Street Fair
Fifth Avenue from 40th 57th Streets

Columbus Avenue Festival
Columbus Avenue from 66th Street 86th Street

Atlantic Avenue "Atlantic Antic" Street Fair
Atlantic Avenue from Hicks Street Fourth Avenue, Brooklyn

Kiwanis Club of Glendale Street Festival
Metropolitan Avenue from 79th Street 73rd

Place, Queens

St. Finbar's Roman Catholic Church Street Festival
Bay 19th Street from Bath Avenue Benson
Avenue, Brooklyn

St. Martin of Tours Bazaar
Knickerbocker Avenue from Hancock Street
Weirfield Street

Greek Orthodox Community of St. Demetrios Festival
152nd Street from 84th Avenue t84th Drive;
and 84th Road from 152nd Street tParsons
Avenue, Queens
September 25-28; 10am-11pm

Transportation Alternatives Street Fair
Fourth Avenue from 8th Street t14th Street
September 27 (Rosh Hashanah); 11am-6pm

The Alliance of Guardian Angels Festival
Seventh Avenue from 47th 57th Streets

Woodside on the Move Street Festival
Woodside Avenue from Roosevelt Avenue t65th
Place; and 61st and 62nd Streets from
Woodside Roosevelt Avenues, Queens

Stephen Siller, FDNY "Let Us DGood" Children's Festival
Vesey Street from North End tWest Street

Muslim Day Festival
Madison Avenue from 23rd Street t26th Street
September 28; 10am-6pm

Broadway Merchants and Professionals Festival
Broadway from Crescent Street to 47th Street, Queens

October

Downtown Visiting Neighbors Street Fair
Wall Street from South Street tWater Street

Federation Preserve Greenwich Village
Greenwich Avenue from 6th Avenue 7th Avenue

Avenue A Adventure Festival
Avenue A from Houston t14th Streets

Chase Corporate Challenge
Park Avenue from 48th 29th Streets

Deepavali Festival
John Street from Water South Streets

N.Y.C. Octoberfes
Lexington Avenue from 42nd t57th Streets

Greenpoint YMCA Street Festival
Manhattan Avenue from Greenpoint tBedford Avenues

North Flatbush Street Festival
Flatbush Avenue from Plaza Street Atlantic Avenue, Brooklyn

Wall Street Community Day Festival Series
Wall Street from Water South Streets

St. Joseph Church Street Fair
Washington Place from McDougal Street Grove Street

Washington Square Festival
Waverly Place from Broadway Fifth Avenue

Our Lady of the Scapular & St. Stephan Festival
Third Avenue from 23rd 34th Streets

Bloomingdale Area Coalition and One Stop Senior Services Festival
W/S Broadway from 96th 110th Streets

Kiwanis Club of Glendale Street Festival
Myrtle Avenue from Cooper Avenue 67th Place, Queens

November

Village Independent Democrats Street Fair
Greenwich Avenue from 6th 7th Avenues

American Diabetes Association Street Festival
Madison Avenue from 42nd 57th Streets

Gramercy Stuyvestant Independent Democrats Festival

Broadway from 17th Street 23rd Street

Women's Democratic Club Street Fair

Astor Place from Broadway Lafayette Street

The Manhattan Republican Club Fair

Park Avenue South from 17th 23rd Streets

Brooklyn Young Republicans Court Street Spectacular

Court Street from Montague Street and Atlantic Avenue

Gay and Lesbian Independent Democrats Street Fair

West 4th Street from Lafayette Street Washington Square East

Independent Downtown Republican Club Fair

University Place from Waverly Place 14th Street

Madison Avenue Holiday Expo

Madison Avenue from 42nd 57th Streets

Tenhouse Family Fund (FDNY) Holiday Market

Wall Street from South Water Streets

December

Christmas in Little Italy
Mulberry Street from Canal Street to Broome
Street

"Miracle on Madison Avenue" Holiday Festival
Madison Avenue from 60th Street 72nd Street

New York

How to get there and other stuff worth knowing

Obviously you need a return airline ticket and a valid passport. Check visa requirements. They differ from country to country ie. For Irish citizens no visa is required if you are not planning to work in the US. At the flight check desk in Irish airports you will receive the relevant visa waiver and customs forms to fill in. You pre clear immigration in Dublin and Shannon.

PASSENGER DATA NOTICE

The United States Government has initiated new legislation requiring all airlines to provide the US customs and immigration authorities with access to data held on an airline's reservation system relating to passengers travelling to or from the United States. Consequently, if your journey involves a flight to or from the United States, any information we hold about you and your travel arrangements may be disclosed to the US customs and immigration authorities.

There is also a requirement for all passengers travelling to the United States to provide an address within the U.S. where they will be staying during their visit. Failure to provide an address may result in passengers being refused entry to the U.S. by immigration clearance.

DEPARTMENT OF HOMELAND SECURITY 'U.S. VISIT' PROGRAM

With effect from January 5, 2004, The U.S. Department of Homeland Security will be implementing the 'U.S. Visit Program'.

This program applies to passengers holding U.S. visas. U.S. Customs and Border Protection Officers will use an inkless fingerprint scanner to automatically read the fingerprints of these arriving visitors. The visitor will be asked to put the index finger of one hand and then the index finger of the other hand on the scanner. The

Customs and Border Protection Officer will also take a digital photograph of the visitor. The biographic and fingerprint data will be used to verify the identity of the visitor and compared against watch lists.

Nota Bene: If you plan to stay with friends and want to bring bacon, sausages or any meat or fish products, your food purchase has to be made at the airport where food is sealed in special USDA approved packages. All food products that do not have this USDA labeling are confiscated by Customs on arrival.

If you plan to rent a car you will need a current Drivers License plus a major credit card. A valid credit card really is a must for a serious shopping trip and/or if you are staying in a hotel. Remember when you check in, the establishment will "reserve" what they feel is an average spend for your stay. Obviously only what you spend will be charged to your account when you check out but you could well find a few hundred dollars tied up from the minute you check in. So check your limit.

Personally I always fly Aer Lingus from Dublin, especially nw that Concorde is gone. The Irish national airline flies to JFK International in Queens. Depending on traffic it can take from twenty to ninety minutes to get to or from JFK and midtown. About fifty minutes is the norm. There are so many different coach, car and limousine services to and from the airport and the new internal rail system, which hooks up with the subway, is now operational. Airfares have never been more competitive but still, do look out for special offers. At certain times you can fly for under €200 round trip. Check www.aerlingus.com or www.lastminute.com

Remember you are allowed 2 pieces of luggage. Don't try to either take or bring home endless hand luggage. There is no room to store half the kitchen sink in the overhead bin. If you book in time you can request your favourite seat and if you fly regularly you will be aware that some seats have more legroom than others. In Premier Class my preference is for 1 A. Row 1 has slightly more legroom than the other five rows but all Premier Class seats have more than ample legroom and the seats are large and particularly comfortable. The configuration in Premier Class is 2 seats window and aisle A and C: two centre aisle seats D and G and two aisle and window seats H and K.

In Economy Class there are eight seats in a row. Rows 12 and 31 in Economy are at emergency exits and have plenty of legroom. The seat configuration is 2 seats window and aisle A and C: four seats center aisle DEFG and two seats aisle and window H and K.

If you have special dietary requirements, you can pre order a special menu. Vegetarian is always good as is Indian, or if you would prefer you can pre order a hamburger, sandwich or breakfast at any time. But remember order at the time you make your reservation.

AIG Insurance

WORLDWIDE

0-5 days	€44.00
6-9 days	€61.00
10-17 days	€70.00
18-23 days	€79.00
24-30 days	€87.00

Over 30 days, extra day rate is €1.50 (per day) max 365 days

Adult (18-69 years)	€135.00

Adult (70-74 years)	€270.00

Adult and Spouse/Partner (both 18-69 years)	€223.00

Adult and Spouse/Partner (one 18-69 years, one 70-74 years)	€358.00

Adult and Spouse/Partner (both 70-74 years)	€446.00

Children under 18 years named on parents' policy are covered at no extra charge. Infants under 2 years are covered for medical and baggage only.

If you are a Voluntary Health Insurance subscriber, bring your VHI World Assistance Card. It lists a number of emergency medical phone lines. It is widely accepted by doctors and hospitals in the United States. It's worth a call to VHI 00 353 1 872 4499 for an update on coverage before you travel.

Duty Free

Allowance from US to Ireland

Tobacco Products

Cigarettes	200
Or Cigarillos	200
Or Cigars	50
Or Grammes of Tobacco	250

Alcoholic Drinks

Alcoholic drinks exceeding 22% Vol
(e.g. Whiskey, Gin, Vodka)	1 Litre

Or (other than still wine) not exceeding 22% Vol
(e.g. sparkling or fortified wines, some liqueurs)
2 Litres

Perfumes

Perfumes (Pure perfumes)
50 Grammes (60 mls)
Toilet Water (Eau de Parfum)
0.25 Litre (250mls)

Other Goods

€142 per adult
€73 per child

Too Much-What To Do

If you exceed the limit either entering the
United States or returning to the Irish Republic
you can elect to pay tax on the surplus.

Getting in to the City

From JFK

Make the connection.
By Subway: to Sutphin Blvd
                    to Howard Beach

By Rail: LIRR to Jamaica

The AirTrain

The newest, fastest and cheapest way into the
city is via the AirTrain. AirTrain is a light-rail
system that links the Howard Beach and the
Sutphin Boulevard subway stations, and LIRR's
Jamaica Station directly to JFK. It takes about
an hour from most parts of the city, and about
15 minutes from LIRR's Jamaica Station - with
no traffic or parking worries ever.
And just like the subway, AirTrain runs 24/7.
AirTrain stations are fully enclosed, heated in
winter and air conditioned in summer. They
feature wide escalators and glass enclosed
elevators. Transfers between the subway and
AirTrain at Howard Beach and between the
Long Island Rail Road and AirTrain at Jamaica
are ADA-compliant; the transfer between the

Sutphin Boulevard subway station and the
Jamaica AirTrain station will be ADA-compliant
when construction is completed later this year.
At the airport, convenient moving walkways
take you and your luggage to any one of nine
connecting airline terminals. Some airlines will
check you in and take your luggage at Jamaica
Station before you board AirTrain.

The Fare
Travel to and from JFK via AirTrain is $5 each
way. Children under 5 ride free. You pay the
fare with Pay-Per-Ride MetroCard at either the
Sutphin Boulevard or Howard Beach station
(unlimited ride cards are not accepted for
AirTrain).
Be sure you add additional money to your Pay-
Per-Ride MetroCard to cover the cost for the
subway and AirTrain.

At the Howard Beach Station
The train stops at Howard Beach every 5 to 10
minutes during rush hours and every 15 to 20
minutes evenings and weekends. AirTrain stops
at Howard Beach every 4 to 10 minutes. Most
subway lines connect to the train. Just be sure
you take the marked "Far Rockaway," NOT
"Lefferts Boulevard." It's about a 12-minute
ride from the Howard Beach station to the
airport.

At the Sutphin Boulevard
station in Jamaica
Trains all stop at the Sutphin Boulevard station
where you connect to the AirTrain Jamaica
Stop. Trains run every 5 to 10 minutes during
rush hours and 8 to 12 minutes evenings and
weekends. AirTrain travels to the airport from
Jamaica every 4 to 10 minutes and the trip
takes no longer than 12 minutes.

At LIRR Jamaica Station
There is an in-station link to the AirTrain
platform - AirTrain travels to the airport from
Jamaica every 4 to 10 minutes. The AirTrain
ride takes about 12 minutes. By 2005, upon

completion of the LIRR's renovation of Jamaica
Station, the AirTrain will be connected to the
Railroad's hub by escalators, elevators, people
movers and an overhead mezzanine bridge.

Sample Travel Times and Costs
(using full $2 subway fare and $5 AirTrain fee)

To JFK Total Cost/Time

From 53 St/Lex Av station via Jamaica
$7 / 50 min.

From Fulton St station via Howard Beach
$7 / 1 hr. 5 min.

From West 4 St station via Jamaica
$7 / 1 hr. 5 min.

From Jay St station via Howard Beach
$7 / 55 min.

Long Island Rail Road
Penn Station to Jamaica via LIRR express train
$11.75* / 35 min.

*$6.75 peak time LIRR fare and $5 AirTrain
fee.
For more AirTrain information, call 877-JFK-
AirTrain or log on to www.panynj.gov

From La Guardia

M60 bus from Manhattan and Astoria
With the M60 bus, you can travel to La Guardia
from the West Side, the East Side or Astoria
(Queens). The M60 runs between 106 St and
Broadway in Manhattan and La Guardia
Airport from approximately 5 am to 1 am,
seven days a week. The M60 serves all airport
terminals. Connections can be made with all
north-south Manhattan subway lines or with the
N train at the Astoria Blvd station.
If you pay your fare with MetroCard, you can
transfer free between the subway and the M60
bus. The M60 also makes convenient

connections with MTA Metro-North Railroad at
the 125 St station. Travel time between
Broadway and 116 St and the Delta Terminal is
approximately 40 minutes.

Q48 from Flushing, Queens

The Q48 provides local bus service between
Flushing and La Guardia Airport. It loops
through La Guardia Airport and makes a stop
at Shea Stadium. Free transfers between the
Q48 any bus or the subway are available if you
pay your fare with MetroCard. The Q48
operates from 4:30 AM to 1:00 AM. Travel time
from the Main St 7 station to La Guardia
Airport is approximately 30 minutes.

Triboro Coach also provides service to La
Guardia via the Q33 bus.

JFK Airport Bus

There are several airport bus services available.
Carey Bus goes to 42nd Street and costs $12.00.
Supershuttle goes to hotels and apartment
buildings all over town. $15.00 Remember
buses trawl all around the airport picking up
passengers from all terminals until the bus is
full. So while the trip, once you leave the
airport, isn't much longer than the cab ride, you
can waste an hour or more in the bus at the
airport.

Supershuttle:

From your hotel, home or office to JFK or La Guardia

Ph: 212 BLUE-VAN (212-258-3826).
Try to give us 24 hr. advance notice.
Or ask the hotel concierge to arrange for your
pick-up.

Upon Arrival At Airport
Follow the signs to the Ground Transportation
Desk near the Baggage Claim area. Ask an
agent to arrange for SuperShuttle service, or,

you can call SuperShuttle direct from the
courtesy phone next to the Ground
Transportation Desk.

Approximate Fares
Rates range from $13 to $22. Discounts
available for additional passengers in the same
party. See On-line reservations for exact
quotes.All fares should be considered
approximate & from a general area.
All fares are subject to change without notice -
please call to confirm.
Groups And Conventions
Contact National Group Sales
@ 1-800-622-2089 or local Sales Director
Phone - 212-209-7000 x224
Fax: 718-482-1982
email:mailto:NYCSales@supershuttle.net
Services and programs available:

Cab

Cabs have a set fair of $35.00 plus tolls and tip
from JFK to anywhere in the city. By the way
there is no toll on the 59th Street Bridge. The
Triborough Bridge toll is $6.00. The Midtown
Tunnel toll is $6.00. If you have more than one
stop in the city, the meter starts running after
the first stop. The recommended tip is $10.00.
Always check the drivers license number and
the cab number, both should be displayed in the
passenger section of the cab.
If you have a complaint call: Taxi and
Limousine Commission: Ph:212 302 8294

Limousine or Town Car Service

There are several Limousine Services that you
can order ahead of time. Most hotels are usually
able to send a car service, but this will be more
expensive than if you order the service yourself.
The fares can range from $60.00 to $125.00
depending on the company you use. A tip of at
least 15% is expected. Always check the drivers
ID. Never accept a ride from the drivers who
tout business in or outside the Arrivals Building.

These cowboys charge extortionate fares and always take the scenic route into town.

I have used the following Limo services and I rate them as follows. The reality is you pay for superb quality.

3Star (about $35.00)
Allstate Car and Limo Service 212 333 3333

2Star (about $35.00)
SABRA 212 777 7171

2Star (about $30.00)
Tel Aviv 212 777 7777

5Star(about $125.00)
Dav-el 212 957 4390

3Star(about $40.00)
Lincoln Limo 212 722 0939

From Newark, New Jersey

Mass Transit trains

Take New Jersey transit trains which go from Newark's Penn Station to New York's Penn Station.
Ph: 1 800 872 724
Ph: 212 935 3560
Or if you are going downtown a bus. #302 or #62 will take you from Newark airport to Newark's Penn Station,.8th Avenue and 41st Street.
Ph: 212 564 8484
From there the PATH train to New York's World Trade Center costs $2.00.

Public Bus Service

Direct buses go to the Port Authority Bus Terminal, Grand Central Terminal at 42nd Street and Park Avenue, Penn Station at 7th Avenue and 33rd Street and World Trade Center Catch Olympia Line for $11.00($20.00

return) from Newark Airport to Grand Central Station at 42nd Street.

Cab

Cabs are metered from Newark and will cost anything from $35.00 to $55.00 plus tolls and tip. Holland Tunnel toll:$6.00 (inbound only) Lincoln Tunnel toll: $6.00 (inbound only) George Washington Bridge toll: $6.00 (inbound only)

Limousine Service

Companies as listed above Rates from $60.00 to $150.00 plus tip and tolls.

The Basic
Big Apple

Manhattan is an island designed on a grid system where avenues go from north to south and streets run east to west. 5th Avenue divides the city into the east and west sides. Unless you are down in the Village it is virtually impossible to get lost.

The Main Areas

- Downtown *from 1st Street to 14th*

- Lower East Side *Houston Street to Canal Street*

- Lower West Side

- Lower Midtown *from 14th to 32nd*

- Midtown *from 32nd Street to 57th*

- Upper east side *from 57th to 96th*

- Upper west side *from 57th to 96th*

Downtown Manhattan Neighbourhoods
- Alphabet City *East of 1st Ave from 1st St.*

- Soho *14th Street to Canal Street*

- Noho *North of Houston to Union Square*

- Tribeca *triangle below Canal bordered by Broadway and West Street*

- Chelsea *8th Avenue to Westside Highway from W 37th to W 14th*

- Chinatown *centered around Confucius Plaza, Canal, Grand, Lafayette, Christie, Bowery.*

- Little Italy Mulberry Street/ Mott Street area

- Greenwich Village

- East Village *runs from E14th south to Houston Street*

- West Village *Avenue of the Americas west to the Westside Highway from W15th to Canal Street*

Getting Around

Public transport

Public transport is the best value in NYC. Buses come very regularly and are safe and clean. Hundreds of millions of dollars have been spent on the Subway system over the past few years. Most stations are now state of the art and very safe. The Subway is the fastest way to get around the City. If you take a few minutes to check where you're going on a subway map, you will find it's easy to identify the train or bus that will take you closest to your destination.

A bus or subway ticket is $2.00. Tickets are interchangeable, i.e. you can transfer from bus to train or visa versa and bus to bus as long as the transfer is within two hours of embarking on the first leg of the trip. Obviously you can't use the ticket to double back on your journey.

For the bus you must have exact money in change... no pennies or dollar bills. Metro Cards work for both Subway and Bus and are available in most newsagents, local delis as well as in Subway stations for values of $4.00 to $80.00. You can pay for up to two fares at one

time on one card. There are also special One
Day Metro cards. For $4.00 you get unlimited
local bus and subway rides all day. Tickets are
for individual use. Seven Day Metro Cards
entitle you to seven days of unlimited local bus
and subway rides for $17.00. Again for
individual use.

Cabs

Cabs can be hailed down anywhere. It really
helps to have the exact address since most
cabbies haven't a clue where they are going and
many don't speak English. It also helps if you
know which side of the street you want to get
out. It's very difficult to get a cab between
3.30pm and 5.30pm, when shifts change over.
That is also the time most people are heading to
the airport for international departures.
Be sure to tip, (about 20%) especially if the
cabbie has been helpful. He won't be shy to
inform you if he thinks you haven't given him
enough.

If a few of you are planning a shopping trip, it
might be an idea to hire a limo and driver.
Usually about $30.00 plus tip a hour but you
can often do a deal. It's good value and great
fun.

Emergencies

For all emergencies Ph: 911

Lost and Found

If you lose your wallet, money, credit cards, the
whole nightmare, first call your credit card
company to cancel your cards. It is possible to
have cards replaced in the relevant New York
offices. If you lose valuables, it's always a good
idea to report the loss to the local police
precinct. I have listed the main precincts. For
insurance purposes it is always easier to make a
claim if you have a police report of your loss.

Police Precincts

Every area has its own police precinct.
Call directory enquiries at 411 for details.
The most centrally situated mid town precinct
is:
17th Precinct
Location
East 51st Street between Lexington and Third
Avenues
Ph: 212 826 3211

24 Hour Emergency Services

Hospital Emergency
Hospitals in Manhattan tend to be found in
clusters in a number of neighbourhoods. Some
of the establishments listed below are
recognized as among the best in the world in
their special areas.

East Side
New York Downtown Hospital 170 William
Street
Bellevue Hospital 462 1st Avenue
Beth Israel Medical Center 281 1st Avenue
New York Eye and Ear 310 14th Street
Hospital for Special Surgery 535 E.70th Street
Lenox Hill Hospital 100 E.77th Street
New York Presbyterian 525 E 68th Street
Manhattan Eye, Ear and Throat 210 E 64th
Street
Memorial Sloan Kettering Cancer Center 1275
York Avenue
Mount Sinai Hospital 5th Ave. @ 100th Street

West Side
St. Vincent's Hospital 153 W. 11th Street
Roosevelt Hospital Center 1000Tenth Avenue
St. Clare's Hospital 426 W. 52nd Street
St. Luke's Hospital 1111 Amsterdam Ave

Dental Emergency
Ph: 212 677 2510

Pharmacies
The following is a cross section of 24 hour

pharmacies in Manhattan.
You can also order on-line at:
www.duanereade.com (a really good site)
or
www.eckerd.com

East Side

Duane Reade 7 World Trade Center 212 912 0998
Duane Reade 24, East 14th Street 212 989 3632
CVS 342 E. 23rd Street 212 473 5750
Genovese 221-225 Lexington Ave 212 252 7410
Duane Reade 300 Park Avenue South 212 533 7580
Duane Reade 485 Lexington Ave 212 682 5338
Duane Reade 866 Third Ave 212 759 9412
Duane Reade 405 Lexington Ave 212 808 4743
Rite Aid 542 Second Avenue 212 213 9887
CVS 1400 Second Ave 212 249 5699
Duane Reade 1279 Third Ave 212 744 2668
Genovese 1299 Second Ave 212 772 0504
Duane Reade 401 E. 86th Street 917 492 8801
Duane Reade 1231 Madison Ave 212 360 6586
Rite Aid 144 E. 86th Street 212 876 0600

West Side

Duane Reade 378 Avenue of the Americas 212 674 5357
Rite Aid 282 Eight Avenue 212 727 3854
CVS 1 Columbus Place (58t @9th) 212 245 0611
Duane Reade 224 W.57th Street 212 541 9708
Duane Reade 2025 Broadway 212 579 9955
Rite Aid 210 Amsterdam Ave 212 787 2903
CVS 606 Columbus Ave 212 787 3303
Duane Reade 2465 Broadway 212 799 3172
Rite Aid 2833 Broadway 212 663 3135

Car Hire

A valid Irish, British or International Driver's license and one major credit card is required.

Avis 1 800 331 1212 www.avis.com
Hertz 1 800 654 3131 www.hertz.com

Alamo 1 877 227 8367 www.alamo.com
Budget 1 800 527 0700 www.budget.com
Enterprise 1 800 736 8222 www.enterprise.com
Thrifty 212 586 4343 www.thrifty.com

All the above have rental offices all over the
New York City. Some companies will collect you
from your hotel and take you to the rental office
to sign the contract. Cars from around $50.00 a
day depending on time of year and/or if you are
a member of a rental company's special
programme. Major airlines often have discount
deals with car hire companies. Weekends during
the summer can be extremely difficult to reserve
at short notice, so book as far in advance as
possible. Advance booking is also advisable for
all US holiday weekends. If you are in dire need
of a car and you can't locate one in Manhattan,
the odds are much better with the major
companies at either La Guardia or JFK airports.

Banks

There are banks on just about every block in
Manhattan. Most of them have a Foreign
Exchange section but do not exchange Euros.
Most of them also have a Cirrus instant
withdrawal service where you can get cash from
your home bank account

Cash Machines

ATMs are located all over the city. Check below
for a cross section of local ATMs. In addition to
the usual ' bank holes in the wall' ATM
machines are available in many department
stores, corner shops, newsagents etc. You can
get cash with American Express, Mastercard,
Visa, and Irish ATM cards with Cirrus facility.
American Express
374 Park Avenue at 52nd Street
Ph: 212 421 8240
Monday-Friday 900am-5.00pm
Saturday & Sunday Closed
Reporting lost/stolen Amex credit card or
traveller's cheques:
Ph: 1 800 233 5432
The company operates an emergency cheque

cashing facility. It is possible to get dollars using your Irish chequebook. For Amex Greencard members the limit is the equivalent of € 500 per 21 days. Amex Goldcard members have a limit of the equivalent of € 1,000 per 21 days. There is no Irish Platinum Amex Card Service. American Express also offers members a PIN number and cash can be obtained from ATMs throughout the city. There is an ATM at the above location.

Allied Irish Banks Visa and Mastercharge Cards In addition to the normal credit card transactions also offers cash withdrawal facilities. With a PIN number you can get the equivalent of € 250 a day from an ATM. Any bank or Bureau de Change displaying the Visa or Mastercharge sign offers a cash advancement service. To avail of this you need your credit card and photo ID. You don't need a PIN number. The amount of money banks will advance differs but all offer the same amount as the ATM (€ 250.00) Others offer substantially more**ATMs and local nuts and bolts.**

In addition to these 'holes in the wall' ATMs are to be found in most department stores as well as in many smaller newstands and corner fruit and veg stores. Fees to use an ATM vary from $1.50-$3.00 per transaction.

Downtown

Fleet 100 Church Street

Lower East Side

Chase 108-109 Delancy St
Fleet 126 Delancy St
Fleet 318 Grand St
Citibank 411 Grand St
Emigrant 465 Grand St.
Chase 302 W 12th St
Chase 156 W 14th St
HSBC 101 W.14th St
Citibank 75 Christopher St
Chase 345 Hudson St

Chelsea

Chase 475 West 23rd Street.
Citibank 322 West 23rd Street
Citibank 111 Eighth Avenue
Chase 238 Eighth Avenue

Tribeca

Bank of New York 233 Broadway
Chase 281 Broadway
Chase 407 Broadway
Citibank 415 Broadway
Citibank 250 Broadway
HSBC 265 Broadway
HSBC 253 Broadway
Fleet 100 Church Street
Chase 423 Canal Street

SOHO

Chase 756 Broadway
Chase 766 Broadway
HSBC 599 Broadway
Citibank 72 Fifth Ave
Apple 145 Fourth Ave
Citibank 262 First Ave
HSBC 245 First Ave
Dime 130Second Ave
EAB 105 Second Ave
HSBC 245 First Ave
HSBC 10 Union Square East
HSBC 1, East 8th Street
Chase 158, West 14th St.

East Village

Chase 255 First Avenue
Citibank 262 First Avenue
HSBC 245 First Avenue
Union 37 Avenue B
EAB 50 Avenue A